The Uses of
LITERARY
HISTORY

MARSHALL BROWN

editor

Published by Duke University Press
Durham and London
1995

With the exceptions of the Preface by Marshall Brown;
"Figures of the Feminine: An Amazonian Revolution
in Feminist Literary History?" by Donna Landry; "Public
Memory and Its Discontents," by Geoffrey H. Hartman;
"The Pedigree of the White Stallion: Postcoloniality
and Literary History," by Rukmini Bhaya Nair; and "Preface
to a Lyric History," by Susan Stewart, these articles
have appeared previously in *Modern Language Quarterly.*

Library of Congress Cataloging-in-Publication Data
The uses of literary history / edited by Marshall Brown.
p.   cm.
Some articles previously appeared in Modern language
quarterly.
Includes bibliographical references and index.
ISBN 0-8223-1704-4 (acid-free paper).—ISBN 0-8223-1714-1
(pbk. : acid-free paper)
1. Historical criticism (Literature) 2. Literature and history.
3. Literature—History and criticism—Theory, etc.
I. Brown, Marshall, 1945- . II. Modern language quarterly.
PN98.H57U82   1996
809—dc20   95-42027

The Uses of
LITERARY
HISTORY

For Magrets,
who knows more about
literary history than
any of us,

with much love,

Pat

ix. 17. 1996

Contents

Literature as History

PREFACE

Marshall Brown

Why literary history? Modernism, it could be said, suffered history in public, and struggled against it in art. Postmodernism renounced or parodied history in public, only to be haunted by it in ethics and in conscience. As the past grows lighter, the future grows weightier and more apocalyptic, and thus the whirligig of time brings in his revenges. Never but in dreams are we free of history. And even dreams are driven by the immediate needs of our lives and the conditions of our dwelling. Having failed to escape metaphysics, we find ourselves enmeshed in physics. Whatever transcendental entity may grant us our existence, a chronotope—a dynamic nature composed of time and force—molds it. These days, history enjoys vast prestige in satisfying a widespread nostalgia for the real.

So I need to restress the question: why *literary* history? Because the real needs a counterweight if we are to enjoy it. Taine's unholy trinity has returned to fashion—milieu, moment, even race—but with what threatens to be an imperial dignity. Time is all-important; too often it seems all-powerful as well. As several essays in this volume argue, historical time needs productive tension with alter egos. Whether it be the material reception by readers and editors, the hermeneutic dialogue of overlooked and recovered voices, or the critical resistance that *otium* brings to occasions, literature provokes time to give itself to us. History looms large—too large to be seen or felt in itself. Human expressions do not so much make history as make history human; it is our texts that shape events, turning them, for better or worse, into the ongoing equipment of our experience.

In the spring of 1993 *Modern Language Quarterly* celebrated its rebirth as "a journal of literary history" with a new design and a special issue. Sixteen position papers addressed "the state of literary history" from a range of disciplinary and methodological vantage points. The present volume contains those essays and four additional ones. The authors were asked to write from the perspective of their specialization and from the experience of their own writing. I encouraged them to develop their ideas from concrete examples. Three of the original authors, Jonathan Arac, Richard Dellamora, and Paul Fry, have amplified their essays; of the additional essays, those by Donna Landry, Rukmini Bhaya Nair, and Susan Stewart are wholly new, while Geoffrey Hartman expands an essay published in *Raritan*.

I conceived this volume as a reaffirmation of the originality of the literary disciplines. Consequently, all the contributors to *The Uses of Literary History* teach in departments of language and literature. I aimed at a broad representation of different language fields, historical specializations, and critical approaches. The first section of the collection concerns methods and problems of writing literary history; the second, the nature of contemporary interest in the literary past; the third, the temporality of literary works and the ways they build their own history. The essays differ markedly in approach: personal narrative, critical exposition, philosophical analysis, review of research, meditation, polemic, exhortation. The tone varies from informational to playful, wistful, introspective, indignant, exalted. Example, system, method, and application all get their due. No single reader will come with interest and knowledge in all the specific areas represented in the collection; rather, readers should take ideas for their own use from all the strategies illustrated here. The multiplicity of literary history and the clash of voices were part of my intention. Indeed, I was delighted that three contributors chose to make counterstatements, featured at the conclusion of the three sections. Literary history has many uses and properly should stir debate.

I think of a collection like this one as an echo chamber. The pleas by Jerome McGann and Marjorie Perloff for accurate reporting of texts and contextual information are seconded by several later essays that call for accurate and pertinent reporting of ideas; at the same time, David Perkins (seconded by Virgil Nemoianu) reminds us that facts without taste are blind. Hartman's view of the artistic heritage as a memorial disclosure links up with the identity constructions discussed by Peter Stallybrass, Denis Hollier, and others; at the same time, Walter Benn Michaels warns us not to take Hartman's "collected memory" (*Gedächtnis*) for individual recollection (*Erinnerung*). Several essays in the final section concern the temporality of literature, and so do Arac's reflections on his experience writing literary history; Fry reminds us that literature can also transcend time, and that timelessness, too, is a use of history. However antithetical in their rhetoric, his readings also renew Meredith Anne Skura's and Annabel Patterson's historicizing critiques of historicism and circle back to Lawrence Lipking's eloquent warnings—all of them concerned to remove the blinkers of inappropriate perspectives so that the past can speak to us directly. A general overview in one essay may intersect a specific example in another, as happens with the complementary discussions of feminism by Howard Bloch and Donna Landry. Stereoscopy promotes depth, as when Doris Sommer's recovery of narrative sophistications concealed by Eurocentric histories responds to Nair's construction of narrative sophistications unimaginable to any purely nationalist history. By sharing topics while differing in approach and subject matter and sometimes disagreeing in evaluation, the essays energize one another. In the festive introduction to the journal issue, unconsciously echoing Charles Altieri's invocation of Antaeus, I wrote that "history is the challenge of a perpetually exhilarated dissatisfaction." I hope the challenge is still felt in this larger collection, tempered with literature's role in anchoring and focusing the exhilaration. What Altieri calls "bootstrapping," rather than leaping, is the road to transcedence.

The people I am most grateful to for this volume are the contributors, who have made it what it is. My coworkers at *Modern Language Quarterly* made it happen: James McNelis and Graham Shutt, who prepared all the materials for the journal issue, and Mike Magoolaghan, who did the same for the book. They performed many complicated tasks thoughtfully, efficiently, and enthusiastically. John Coldewey, longtime editor of *MLQ* and coeditor for the special issue, was the sine qua non—friend, confederate, and corrective to my excess zeal. Richard Dunn and Tom Lockwood saved the journal when it was in trouble from above. The Journals Division of Duke University Press is full of dedicated workers and allies; it has been my pleasure to meet them several times and to see how much work they do that remains invisible to the rest of us, and how well they do it. I list alphabetically the ones I know: Marc Brodsky, Mike Brondoli, Steve Cohn, Paula Dragosh, Sue Hall, Annie Kao, Chris Mazzara, Trish Thomas, Angela Williams. The index was prepared by Alan M. Greenberg. It was Anne Keyl's idea to make a book of it all.

Literary History

A Trout in the Milk

Lawrence Lipking

Literary history used to be impossible to write; lately it has become much harder. The main problem is the decreasing weight of *literary*. Not long ago, the impossibility of writing literary history stemmed from the struggle to do equal justice to both halves of the phrase, to write a narrative that would take account at once of the relatively timeless, formal, autonomous world of works of art and of their contingent, fact-strewn, wandering passage through time. True literature had no history; true history ignored the category literature-as-such. This led to a comfortable division of realms. Team teaching with a historian, I could take it for granted that he or she would fail to appreciate the art of the text and force it to be an example of something or other, and she or he could take it for granted that I would fail to comprehend its larger social and historical context. In this way we got along, correcting each other. Most literary histories represented a similar collaboration. Never quite satisfactory in focusing on works of art—too much *background* had to be included, too many sources and happenstances and catalogs and genealogies—they were also not quite right as history: no matter how informative, texts were excluded if nobody thought they were *good*. Hence the genre of literary history was always already compromised, neither one thing nor the other. Even the best works of the kind were impossible. But that did not prevent them from being useful. In general, most of the standard English literary histories appeared at a time when the opposition between the literary and the historical seemed particularly bitter, and critics and historians sparred with each other. C. S. Lewis, Douglas Bush, George

Sherburn et al. did not solve the dilemma. But their well-thumbed books have yet to be replaced.

Today the problem of balance seems rather outmoded. Not many scholars spend time defending the literariness of literary works, nor do they imagine a realm of art divorced at least in part from history. In 1952, when the Modern Language Association published a report entitled "The Aims, Methods, and Materials of Research in the Modern Languages and Literatures," René Wellek pointed out that "either we conceive of 'literary history' as a branch of history, especially the history of culture, for which we use works of literature as 'documents' and evidence; or we conceive of 'literary history' as a history of art, and study works of literature as 'monuments'";[1] but he also insisted that the two aims and methods were not mutually exclusive and that a good literary historian had to be a good critic. By 1963, in a new version of *The Aims and Methods of Scholarship in Modern Languages and Literatures*, Robert E. Spiller was warning against such eclecticism. As an independent discipline, literary history needed to be distinctively *literary*: "It deals with the materials of literature and therefore should not be written in any idiom but that of literature; and it is itself a form of literature and is therefore an art and not a science."[2] But times have changed. In the 1981 *Introduction to Scholarship in Modern Languages and Literatures*, "Literary History" was replaced by "Historical Scholarship," whose author, Barbara Kiefer Lewalski, notes that the new title "intends to recognize that the province inhabited by the contemporary historical scholar is more extensive and at the same time less clearly demarcated from its neighbors than the territory Spiller mapped out."[3] Here the literary takes a back seat. But not back far enough by current measures. In the recent, much-expanded second edition of *Introduction to Scholarship* (1992), Annabel Patterson observes that, despite the change of title, "Lewalski's categories of historical inquiry were still predomi-

---

[1] Wellek, "Literary History," *PMLA* 67 (October 1952): 20.

[2] Spiller, "Literary History," in *The Aims and Methods of Scholarship in Modern Languages and Literatures*, ed. James Thorpe (New York: Modern Language Association, 1963), 45.

[3] Lewalski, "Historical Scholarship," in *Introduction to Scholarship in Modern Languages and Literatures*, ed. Joseph Gibaldi (New York: Modern Language Association, 1981), 53.

nantly 'literary,'" and she goes on to announce that the new historical scholarship will occupy the social and cultural territory once relegated to "contexts." After Foucault, "all texts were now equal."[4] The old tension has gone. Though Patterson does use the word *literary* quite often—literary criticism, literary elements, the literary text—it is clear that in using it she does not mean anything special.

In this she speaks for a present-day consensus. If literary history has not disappeared, it has certainly been redefined. In practice, it seems to stand for nothing more than the sort of history written by people employed in language departments. A high proportion of current studies in the field pay more attention to issues of culture than to matters of art, and many deny that "art" has meaning except as an instance of culture. To be sure, most scholars in English and French and German and Spanish departments continue to write about plays and novels and poems. But that behavior might itself be viewed as a cultural practice, the result of habit and training. The center of interest lies elsewhere. The graduate students whose work I supervise now write about print culture and slavery and commodification and historiography and copyright law and nationalism and the body, not to mention race, class, and gender. Sometimes they illustrate their theses with well-known "literary" texts; sometimes they do not. But neither they nor I consider this preference crucial. Nor do they seem oppressed by any tension in balancing the claims of literature against the claims of history. By some older standards, then, they seldom write literary history; to satisfy Spiller's terms would be not only impossible but unimaginable. And who would *want* to write that sort of history?

Yet the redefinition of literary history has not made it easier to write. Notoriously, theses take longer and longer to finish. If the turn from art to culture has eliminated the need to dwell on the literary, it has also introduced a new set of problems. Three of them strike me as crucial for current practice: choosing a significant topic, searching for evidence, and working out a relation to theory. All are simple, familiar issues, but they have never been harder to cope with than now. Each deserves a longer look.

[4] Patterson, "Historical Scholarship," in *Introduction to Scholarship in Modern Languages and Literatures,* 2d ed., ed. Joseph Gibaldi (New York: Modern Language Association, 1992), 183, 186.

In one respect, the way that literary historians fix on a topic has changed very little: most scholars write about the sort of thing about which other scholars are writing. Choosing a subject, like choosing a name for a child, is an individual, deeply personal decision that usually just happens to coincide with everyone else's. Some topics are in the air. After centuries of silence on Samuel Johnson's working relations with women, four articles on that theme crossed my desk in a single week. Their authors were by no means unoriginal. Each had hit on the idea independently, each had found some new material, each arrived at thoughtful conclusions. Yet somehow the age had decreed that all of them should work on that topic. The projects of literary history are conceived in historical time. Nor should one forget how many are assigned or commissioned by advisors, publishers, or series editors. Years ago I heard the distinguished scholar Joyce Hemlow describe the exact spot in Harvard Yard where her long lifework had been prognosticated. After she mentioned a budding interest in Fanny Burney, George Sherburn said, "Yes," and paused; ". . . and you might edit the letters when they become available." Such sentences still determine the course of many careers.

Nevertheless, the new possibilities of literary history have also created new burdens. Once historical scholarship shed the obligation to be demonstrably "literary," a vast, uncharted field opened. What historical topics or texts are *not* suitable for investigation by scholars in language departments? The question seems unanswerable. As soon as I think of an outcast text—a railroad timetable, a valentine, a laundry list—I think of some project for which it would be the ideal document. The new literary history seems potentially free and wide as the world. This situation is undeniably exhilarating and accounts for the sense of liberation that many contemporary literary historians convey so well. Moreover, the old tight rein on the "literary" encouraged some palpable injustice—for instance, the notion that a few genres cultivated in England by Englishmen educated in the classics were worthy of an attention not to be paid other writings in English that had the bad taste to be composed abroad, in the wrong forms or by the wrong sorts of people. Today we have the freedom to choose. But freedom can also be intimidating. Perhaps the timetables will not check out; perhaps no one else will find them interesting. The study of any document connected to Shakespeare retains some interest because of that association. Documents unrelated to a famous name or literary text hold no such guarantee. Hence the new historical scholarship plays with risk. It searches for significance in very unlikely places and tries to find new ways of being important.

The hunt for importance leads to other problems. Perhaps the most obvious is a runaway rhetorical inflation, observable not only in scholarly essays but in such professional genres as reviews, dust jacket blurbs, applications for grants, and the prefaces and afterwords to books. At one time literary historians enjoyed a reputation for modesty. Today, if one trusts what one reads, they produce paradigm shifts with the regularity of hens laying eggs or roosters welcoming the dawn. I sympathize, not with the rhetoric but with the professional strain to which it testifies. In the absence of any agreement about the *center* of literary history—whether a canon of works or a conception of art—no one wants to be left out in the cold of the margin. Indeed, the former margin has infiltrated or supplemented the center, at least in some circles. Importance itself now has to be contested. No wonder that the choice of a topic in literary history often involves the raised voices of fierce self-promotion.

Nor should one overlook the accelerating pace of change. Patterson's new introduction to historical scholarship, in a book intended for beginning graduate students, covers only the last ten years. As more than one of my own students have pointed out, ten years is about the average time required to complete a literary historical project. Therefore their up-to-date schemes, when finished, will probably already seem unfashionable, if not obsolete. The same might be said about most of the pieces, including this one (written in 1992), in this book; in the lag between writing and publication, they will have fallen behind. I wish that I were joking. In fact the problem is real. As the age of hypertext looms, the relatively relaxed schedule of the older literary histories, often in love with the past and fond of lingering on it, has succumbed to the quicker beat of generational conflicts and tenure decisions. Thus projects must now be planned with one eye on the future. Like the Red Queen in *Through the Looking-Glass*, many contemporary literary historians have to run as fast as possible just to keep in the same place.

They also have to find new ways to test their arguments. If the choice of a topic no longer distinguishes literary history from historical scholarship in general, the choice of evidence is usually revealing. Most historians pass through a course of training quite different from that of literary scholars, and entertain a different set of expectations. Traditionally they deal with records and documents, not with works, and ask questions whose answers depend less on close reading than on circumstantial traces, statistical projections, and skillful inferences. A good historian finds the trout in the milk.[5]

Not every student of literature knows how to catch the trout or what to do with it after it is caught. Many of my undergraduates, in fact, initially miss Thoreau's point. Some are fascinated by the image itself, an incongruous symbol; some lack the historical background or imagination to picture what might happen to milk on its journey from cow to container. But the main problem, doubtless, is that they are taking an English course, where handling circumstantial evidence is not high on the list of priorities. They read for other kinds of insight and pleasure, for following their own special trains of association. Some of these students are destined to be literary scholars.

I do not mean to sound like a prophet of doom. But standards of evidence do seem to me in a state of disrepair, maybe even of crisis, in much current literary history. Once again the enfeeblement of "literary" criteria makes a difference. One peculiarity of the older literary history was its reliance on a consensus of informed readers, whose agreement about the proper interpretation of texts provided the most convincing evidence for any argument. The scholar offered a context in which to understand some literary work; the reader tested whether it made sense by reading the work again. This method was at once the strength and weakness of literary studies—the strength because the decisive evidence for any hypothesis lay out in the open, available to anyone willing to read; the weakness because it depended on something as fragile and fickle as the experiences of individual human beings. Nevertheless it served. When Lewalski tries to define the forte

[5] "Some circumstantial evidence is very strong, as when you find a trout in the milk" (quoted from Thoreau's unpublished manuscripts by Ralph Waldo Emerson, "Thoreau," in *Lectures and Biographical Sketches* [Boston: Houghton, Mifflin, 1904], 482).

of a good literary historian, she keeps returning to "a sense of relevance" and "tact." These are hardly absolute values. Rather, each is underwritten by its respect for the primacy of works of art: "a firm sense of relevance and proportion, so that the context does not engulf the literary texts," and "tactful, judicious, and balanced application of the insights gained in a manner that preserves the integrity and complexity of the literature"(63). The literary historian, on this model, must recognize the special qualities of texts; this recognition will in turn be recognized by competent readers. The test of such evidence is always communal and intersubjective. It works so long as readers say it does.

Today it does not seem to work so well. Not many literary historians now boast about their sense of relevance and tact. Obviously the readership has changed. Just as the subject matter of historical scholarship encompasses many texts outside any literary canon, so scholars and readers currently belong to centrifugal and incompatible communities. Our politics of reading is democratic, unafraid of irrelevance and tactlessness. Indeed, much of the New Historicism actively seeks out the most unlooked-for contexts, hoping to make familiar texts look strange in a shock of unrecognition. At their best, such historians, like Stephen Greenblatt, contrive the "perspective by incongruity" recommended by Kenneth Burke.[6] Their milk is full of trout. Hence literary history now teems with interesting new flavors, with abundant evidence that need not conform to any standard reading or sense of appropriateness. Cumulatively, this sort of evidence denies that the interpretation of texts can ever be uncontested or self-evident; one use of the trout might be to shake the assumption that the natural goodness of milk can be taken for granted. Nor are Thoreau's criteria decisive. The link between fact and inference is always factitious, if not arbitrary; even the strongest circumstantial evidence might turn out to be misleading. Thus evidence itself must go on trial.

What standards of evidence, then, do literary historians currently accept? I am not at all sure. When historical narratives followed chains of cause and effect, the logic of the historian's argument could claim to reproduce the logic of events. A led to B, and Homer to Virgil, in a

[6] Burke, *Attitudes toward History* (Los Altos, Calif.: Hermes, 1959), 308–14.

continuous process. Now discontinuity has come into style. In a good deal of recent literary history, the relation between the argument and the evidence, or even between one paragraph and the next, has become quite elastic; witness the popular New Historicist transition, "Now I want to talk about something else." Thus readers as well as writers must use their imaginations to trace a connection. In this respect the models of evidence for literary history no longer resemble those of historical scholarship but those of psychoanalysis or archaeology. Such models assume that most of the past is hidden; the clutter of surface features only distracts the scholar from underlying, deeper structures. Hence bits of evidence must be magnified, through daring hypotheses, to reconstruct the essence of a psyche or a civilization. The influence of Benjamin and Foucault supports this use of evidence. But the same line of thought can be turned against the use of any "legitimating scholarly apparatus."[7] In some recent studies the notion of evidence itself seems to be the target, one more example of the repressive institutions that continue to haunt our world even after their authority has dissolved. What institution might replace them remains to be seen. Meanwhile, many scholars search for a new kind of proof, neither the inferences from data favored by historians nor the plausible readings approved by older literary scholars, but a tertium quid.

The question "What counts as evidence?" cannot be answered, however, by citing evidence alone. It is partly a matter of history and partly a matter of theory, and the intertwining of history and theory is another reason why literary history has become harder to write. At one time many historical scholars proudly defined themselves as the antitheses of theorists if not their scourge. Some still do. But the rising tide of theory has flooded many of the old retreats and forced most younger scholars to bob along in the current of discourse. In practice, a great many contemporary literary histories argue for an explicit the-

---

[7] The phrase comes from Eve Kosofsky Sedgwick, "Jane Austen and the Masturbating Girl," *Critical Inquiry* 17 (1991): 835. Sedgwick is commenting on her use of a document dated 1881 and reproduced without documentation in 1981 in *Semiotext(e)*, as a context for "the bedroom scenes" of *Sense and Sensibility*. Not only this article but the *Critical Inquiry* series "Questions of Evidence" in which it appears exemplifies the contested and unstable function of evidence in current literary history.

oretical position and often present their historical research as an example or vindication of that theory. Indeed, some scholars maintain that such theoretical self-consciousness is the defining characteristic of the new literary history. To *do* history no longer seems enough; one must also see through it.

But what exactly is theory? Today no one quite knows. A decade ago some fierce debates raged around the word, and many theorists seemed convinced that only one enterprise deserved the name and that others who called themselves theorists were only pretenders. "The resistance to theory," in Paul de Man's terms, resisted a paradoxical but inescapable "theoretical project of rhetorical analysis,"[8] and resisters paid tribute to that project, whether they knew it or not. Lately, such imperial confidence has softened. In the recent *Introduction to Scholarship,* for instance, Jonathan Culler suggests that literary theory "is not a set of methods for literary study but an unbounded corpus of writings about everything under the sun, from the most technical problems of academic philosophy to the body in its relations to medical and ethical discourses."[9] Perhaps even this generous description understates the equivocal meaning of the term. Theory refers, in current usage, to all-encompassing systems of thought ("Grand Theory"), to ideologies, to methods, to any assumptions or presuppositions (even unconscious ones), to hermeneutic suspicion, to hypotheses or bright ideas, to any level of generalization, and often to no more than a preferred vocabulary into which all phenomena might be translated. The enemies of theory like to characterize it as a single, fatal movement. Those who subscribe to theory no longer assert that it is any one thing.

The eclecticism of contemporary theory offers a great wealth of opportunities to literary historians. It also raises some serious problems. The most obvious is the difficulty of deciding which theory might

---

[8] De Man, *The Resistance to Theory* (Minneapolis: University of Minnesota Press, 1986), 17. The essay was originally intended for the 1981 edition of *Introduction to Scholarship* but was rejected by the MLA Committee. As the writer of the complementary essay "Literary Criticism" in the same volume, I consulted at length with de Man on his plan for "Literary Theory" and witnessed his own resistance to surveying other sorts of theoretical projects.

[9] Culler, "Literary Theory," in *Introduction to Scholarship,* 2d ed., 203.

be most cogent or useful. The training of literary historians seldom prepares them for the sort of rigorous analysis to which Grand Theory aspires, nor do they ordinarily impress philosophers with the acuteness of their thought. Hence much of the theory applied in historical scholarship seems unavoidably secondhand or homemade. At best it exhibits a conscientious assimilation of ideas imported from some other discipline; at worst it relies on a patter of magical passwords—the Other, logocentrism, hegemony, discursive formations, and paradigm shifts—that procure an illusion of mastery at very little expense. Much current literary history grapples, not always successfully, with this problem. Not every theory pays off.

Moreover, the aggressive use of theory tends to introduce historical distortions. Ideas are general and texts particular. I have never written an extended piece of literary history without being conscious of a tug-of-war between two imperatives: proving my hypothesis and telling the whole truth. Never having satisfied myself on this score, I am of course not easily satisfied by other people's clever ideas and selective facts. But lately the tug seems more shameless. To the scholar in the grip of an attractive theory, as to Blake, the Outward Creation "is as the Dirt upon my feet," and as lightly cast off. Hence unresponsive facts or texts are often treated like dirt. One popular school of literary history warns against the danger of succumbing to the ideology of romantic poems in the process of reading them sympathetically. To resist the authors' own ways of seeing is thus a point of honor. Some scholars refuse to pronounce *Juan* with Byron's hard *J* and disyllable; the tongue and teeth themselves rebel against the implicit ethnocentrism and colonialism of the poet's rhymes. Many theories induce a similar suspicion and resentment of the motives of the text. No theorist ever loses this battle. Strong theories are self-reinforcing and not to be contradicted by anything so vulnerable and ambiguous as a literal meaning or an author's intention. But texts and histories offer their own resistance. They stick in the eye of theory like pieces of dirt and never stop smearing its visions.

Nor do theory and history ever seem likely to make a perfect match. Even the best recent efforts of theorists to account for the workings of literary history have run up against two sources of tension. The first is disciplinary. Not every mode of thought accommodates the past.

When literary scholars adopt ideas and terms from anthropology, for instance, they also take on the extreme discomfort with history that has long been the anthropologist's burden. Forty years ago, in an undergraduate introduction to anthropology, I studied *Our Primitive Contemporaries*.[10] There time was out of joint. The title of the book contrasts two ways of life, one prehistoric and timeless, the other advanced and progressive—"our" way. Nor could these ways of life be allowed to mix; to preserve such cultural fossils, it was necessary to quarantine them from history. This was of course a losing game. Much recent anthropology has sought a less patronizing and ahistorical meeting ground with the Other.[11] Yet the difficulties remain. The discipline of history only compounds the problem by subjecting past cultures to modern perspectives. Even the dates in the scholar's notebook impose a foreign code or calendar on the time frames of other people. An anthropologist might want to erase those dates; a historian cannot afford to. Thus literary historians lose track of time when they try to think like anthropologists. A similar disorientation is provoked by postmodernism, whose mélange of styles from the past reshuffles the orderly sequence of cause and effect on which historians traditionally rely. The daring of such radical games with time stirs up exciting possibilities, new combinations of data and thought. Whether they will prove compatible with plausible versions of literary history, however, is open to question.

Moreover, theorists tend to be in love with the future. That is a second source of tension with the historian's trade. Almost without exception, modern literary theories promise a method whose fruit has yet to come, a history still to be made. Theory depends on its future applications. Consider some well-known remarks by Paul de Man. "*Allegories of Reading* started out as a historical study and ended up as a theory of reading. . . . This shift, which is typical of my generation, is of more interest in its results than in its causes. It could, in principle, lead to a rhetoric of reading reaching beyond the canonical principles of liter-

[10] George Peter Murdock, *Our Primitive Contemporaries* (New York: Macmillan, 1934). Murdock's comment that "all cultures, including our own, are built according to a single fundamental plan, the so-called 'universal culture pattern,'" reflects the "timeless" nature of his enterprise.

[11] See, for instance, Johannes Fabian, *Time and the Other* (New York: Columbia University Press, 1983).

ary history which still serve, in this book, as the starting point of their own displacement."[12] This is an artful and disingenuous statement. By deflecting attention from the causes to the results of his inability to write a historical study, de Man fends off a relevant question: did his theory itself preclude a historian's way of thinking? Suppressing this question allows him to suggest, in the final sentence, that somehow his rhetoric of reading already implies a new literary history. He has reached beyond the old principles, in principle; this fox will have nothing to do with rotten grapes. But *could* someone write a comprehensive and persuasive literary history on de Man's principles? I do not think that anyone has done it yet. In this regard his shift is indeed typical of two decades in which the displacement or revitalization of literary history has been promised but not performed. Even the most thoughtful efforts to imagine a more theoretically sophisticated history tend to point to a promised land they have yet to enter.

Meanwhile good literary histories still bumble on. For the impossibility of writing them does not stop scholars from trying and often succeeding. Despite the uncertainty of its terms and its grounds, the writing of literary history remains a fascinating and deeply satisfying practice. It provides an opportunity to imagine how past times imagined themselves and even to intervene in shaping the past. That satisfaction does not seem about to go out of style. Nor does the weightlessness of "literary" values or the hopelessness of grasping "history" as a whole discourage a thousand modest and useful ventures. Those ventures are all around us. If contemporary literary historians have trouble deciding what texts to exclude from their field, they show their ingenuity by turning up texts to put in. One after another, forgotten texts return, and with them the lives of the unsung people who wrote them. They will survive when the manifestos have faded. The reward of reading literary history at this moment is not a sense of knowing where we are but a sense of surprise, delight, and the unexpected—like finding a trout in the milk.

[12] De Man, *Allegories of Reading* (New Haven, Conn.: Yale University Press, 1979), ix.

LITERARY HISTORY: SOME ROADS NOT (YET) TAKEN

Virgil Nemoianu

I t is more frightening than amusing to observe the relentless scholarly stampede once a theoretical paradigm has been erected, along with the blind allegiance that it comes to command. Thus the left Nietzscheanism currently hegemonic in the literature departments of North America, with its postulate that adversarial power is the center of human beings and relationships, has generated an enormous amount of research and has insinuated itself into virtually all of our reflections on literature, sometimes hampering other kinds of critical reading. It is in the nature of things that a good many of these materials are futile, while some may even come to seem ludicrous or unethical.

A good parallel to such paradigm worship is the following. In the last four decades (in North America and elsewhere), vast resources in economics, sociology, and political science were applied to explore the best strategies for transition from "capitalism" to "socialism," or to devise paths for some convergence of the two. All this research effort was predicated on the proposition that Leninist-type societies were viable and justifiable constructs. Literally no research at all was dedicated to transitions from "socialism" *to* "capitalism"; indeed the mere exploration of such a possibility was sternly frowned upon by both intellectuals and officialdom. When, within a few short years, the illusion of a tenable utopian collectivism collapsed, hundreds of millions of people (not only in Eurasia but also in Africa and South America) found themselves devoid of the most elementary kind of guidance in coping with transition and progress and guiltlessly sentenced to uninformed, groping, blundering empiricism.

It seems chillingly probable that the academic complacency in a world of "revolutionary" ivory towers in the humanities will have similar results. The humanities, as currently conducted, leave individuals and groups (above all minorities and postcolonial societies) disarmed and helpless in the face of emancipatory change and of its real, cruel traumas. They fail at precisely the tasks they ostensibly pursue—preserving otherness, maintaining a dialectic of local textures against unifying and homogenizing pressures—and they show themselves incapable of devising an authentic criticism of society.

Professional ethics should, of course, impel some of us to ruminate on the feasibility of a new orientation for the humanities, but this is not my purpose here. I will simply outline some thoughts on alternatives to paradigm worship in literary history.

1. Multidimensional realities. It has been widely noted that the breakdown of New Criticism and of the premise of aesthetic intrinsicality did not bring with it a disappearance of textual analysis. On the contrary, it enhanced and intensified the dissective urge up to deconstructive dimensions (a super New Criticism). Likewise, the subsidence of the Marxist family of thought generated an intensified historicism: a blending of the infinitesimal detail (or the insignificant context) with the grand unified theory, often under the sign of (how shall I say this?) aesthetic whimsicality. This, as I see it, is what we call New Historicism, an enterprise behind which one always feels a slightly nervous grasping for a vanished certainty. Surely, it ought to be possible to provide a somewhat more balanced formula, that is, to place ourselves in an area equidistant from these two kinds of (almost morbid) intensification.

Human beings, under whichever shape history or geography presents them to us, are founded upon, and have to deal with, a few common tensions or polarities, among them male versus female, old versus young, individual versus group (or society), self versus other, Godhead versus creatureliness, inborn versus acquired (and/or imagined) dimensions.[1] Simply keeping this indisputable fact in mind (without

---

[1] I take a page from George Steiner's splendid *Antigones* (1984; rpt., Oxford: Oxford University Press, 1986), 234–67.

necessarily dwelling too much upon it) can protect us from the exces-
sive burdening of *one* single oppositional axis with the entirety of
human existence (e.g., the merely intersocial, the "Never trust any-
body over thirty" of yesteryear, gendering as of today, and others yet)
or with all textual options. An initiative in literary history, more than a
merely critical piece, ought to incorporate these multiple polarities
(or, to lower my pretensions farther, to indicate an awareness of them);
otherwise it will end up by quickening its own obsolescence.

The discourse of public communication media is based upon binary
adversariality, both in its relation to most other public institutions and in
its own rhetoric. Binary modes of thinking are deleterious in many ways,
but they also clearly respond to certain contemporary social needs. By
extrapolating from this type of media discourse and trying to replicate it,
however, our profession loses the nuance, complexity, and thickly layered
organization that enable it or justify its existence in the first place. Any
genuine exercise in scholarly reflection, with all its qualifying, evasive, and
refining strategies, subsists only as a repudiation (or call it an undermin-
ing) of public media communicative acts, even though in the long run it
may help rather than wound the right functioning of the latter.

2. Cultural morphology. This is a mode on which authors as different as the early Jameson and the later Raymond Williams could at least
in part agree with Spengler and Friedell, with Sengle and Kenner, with
Taine and Van Wyck Brooks. The obvious advantage of the method is
that it allows for ample tumbling space to the multiple negotiations
and metamorphoses of discourses and behaviors without necessarily
privileging one factor over the other.

But there are two preconditions. One is that cultural morphology,
to avoid becoming tedious and mechanical, must be quickened by
asserting once in a while the diagnostic and therapeutic role of literature inside a given cultural model. I am optimistic enough to believe
that literariness can be posited both as the mere symptom of a socio-
cultural matrix and (more arrogantly) as its playful raison d'être: creation as the genetic code of human existence.

The other precondition is the abundance of contextualization, on
which, in principle, everybody agrees. And yet, what we get in practice
is a kind of utopian allegory: what if a state of affairs obtained where
the literary was an immediate consequence of socioeconomic materi-

ality (power urges and economic and/or sexual acquisitiveness)? The veritable contexts of literary activity are, of course, different, whether negative (shame, fear, envy, and competition) or positive (cognition and contemplation, generosity and gratuitousness, play and unsuppressible creativity). Fashions and mentalities, giddy imitations, scientific hearsay, religious impulses, the grammar of sentiments, arbitrary subjectivity, hazy personal ambitions—these are the amniotic waters of the literary text. Bare socioeconomic and political-ideological events or attitudes are at one remove, and they are mediated, as well as (usually) massively distorted, by these turbulent immediate contexts.

3. Cognition over coercion. Is it true that, as some historians of science say, humans are at bottom information-gathering and information-processing entities? Is it true at least in part? Can we read the history of mankind as a narrative of epistemological accumulation, expansion, and growth? I do not know the answer to these questions, but I do know that they are taken quite seriously in some quarters. If so, a literary history (one at least!) that treated literature as the effort to package and transmit cognitive materials would be quite exciting. Umberto Eco has argued eloquently that the function of literature is to cultivate faculties such as perceptual alertness, rapid induction, the ability to construct hypotheses and posit possible worlds, moral sophistication, linguistic proficiency, and value awareness.[2] I would go a little farther and claim that the actual transmission of information (learning) in palatable forms would also be part of such a putative history.

Putative? In some of the most exciting and promising critical writing (in America, in France, in Germany also, I believe), literature and science (sometimes infused with eclectic spirituality) already interact and teach each other: Michel Serres, Henri Atlan, Frederick Turner, Katherine Hayles, William Paulson, Mihai Spariosu, and Paisley Livingston are just some of the names that come to mind.[3] I find in many

[2] Eco, *The Role of the Reader: Explorations in the Semiotics of Texts* (Bloomington: Indiana University Press, 1979). See the comments of Thomas Pavel, *Fictional Worlds* (Cambridge, Mass.: Harvard University Press, 1986), 141.

[3] See, for example, Turner, *Beauty: The Value of Values* (Charlottesville: University Press of Virginia, 1992); Hayles, *Chaos Bound: Orderly Disorder in Contemporary Literature and Science* (Ithaca, N.Y.: Cornell University Press, 1990); and Paulson, *The Noise of Culture* (Ithaca, N.Y.: Cornell University Press, 1989).

of these critics a certain joyous agreement with the world and an exuberant sassy usage of its surplus of meanings. But will this history not be just another "utopian allegory," another reductive game, merely hypothesizing on a state of affairs in which the beautiful is subservient to the true, rather than to the good, as in sociopolitical criticism? Not having read it yet, we have no way of knowing; perhaps it will, perhaps it will not. Presumably an epistemological history of literature will not shut out an awareness of the multiple definitional axes of our common humanity. Ernest Gellner writes precisely of the ways in which cognition, coercion, and production influence and interfere with each other.[4] There is no reason why a variant of his approach could not exist in literary history also.

4. Reciprocity and gift making. An even more radical departure from current practices of literary history and criticism would be to interpret the gesture of literary production not primarily as part of the "market" or of "social command," but as an archaic survival of an earlier type of socioeconomic relationship based upon reciprocity and gift making. (This would correspond to Karl Polanyi's first stage or type of economy.)[5] Similar suggestions have been made by very different critics, from Wayne Booth (the friendship metaphor for books) to Raimonda Modiano, or to the intricate and detailed model of Georges Bataille.[6] This approach has solid factual bases in the large literature of direct address (dedications of poems and other works, the I-you insertions in works of fictions and others, etc.). It is not difficult to imagine a more general model of literary history and criticism in which writing is deliberately taken as a gift to others (friends, "the neighbor," "the Other," or "mankind"), or as an exercise in generosity, and where this feature is energetically foregrounded. In such a reading the theme of communication (reaching out to those known and those unknown alike) interlaces in paradoxical and sweet ways with the theme of love.

---

[4] Gellner, *Plough, Sword, and Book: The Structure of Human History* (Chicago: University of Chicago Press, 1988), is a truly seminal work as yet little read by humanities scholars. Gellner uses terms such as *predation* or the more habitual *political power* alternatively with *coercion*.

[5] Polanyi, *The Great Transformation* (1944; rpt., Boston: Beacon, 1985).

[6] See Jean-Michel Heimonet, *Le Mal à l'œuvre: Georges Bataille et l'écriture du sacrifice* (Marseilles: Parenthèses, 1986).

Literary history would be on the one hand the record of loving gestures, but on the other, critically, an exercise in love (whether as mere Diltheyan *Einfühlung* or as Susan Sontag's "erotics"),[7] which could become the preferred avenue for text cognition. The difference between love and the possessive, self-gratifying "desire" need not be elaborated here, I trust. The former as opposed to the latter is endowed precisely with those connotations of disinterestedness that are spurned by a good part of our academic hierarchies. Values such as gratitude and praise, politeness and attention, would receive their due, and the substantiality of leisure could be reconsidered.

5. Taste. There is, of course, something defiantly and vexingly old-fashioned or sentimental in the idea of giftedness, of "love," and of literature as survival of an older, discarded phase of human evolution. But why not? If anything, such a viewing mode can only be sharpened and vindicated in light of the widely circulating postulates of otherness and marginality. (David Perkins alludes to this mode of thinking in the last and best chapter of a recent book, and I myself have outlined it elsewhere.)[8] Undoubtedly, even a jaded public overburdened with information might sit up and listen to a literary history dedicated to bringing out, without squeamishness, without resentment, the counterhistorical and the counterprogressive action of literary discourses.

The approach can be defended, briefly, as follows. The thickness of history, its substantiality, can be rendered only by acknowledging contrast and opposition. There is no more striking opposition to the ideological topoi of the present than the reading of Milton and Dante, for instance. By the same token, the education for otherness can find no more excellent foundation than a glance at the redoubtable values of aesthetic pastness. If multiplicity and adversarial virtues are to be cherished and cultivated, as essential preconditions for the improved polities of the future, then it is precisely the dialectics of the unlikable and of the counterprogressive that must be studied and practiced. A

---

[7] Sontag, *Against Interpretation* (New York: Farrar, Straus and Giroux, 1966), 3–14.

[8] Perkins, *Is Literary History Possible?* (Baltimore, Md.: Johns Hopkins University Press, 1992), 184–86; and Nemoianu, *A Theory of the Secondary: Literature, Progress, and Reaction* (Baltimore, Md.: Johns Hopkins University Press, 1989), 3–25, 173–203.

"politically correct" attitude, honestly thought through to its true ends and complete implications, will result in a careful and loving study of the reactionary, not as an enemy but as an indispensable co-actor.[9] By contrast, denying the dignity and the autonomy of the past (erasing the outrageous pastness of the past) is a very chancy enterprise: it opens the door wide to any and all denials of otherness. Finally, a counterhistorical approach has the advantage of being less "elitist" and more democratic, by extending rights of participation (ideally voting rights) to societies and human structures of the past.

6. Hypocrisy. I am not much interested in or worried about the representation value of literary history (or of any history, for that matter), of its mimetic merits, of its "possibility," or veridicity. Like any good neo-Leibnizian, I take it for granted that in a strong and definitive sense such pristine veridicity is quite impossible, but that in a much weaker epistemological sense (as plausibility, probability, credibility) it is readily available to us.

I also look with some fatalistic indifference toward the overly feared and denounced prejudgments of each and every literary historian. Recognition of prior decisions does not prod me toward hopeless relativism and embracing of blunt ideological constraints, but rather provides me with arguments in favor of such old-fashioned things as empathy, taste, and common sense. A literary history founded upon common sense will be no less (and no more!) biased than other histories, no less reliant upon gaps, guesswork, and arbitrary formulations. It will instead have the compensatory advantage of talent, by which I mean an ability to perceive and to process associations and analogies more quickly, that is, to allow one's mind to function in ways derived from and more germane to the dynamics of literary production itself. In this sense, much like the skills and abilities of Olympic champions, critical talent is nothing more than the interface between some innate endowments and purposeful hard effort.

I am fully aware of the usual objection that what we call common sense and taste are nothing but internalized sets of prejudices and

---

[9] In all fairness it should be said that it is usually Marxist critics—Adorno, Bloch, and more emphatically Fredric Jameson, for example, in *Fables of Aggression* (Berkeley: University of California Press, 1979) and *The Political Unconscious* (London: Methuen, 1981)—who have advocated and/or practiced this line of inquiry.

received, unexamined values, but I respond to it in two ways. First, any-body who thinks that intuitive, "synthetical" responses of the mind are uncritical and simple betrays a woeful ignorance of how the mind works. Intuitive and "irrational" reactions are based upon thick and multifarious internal processings and are not less but more likely to be complex and dialectical than the "unpacked" and reductive explica-tions of "critical" reasoning. Second, assuming that ideological bias is inevitable, it still remains true that an openly and cynically acknowl-edged tendentiousness in the guise of enforceable dogmatic impera-tives is ethically inferior to and rhetorically less efficient than a coyly disguised or indirect form of prejudgment. The management of insin-cere discourse imposes refinements and counterbalances that limit the scope of pure ideological prejudice and allow somewhat better access to factuality. Illusion, indirection, and, yes, hypocrisy can often be beneficial factors.

Should literary history be subordinated to the goals of social action; should it be a brave and disciplined soldier in the battle of social indoctrination, as is so often suggested to us nowadays? From all I said above it is clear that I do not believe so. Still, I do not find it hard to concede that ideological options ought to be part of any comprehen-sive reflection on literary history, albeit *only* a part of it. If such a reflec-tion or debate is to be fruitful at all, it will have to be conducted in ways that are (mutually) beneficial to the discourses of postmodern societies, rather than to bow either to the compulsions of utopian desire or to a worldview in which the insistent presencing (no, the ontologizing) of negativity ensures a hopeless disorientation.

Among the circumstances of historical postmodernity, two are most pertinent to the discourses that shape literary history. One is the globalization of human affairs. A "being with other cultures" makes the Western literary past more rather than less relevant and immedi-ate, and here is why. An autistic Western civilization intent upon splen-did isolation and supremacy could well be indifferent to Homer and Chaucer and deal instead with its own contemporaneity. By contrast, a Western civilization aware of its synchronicity with and responsibility toward the southern and larger tiers of our planet (from Islam and China to sub-Saharan Africa and Catholic/pagan Latin America) cannot possibly throw overboard a literary history whose concern was never phallogocentrism, of course, but rather the pains, joys, and dilemmas of emancipation and transition. Attempts to allay the brutality of progress, dramatic enactments of options and scenarios in negotiating change—this is what the key patterns in Western literary history engage their readers in. (That is also, and overwhelmingly, though in infinite variations, the sociopsychological theme of non-Western and postcolonial societies.) Willfully to disremember them is to deliver younger generations (in the West, no less than globally) gagged and bound into the hands of the present and the future. My impression (and I wish I would be proved wrong) is that current discourses in literary history and academic criticism do nothing to soften the sandpaper harshness of postmodern history and to empower the individual in any transactions with it.

The second relevant ideological circumstance is the battle around the proper definition of liberalism. Even though it has not yet been noticed by many in literature departments, the major political-economic debate in the real world is no longer waged among those whom Henri de Lubac once called "the spiritual posterity of Joachim of Fiore" (as it has been throughout much of the twentieth century).[10] We are dealing now with the spiritual posterity of Montesquieu. The conflict unfolds on a much narrower strip of ideological land, and it has to do with setting the landmarks and formulating the values of liberalism. Can the tradition that goes from Burke to Burckhardt be included in it? Should we bet on Mises or on Polanyi? Can Rawls or Nozick be a better advisor? Are Rousseau, are Herder and Cobbett indispensable to the canon of liberalism? How well is Tocqueville compatible with John Stuart Mill? Have Edward Shils and Stephen Holmes anything in common? These are some of the real ideological

---

[10] Lubac argues that modern secular utopianisms, as well as totalitarian, social, and revolutionary doctrines, derive from Joachim's twelfth-century philosophy of history (*La Postérité spirituelle de Joachim de Flore*, 2 vols. [Paris: Lethielleux, 1981]). The view that utopianism and totalitarianism are essentially secularized versions of religious vision is widely held in the field by quite various people, such as Karl Löwith, J. L. Talmon, and Karl Mannheim, Frank and Fritzi Manuel, Thomas Molnar, and Norman Cohn, to name a few. Lubac differs from them chiefly in assigning the role of direct and essential source to Joachim's theory of the "third empire" (the phase, or the *Reich*, of the Holy Spirit).

questions of the 1990s, when we are all inhabitants of a debating space outlined by Weber and Durkheim. At this point, it is abundantly obvious that Western literature in its evolution, which has been dealing with these issues all along (not only in the last two hundred years but, for the careful reader, earlier), becomes—because of this second circumstance also—highly relevant. A literary history in which Fenimore Cooper, Manzoni, and Goethe, Germaine de Staël, Scott, and Chateaubriand are principal actors is one that can intervene creatively in the real ideological debates of the late twentieth century. The insights of literary history are enormous, and they can nurture and guide sociopolitical quandaries toward fuller, more flexible, and more compassionate social responses.

WHAT IS THE HISTORY
OF LITERATURE?

Jonathan Arac

The Object of Literary History

The history of literature is part of history "proper" and therefore is defined by two crucial features. The first is referential falsifiability. Unlike some other kinds of work, history is not judged exclusively by internal coherences, such as those of logic, method, or tone. It is considered legitimate to relate materials textually present within the history to materials textually absent from it, and there are (contested) standards of correctness by which such relations are discussed. The second feature is the fundamental doubleness marked by such formulations as those of Adam Ferguson (history results from human action but not from human choice) or Karl Marx (people make their own history but not under conditions of their own choosing). This doubleness produces such oppositions as agency and circumstantiality, subject and structure, humans and institutions. These first two crucial features have already revealed a second fundamental doubleness. The history of literature involves both historiography ("subject".) and historicality ("object"?).

As historiography, the history of literature is an activity in the present. It is determined, that is (as Raymond Williams has glossed the term), both pressured and limited, by its readership and its predeces-

This little piece owes large debts, especially to Paul Alpers and the Townsend Center for the Humanities at the University of California, Berkeley; to Winfried Fluck and the John F. Kennedy Institute for North American Studies at the Free University of Berlin; to Lauren Berlant and the MLA Division on Nineteenth-Century American Literature; and to Marshall Brown.

sors.[1] The predecessors have prepared a readership to greet any new work with certain expectations, and they have provided the historian with certain conventions by, or against, which to work. The Harvard *New History of French Literature* (1989), for example, covers 1,150 years of history in 1,150 pages, but it is not a homogeneous chronicle. In an emphatically meaningful tilting, the midpoint of its page count comes over 900 years on, near the beginning of the French Revolution. More strikingly, each of its 199 short essays is cued to a date and headline. This self-consciously postmodern organization presupposes a solidly established tradition of French literary history that gives the implicit background against which the new undertaking is comprehensible in its difference.

The historiography of literature is also determined by its materials. Much of the long-standing discontent—from René Wellek to Paul de Man—with traditional, positivist and philological, literary histories comes from their failure actively to read the materials they name and order, even though the materials, as literature, demand to be read, not only cited. The agenda, as I understand it, of what Ralph Cohen taught a generation to call "new literary history" comes from various attempts to bring reading into the historical process, whether in the mode of integration or disruption. In the history of literature the renegotiation of the canon links determination by audience and predecessors with determination by materials. Readers expect to see certain things treated, while the historian departs from predecessors by finding new materials to be treated. In recent years, we expect such innovations to be organized in relation to gender or race, but Alastair Fowler's *Short History of English Literature* surprised readers by its emphasis on the persistent force of the georgic mode.

From the perspective of historicality, a crucial feature of the history of literature is that its object itself is historical. Consider the difference between political history and the history of democracy, between economic history and the history of capitalism, and so between cultural history and the history of literature. In the last two

---

[1] This sole acknowledgment stands for a great debt to Raymond Williams's work. See especially "Base and Superstructure in Marxist Cultural Theory," in *Problems in Materialism and Culture* (London: Verso, 1980), 31–49.

decades it has become increasingly important to acknowledge that literature and the literary are themselves historical transformations, rather than either fulfillments or invariants. This acknowledgment has typically been intended to combat the idealization of literature; it has had the somewhat paradoxical effect of empowering literature by treating it as a means of historical agency, not merely as intransitive. This recent turn to reading literature in(to) history stands against the philological tradition of reading history out of literature, which in diverse ways made possible the work not only of Curtius and Spitzer but also of much Anglo-American formalism, from the New Criticism to the Yale critics. These close-reading, supposed formalists all also generated historical claims from their readings.[2]

The Shape of a Literary History

These preliminary observations help focus my own recent work as a historian of literature. A literary history cannot simply find its objects and lay them out in order. It must actively define and organize its materials, and there are strategies, problems, and consequences that arise from the various possible choices made in organizing. I have completed a portion of the new *Cambridge History of American Literature* on mid-nineteenth-century prose narrative.[3] The intended readership was defined by the publisher as global and general, entailing certain stylistic protocols (no footnotes, minimal use of technical terminology). The assigned topic of "prose narrative" was inspired in part by my own earlier work in interrelating the writing of history and fiction,[4]

---

[2] For one example, see Cleanth Brooks's position-defining "Literary Criticism," criticized by theorists because it is simply a reading of Andrew Marvell's "Horatian Ode." Brooks concludes, "If we do read the poem successfully, the critic may on occasion be able to make a return on his debt to the historian" (*English Institute Essays, 1946: The Critical Significance of Biographical Evidence; The Methods of Literary Studies* [New York: Columbia University Press, 1947], 155).

[3] Jonathan Arac, "Narrative Forms," in *Prose Writings, 1820–1865*, vol. 2 of *The Cambridge History of American Literature*, ed. Sacvan Bercovitch (Cambridge: Cambridge University Press, 1995), 605–777.

[4] Jonathan Arac, *Commissioned Spirits: The Shaping of Social Motion in Dickens, Carlyle, Melville, and Hawthorne* (1979; rpt. with new preface, New York: Columbia University Press, 1989).

and it defined the materials in ways that offered important possibilities for difference from preceding accounts that focused attention on single authors, by means of chapters entitled "Hawthorne," "Poe," and "Melville."

In defining my procedures, the most important predecessor was the *Literary History of the United States* (1948), which links author, art, and nation, in an expressive identity with the historian and reader, by means of the first-person plural pronoun. Even the avowedly postmodern *Columbia Literary History of the United States* (1988; begun about the same time as the new *Cambridge History* but completed sooner) shares with the earlier *Literary History of the United States* and the original *Cambridge History of American Literature* (1917) the compositional model of twenty-page chapters titled either by topics or by authors. My work attempts to reshape the field of inquiry by taking a distance from the materials. Schematically, this distance is produced by four choices: to avoid the first-person plural; to make of the nation a problem rather than a presupposition and a goal; to take as the fundamental unit of intelligibility not the author but the generic system; and to chart the emergence of the literary as an event within the generic system which responds to specific problems of nationality.

Here is the plot of this piece of history. The starting point comes equally from Raymond Williams and Michel Foucault: it is the transformation of the notion of literature. In the late eighteenth century, *literature* meant all culturally valued writing, including what would now be distinguished as *nonfiction*, such as history, travel, philosophy, and science. By now, in the United States of the late twentieth century, the most widely accepted meaning of *literature*, as may be witnessed in innumerable bookstores nationwide, is fiction that does not fit any defined marketing genre (science fiction, western, crime, romance, etc.). In the U.S., mid-nineteenth-century prose narrative was a crucial place for the emergence of a new meaning—imaginative belles lettres—that is now becoming residual. As a result of this transformation, by which literature came to be understood as countergeneric and as existing in an imaginative space distinct from that of publicly shared life, it is now expected that literary culture and national culture will stand at a tense distance from each other. This historically limited conception of literature as a "world elsewhere" often makes it difficult to understand the value of works that enact differing relations to the national.

The event that shapes my literary history of mid-nineteenth-century American prose narrative is the emergence, around 1850, of works, preeminently *The Scarlet Letter* and *Moby-Dick*, that still count as *literature* for many readers of the late twentieth century. Other important prose narratives of the time, such as *Uncle Tom's Cabin*, still trouble many readers because there is no valued conceptual category into which they fit ("It's not literature, it's propaganda"). The history's fourth chapter addresses the newly emerging genre of literary narrative. Chapters 1 through 3 define the competing, earlier generic types in relation to which the specificity of literary narrative may be understood, and chapter 5 sketches the fate of literary narrative in the period of its first emergence. Although literary narrative dominates late-twentieth-century views of this period, the works that are now valued did not establish themselves immediately, and the very genre of literary narrative almost disappeared in the intense national crisis of the Civil War.

The dominant narrative type that preceded literary narrative, and which continued to flourish after literary narrative had appeared, I call "national narrative." From the standpoint of America's present existence as an independent union, national narrative told the story of America's colonial beginnings and looked forward to its future as a model for the world. This story, which still has much force in the United States—but not in what is now considered *literature*—began to take fully articulated form around the presidency of Andrew Jackson. It could be told with equal power through fiction, especially in the work of Fenimore Cooper, beginning in the 1820s, and through history, especially in the work of George Bancroft, beginning in the 1830s. When it first took shape, there was no fully operative national culture. National narrative was part of the process by which the nation was forming itself, not merely a reflection of an accomplished fact, yet it defined the ground against which the other major narrative types stand out.

Articulated in contrast with national narrative, two important smaller types flourished and competed with it. First, in the 1830s, came what I call "local narratives." These are more restricted than national narrative, either geographically or in the scale of human experience that they deal with. Following the example of Washington Irving's New York sketches, local narratives include the "southwestern humorists," the northeastern tales of Nathaniel Hawthorne, and the works of Edgar Allan Poe, which began to define the city as a new American locale. In the 1840s, what I call "personal narratives" became prominent. Rather than the collectivity of a nation, these works foreground a single first-person narrator. Yet contrary both to Puritan tradition and to twentieth-century expectations, this "I" is a rather extroverted reporter, not so much exploring inwardness as bringing news from the margins of the dominant culture. This form includes work by travelers, such as Herman Melville, Richard Henry Dana, and Francis Parkman, and also narratives by escaped slaves, such as Frederick Douglass and Harriet Jacobs.

Literary narrative emerged around 1850, together with a political crisis over slavery which threatened the Union's existence and produced a compromise intended to subdue controversy. At this moment, Hawthorne and Melville newly emphasized certain elements from their own earlier work and that of Poe and set their work apart from national narrative. The "Custom-House" introduction to *The Scarlet Letter* illustrates this distancing from national concerns. In contrast to national narrative, but also to local and personal narratives—all three forms both addressed and reflected the concerns of everyday public life—the literary narrative of *The Scarlet Letter* turned away to develop a freely imaginative space. This turn of American literary narrative was not unique. Since the late eighteenth century, romantic writers in England and Germany had elaborated a new understanding of the place that highly skilled writing occupies within a culture. Conceptions such as *originality, genius,* and *imagination* defined literature as independent from the public world rather than interrelated with it, and the notions of *psychology* and *development* defined new areas of attention and new techniques.

Such works not only differed from but seemed also to transcend and, implicitly, to criticize the world of common, public life. Yet their critical authority depended on their limitation to elite audiences, esoteric subjects, and indirect means. The possible glory of forming a "world elsewhere" through writing was often felt by the authors themselves as the deadening activity of repetitive, solitary labor. This moment in which the "literary" writer was redefined as an artist marked a crisis in the relation of narrative to its public, for the work of the artist was understood to draw its primary value from its private relation to the writer's self.

The fifth chapter is entitled "Crisis of Literary Narrative and Consolidation of National Narrative." This chapter immediately follows extended discussions of *The Scarlet Letter* and *Moby-Dick* at the conclusion of chapter 4, "Literary Narrative." Chapter 5 begins with a section on national narrative in 1851, which treats at some length Francis Parkman's *Conspiracy of Pontiac* and then *Uncle Tom's Cabin*. The next section, "Uncle Tom's Echoes," argues the impact of Stowe's alternative national narrative across the generic system: on personal narratives such as Frederick Douglass's *My Bondage and My Freedom* and Harriet Jacobs's *Incidents in the Life of a Slave Girl*; on local narratives such as Rebecca Harding Davis's "Life in the Iron Mills"; and on literary narratives such as Melville's *Pierre*.

I have argued that organization has consequences, and here is one example. This sequence across the two chapters, some twenty thousand words, places in a single plane of discourse and a single argumentative frame, at comparable levels of attention and detail, works that have, I believe, been separated for the whole history of American culture, so different have their generic and canonical values seemed. From this result, other results may follow as an audience encounters something that runs counter to previous practice and to expectation. I anticipate controversy from readers who will charge me with promiscuously mingling masterpieces with matter of purely historical significance, and from readers who will charge me with homogenizing works of very different political valences. When I have sketched my approach in lectures and conferences, aesthetic readers have felt that I favored the national, while political readers have felt that I favored the literary. These responses encourage my hope that I have produced, through such unease, a historical distance from these categories which may aid in producing alternatives for us now.

Literary Historical Memory: The Case of *Huckleberry Finn*

One alternative has been to rethink the cultural place of what I take to
be by far the most strongly canonized work of American literature,
Huckleberry Finn. This rethinking springs from the distinction, which I
first developed in the work discussed above on antebellum narrative,
between national and literary narratives. For literary history, in defining
a relation of our present to a past, functions as a mode of social memory, and the different generic categories define differing modes of
memory, as they specify what values we associate a work with in remembering it and what other materials we link it with in our remembrance.

We remember *Huckleberry Finn*, even as the book itself seems an
act of memory. *Huckleberry Finn* is the "most remembered" work of
American fiction; among the few hypercanonized texts, it is at the
top;[5] and its subject matter is, to take a term from Shakespeare editors, Mark Twain's "memorial reconstruction" of the small-town and
river life Samuel Clemens knew in the 1840s and 1850s. These two
memories are connected. One reason *Huckleberry Finn* has become
canonically remembered is the shape its remembering gives to the
largest ongoing felt problem in the modern history of the United
States: What human relations, and what legal relations, are possible
and desirable between people socially defined as different in "race"?

From its publication in 1885 into the 1930s, *Huckleberry Finn* was
greatly admired by leaders of advanced literary practice and opinion
(for example, William Dean Howells, Sherwood Anderson, and Ernest
Hemingway), but it became a universal school text only after the Second World War. The first college-text edition of *Huckleberry Finn* was
introduced by Lionel Trilling, who opened a wholly new interpretive
field when he characterized Huck and Jim as forming a "community of
saints."[6] I take the meaning of the new moral value thus attributed to

---

[5] On hypercanonization see Jonathan Arac, "Nationalism, Hypercanonization,
and *Huckleberry Finn*," in *National Identities and Post-Americanist Narratives*, ed. Donald
E. Pease (Durham, N.C.: Duke University Press, 1994), 14–33. This piece and my
observations on Twain below both contribute to my book in progress, *"Huckleberry
Finn" and the Functions of Criticism*, forthcoming in Frank Lentricchia's American
Writers series.

[6] Trilling, introduction to *The Adventures of Huckleberry Finn* (New York: Rine-
hart, 1948), ix. The authority and visibility of this introduction were both greatly

Huckleberry Finn to be the following claim: "We Americans have spiritually solved any problems involved in blacks and whites living together as free human beings, and we had done so already by the 1880s; all that remains is to work out the details."

Using the organizing generic terms developed in the *Cambridge History*, I judge that this appropriation of *Huckleberry Finn* makes it into a national narrative but that Twain wrote it as a literary narrative. As a literary narrative *Huckleberry Finn* did not directly address the concerns of its time with race and nation, as for example George Washington Cable did in his national narrative *The Grandissimes* (1880), and precisely the obliquity of *Huckleberry Finn*'s relation to its own time has made it more readily amenable to our time's reshaping remembering of it. Such reshaping remembering, what I call the "nationalization of literary narrative," is a tremendously useful ideological practice for empowering a national first-person subject—the "we Americans" that I ventriloquized in the preceeding paragraph deeming themselves to have spiritually solved the problems of race. The wish for such a discursive location, a national-cultural first-person plural subject, can be found across a wide range of commentators on the current life of the United States, from the neoconservative English professor James Tuttleton to the liberal pragmatist post-philosopher Richard Rorty to the Ph.D. in history who is the Speaker of the U.S. House of Representatives.[7]

In its standing as "our" most beloved and admired book, *Huckleberry Finn* is not only a cultural treasure but a resource for power. It permits a nationally honored memory of slavery. Through an interpretive tradition now extending some fifty years, the enslavement of African Americans is associated with the morality, humor, and beautifully articulated vernacular voice attributed to Huck, rather than understood as an unspeakable horror that fractures both verbal regis-

---

enhanced through its republication as the essay "*Huckleberry Finn*" in Trilling's generation-defining collection *The Liberal Imagination: Essays on Literature and Society* (New York: Viking, 1950); it has also been frequently reprinted in anthologies of criticism on Twain as "The Greatness of *Huckleberry Finn*."

[7] See Tuttleton, "Rewriting the History of American Literature," *New Criterion*, November 1986, 1–12; Rorty, "The Unpatriotic Academy," *New York Times*, op-ed, 13 February 1994, 15; and "G.O.P.'s Rising Star in the House Pledges to Right the Wrongs of the Left," *New York Times*, 10 November, 1994, B3.

ters and linear emplotment, as in the gothic plot contortions of Faulkner or Morrison, whose prose adds lush extravagance, but also silence, to the register of plainspoken eloquence.

The dedication of *Beloved* to the "sixty million and more" asserts that the scale of inhumanity in the centuries-long, circumatlantic process by which Africans were enslaved and brought to the Americas fully merits comparison with that of the inhumanity practiced by twentieth-century totalitarian regimes, even though in the United States the overall conditions of life permitted enslaved African Americans to flourish demographically (a perspective that *Beloved* would tend to identify with the brutal figure of Schoolteacher). *Huckleberry Finn* has been put to work in the public culture of the United States as the attempt to transform haunt into idyll. Huck's decision in chapter 31, "All right, then, I'll *go* to hell," has been authoritatively read for decades as the cry not of a demon but of Trilling's saint, a holy fool.

That moment of decision, the most hypercanonical moment in *Huckleberry Finn*, is also the most powerful moment of memory in the book, for the decision is motivated by Huck's vivid recall of his times with Jim, set as counterweight to the voice of conscience, which speaks for the practices and values of a culture that regularly and resolutely enslaved African Americans. You may recall that conscience tells Huck, "There was the Sunday School; you could a gone to it; and if you'd a done it they'd a learnt you, there, that people as acts as I'd been acting about that nigger goes to everlasting fire." It's a strange kind of memory, for conscience tells Huck what he would have learned if he had gone to school, but apparently he knows anyway. Twain here offers a model of something that might be called "cultural memory." Such memory need not arise directly from the individual experience of the persons whose memory it nonetheless forms part of; it is an intimate part of the person, so much so that it may manifest itself unbidden, and yet it is a part that one may debate with or even override.

It seems necessary to underline the structure of this model because of recent, brilliantly provocative work that I value for having set itself to challenge the national-cultural first-person plural but that I also find misleading. Walter Benn Michaels has argued that the pluralist notion of culture, as introduced in the 1920s and long since a liberal, or even radical, dogma, logically is inseparable from the racism that it believes itself to overcome. For, he argues, only the fiction of race can effectively join me to past others in a "we."[8] The polemical force of Michaels's position depends on the utter discrediting of racism as a respectable intellectual position brought about by the revelation of Nazi crimes against humanity, the terrible and terrifying example that helped transform the terms on which *Huckleberry Finn* was valued in American culture, and which may help explain what is otherwise baffling, namely, why it should have been the Jewish Lionel Trilling whose essay marked this transformation.[9]

I believe that Michaels and I differ over issues of politics, as opposed to culture; over issues of identification (a process), as opposed to identity (a condition); over distinctions between the verb *to remember* and the noun *memory*; and over what I find his strangely all-or-nothing definition of culture; but his work further illustrates the intense and complex controversiality at stake in the discursive protocols of "we" and "us," a controversy I had already entered in deciding to avoid the first-person plural address of the 1948 *Literary History of the United States.*

The history of literature, in its own history, has been inseparable from the emergence of the modern nation-state around 1800 and the subsequent proliferation of nationalities-in-formation through collective scholarly and public practices that have produced national selves capable of being aware of their own, newly defined, shared accomplishments and heritages. The organizational and discursive choices I have made in constructing my literary history constitute an attempt, against the grain of both tradition and many current voices, to define a practice of literary history that can write about the United States without participating in the ideology of the "American."

---

[8] For the fundamental statement of this argument see Michaels, "Race into Culture: A Critical Genealogy of Cultural Identity," *Critical Inquiry* 18 (1992): 655–85. Michaels's essay in the current volume seems part of the same project.

[9] Only after completing this essay did I learn that a literature exists on Trilling and the Holocaust. See Emily Miller Budick, "The Holocaust and the Construction of Modern American Literary Criticism: The Case of Lionel Trilling" (Working Paper 61, John F. Kennedy Institute for North American Studies, University of Berlin, 1993).

The Once and
Future Middle Ages

R. Howard Bloch

The study of medieval literature and culture has never been more alive or at a more interestingly innovative stage. The institutional signs of a New Medievalism are everywhere: in the appointment of medievalists at major university centers, many of which remained without specialists in the Old French field after the deaths or retirements of the dominating philological figures in the forties, fifties, and sixties; in renewed interest among graduate students, many of whom are returning even to earlier questions having to do with the material conditions of the medieval text; in a number of recent scholarly gatherings pitched to new understandings of the Middle Ages or to plotting the future of medieval studies; in new book and monograph series; in the founding of scholarly journals like *Assays, Exemplaria, Médiévales,* and *Envoi* that are devoted to the Middle Ages; in special issues of established reviews like *Yale French Studies,* the *Romanic Review, Esprit Créateur, Littérature;* and—*mirable dictu* —in the recent appearance of an issue of *Speculum* devoted to the so-called New Philology.[1] Then, too, a renaissance of interest in the Middle Ages can be seen in the symptomatic self-consciousness that has begun to creep into the discipline. By this I mean a certain belated thinking about just what it means to study medieval culture in our own fin de siècle.

Questions that have in the past simply been taken for granted as being the immutable and natural defining issues of the field have begun to seem increasingly opaque. Indeed, those who write about the

---

[1] See Marina Brownlee, Kevin Brownlee, and Stephen G. Nichols, eds., *The New Medievalism* (Baltimore, Md.: Johns Hopkins University Press, 1991).

millennium between the Fall of Rome and the discovery of the New World have come more and more to see that their assumptions regarding this period are as historically determined by the framing perceptions of the last century as they are by the artifacts of the medievalist's study. In this the field of medieval studies is not alone but part of a larger movement: almost every discipline within the social sciences and the humanities is wallowing in the question of its origins. So, too, medievalists have begun to write the external history of the discipline from a perspective, or I should say perspectives, that would have been unthinkable twenty years ago. Here, one can identify several stages, which are in reality more logical than chronological.

The first stage can be seen in the attempt to write the history of medieval studies from within the perspective of the discipline itself, that is, from a point of view implying a minimum of distance between the historian and the object of study. The Iordan-Orr history of romance philology, of course, springs immediately to mind. Its highly narrative structure, based upon intellectual genealogies of who did their theses with whom, merely repeats the movement of the philologist's desire for origins, which, as I have maintained elsewhere, also mirrors medieval thinkers' own obsession with etymologies and genealogies. Janine Dakyns's long book on medievalism in nineteenth-century France, which includes the assimilation of medieval material in both primary literary works and criticism, and which seeks to define not a single but a multiplicity of Middle Ages according to the political motivations of particular classes and regimes, represents an important step beyond the old history.[2] So, too, the first chapter of Lee Patterson's recent book offers a more sophisticated version of Dakyns's undertaking within the realm of Middle English studies.[3]

A second stage implies, indeed is defined by, a recognition of and insistence upon a certain identity between the medieval period and our own. The disparate articles and books that have appeared and lectures delivered over the last twenty years are united by a certain sense of wonder at the discovery of how familiar the Middle Ages seem

[2] Dakyns, *The Middle Ages in French Literature, 1851–1900* (London: Oxford University Press, 1973).

[3] Patterson, *Negotiating the Past: The Historical Understanding of Medieval Literature* (Madison: University of Wisconsin Press, 1987).

within the context of the contemporary discourses of cultural criticism, and thus by a sense of relief that those who studied medieval texts were not as irrelevant to the present as many of our own teachers perhaps had hoped we would be.[4] Many of us were no longer content merely to hide behind the foil of philological expertise, which for decades in the academy had served not as a tool to make medieval literature accessible but as a prophylactic to prevent the reading of such works and thus to inhibit dialogue between medievalists and specialists in other fields.[5]

Finally, for some time now a number of medieval historians, art historians, philologists, and specialists of almost every national literature have felt the need for some more sustained external history of the various disciplines of medieval studies, which, in fact, is already under way. Brian Stock has written a brilliant article on Erich Auerbach; Hans Aarsleff, one on Joseph Bédier; Hans Ulrich Gumbrecht, a ground-breaking essay on Friedrich Diez, Gaston Paris, and the development of romance philology in both Germany and France.[6] In 1989 Bernard Cerquiglini published a monograph-length synthesis of the relation between medieval textual practice and medievalism.[7] This phase of the New Medievalism thus places in historical context the cultural appropriations of the study of the Middle Ages as it has been

---

[4] See Eugene Vance, "The Modernity of the Middle Ages in the Future: Remarks on a Recent Book," *Romanic Review* 64 (1973): 140–51; Peter Haidu, "Towards a Problematics of Alterity: Making It (New) in the Middle Ages," *Diacritics* (1974): 1–10; Hans Robert Jauss, *Alterität und Modernität der mittelalterlichen Literatur* (Munich: Fink, 1977); Stephen G. Nichols, "A Poetics of Historicism? Recent Trends in Medieval Literary History," *Medievalia et Humanistica* 8 (1977): 77–102; Paul Zumthor, "The Modernity of the Middle Ages" (Lectures given at the Pompidou Center, Paris, January 1979); Alexandre Leupin, "The Middle Ages, the Other," *Diacritics* (1983): 22–31; and R. Howard Bloch, *Etymologies and Genealogies: A Literary Anthropology of the French Middle Ages* (Chicago: University of Chicago Press, 1983).

[5] On this question see Lee Patterson, "On the Margin: Postmodernism, Ironic History, and Medieval Studies," *Speculum* 65 (1990): 87–108.

[6] Stock, "Literary Discourse and the Social Historian," *New Literary History* 8 (1977): 183–94; Aarsleff, "Scholarship and Ideology: Joseph Bédier's Critique of Romantic Medievalism," in *Historical Studies and Literary Criticism*, ed. and intro. Jerome J. McGann (Madison: University of Wisconsin Press, 1985), 93–113; and Gumbrecht, "Un souffle d'Allemagne ayant passé: Friedrich Diez, Gaston Paris, and the Genesis of National Philologies," *Romance Philology* 40 (1986): 1–37.

[7] Cerquiglini, *Eloge de la variante: histoire critique de la philologie* (Paris: Seuil, 1989).

practiced since the middle of the eighteenth century. And this seems
to point to what I see as a subject worthy of still further study.

One could imagine, for example, a history of medievalisms aimed
at exploring the ways in which medieval studies have been determined
by the specific ideological or local, nationalistic or religious, political or
personal, interests—including the class, race, and gender—of those
who have shaped them. Such a history might consider questions normally excluded from the canon of traditional or of high medieval studies, like connoisseurship, professionalization, and popularization; the
relation of philology to other disciplines and to semiology and linguistics; the role of collections, journals, bibliographies, textual series, and
authoritative manuals like the *Grundriss*. It might include the effects of
presuppositions about paleography upon editions and hence upon the
interpretation of medieval texts; important figures, schools, and movements; defining questions and debates (that would not simply rehash
the terms but contextualize the stakes and motivations) and even the
scholarly quarrel as a form of communication conceived to be productive of knowledge; the logical, philosophical, epistemological, and
even moral presuppositions implicit to the notion of knowledge
about the Middle Ages; the effects of anecdote, rumor, personality,
historical events; the role of academic, nationalistic, religious, and
professional associations and institutions (including the university,
the Société Arthurienne, the Société de Roncesvals, or the Medieval
Academy); the place of secular theology in medieval studies; the role
of congresses and seminars; the politics of specialization, of edition,
and of reviewing; the relation of medieval studies to other disciplines
within the liberal arts curriculum. Then, too, one might seek to eval-
uate the current rationale for the study of the Middle Ages as well as
to assess the potential effects of the study of medieval concepts, theories, and texts upon contemporary criticism, upon the canon, and
upon such modern disciplines as psychoanalysis and semiotics—the
work of Jacques Lacan and Umberto Eco, for example. In what ways
can the study of the Middle Ages teach us to historicize the field of critical theory?[8]

[8] Stephen G. Nichols and I have edited such a volume, *Medievalism and the Modernist Temper: On the Discipline of Medieval Studies* (Stanford, Calif.: Stanford University
Press, forthcoming).

Which is another way of measuring the extent to which our own strategies and desires determine the questions we pose and the answers we give. Medieval studies, again, is merely part of a larger trend within both the humanities and the social sciences, which entails some recognition of the specificity of the inquiring subject in what has been since the Renaissance an enterprise assuming the disinterestedness of knowledge, the objectivity of philological science.

Along this route one can identify a landmark in Paul Zumthor's *Speaking of the Middle Ages*, which not only treats eloquently of what it means to study the medieval past in the twentieth century but does so, unapologetically, in the first person singular: "This is not a stylistic device, but an intellectual necessity. . . . It is not a question of speaking about oneself, still less of retreating into a den of memories. It is a matter of choosing . . . the most directly accessible reference point."[9] Zumthor's personalized voice is justified by what he rightly points to as a crisis of method in the social sciences, especially in the field of medieval studies, coupled to "the weight of mental habits" inherited from the nineteenth century: "a sort of inability to tear ourselves away from an unexamined positivism," which forms the basis of the prejudice called "objectivity."

One result of this increased consciousness of the role of individual and even collective agency in the production of what we know as the Middle Ages, in particular the flattening typographical effect of nineteenth-century editions, has been a powerful return to the study of the material conditions of medieval manuscripts. What is at stake is more than the traditional considerations of the relation of multiple manuscript versions of a same text, the relation of manuscript illustration to writing, or the relation in the late Middle Ages of script to print; rather, we are witnessing a radical rethinking of the physicality of the manuscript within medieval culture—the means of production of both writing and image, the relationship between how a manuscript is laid out and its meaning, the effects of the manuscript as privileged object within the broader culture. Here one thinks of the ground-breaking work of Amelia Van Vleck and Laura Kendrick on troubadour man-

---

[9] Zumthor, *Speaking of the Middle Ages*, trans. Sarah White, foreword by Eugene Vance (Lincoln: University of Nebraska Press, 1986), 3–4.

uscripts, of Sylvia Huot on the trouvères, and, more generally, of Michael Camille on the relationship between the manuscript as cultural object and a certain medieval horror of representation, in *The Gothic Idol,* and more recently on the relationship between social marginality and manuscript margins, in *Image on the Edge.*[10] The trend toward reconsidering the original object itself will only intensify as the new technologies for reproduction, storage, and enhancement as well as manipulation of manuscript images make the "original" increasingly accessible.

The introduction of the subject into the heretofore supposedly objective field of medieval studies and the return to the material conditions of the object of study are the symptoms of a warming of the discipline, which has traditionally considered itself sufficiently detached and coldly other to prevent the kind of identification of the scholar with the others under study, or the kind of identification that, for example, makes the Renaissance and subsequent periods seem more transparent and familiar. And this brings me to what I see as the second feature of a future that is already under way. For the first time since the nineteenth century medievalists are now obliged to enter the mainstream of the university. Consequently, they must know not only their specialty but, more generally, the disciplines of the sciences of man—history, linguistics, philosophy, anthropology—with respect to which they can no longer feign neutrality or disinterest. On the contrary, the present moment offers a golden opportunity to renew the conviction that many pressing issues of modernism have a long and complex history in the Middle Ages. The best work in medieval studies is already and in the future will be truly interdisciplinary, but not in the sense that deans dream of or in the sense merely of the tendency to contrast and compare more than one national literature. The isolation of national literatures from each other or from the study of Latin culture will, in my

[10] Van Vleck, *Style and Stability in Troubadour Lyric of the Classic Period (1160–1180)* (Berkeley: University of California Press, 1982); Kendrick, *The Game of Love: Troubadour Wordplay* (Berkeley: University of California Press, 1988); Huot, *From Song to Book: The Poetics of Writing in Old French Lyric and Lyrical Narrative Poetry* (Ithaca, N.Y.: Cornell University Press, 1987); Camille, *The Gothic Idol: Ideology and Image-making in Medieval Art* (Cambridge: Cambridge University Press, 1989); and Camille, *Image on the Edge: The Margins of Medieval Art* (Cambridge, Mass.: Harvard University Press, 1992). See also Stephen G. Nichols, "Commentary and/as Image," *South Atlantic Quarterly* 91 (1992): 965–92.

opinion, no longer be viable in the Europe of the 1990s. Nor would I wager that the narrow specialties that historically have isolated the study of Old French from the broader culture of the Middle Ages will survive within the university of the twenty-first century. Which is less a grim prospect than an opportunity. Indeed, there has never been a moment more ripe for the teaching of the works of philosophers, historians, and poets who themselves imagined the possibility of what Dante termed the *Imperium*, the known world unified under one rule. Medievalists should exploit the development of the European community to press upon the university curriculum the universalizing aspects of medieval culture. But they will no longer be able to pretend to be beyond, or below, or outside what for better or worse has become the metalanguage of cross-cultural study—that is, literary theory. This assertion is not alien to the spirit of the Middle Ages, for Old French literature contains always a certain imbrication of theory and practice. If one looks carefully, almost every work contains a sophisticated indication of how it should be read and of how literary works signify more generally. Conversely, as the "Arts Poétiques" of the thirteenth century make clear (Mathieu de Vendôme, Geoffroi de Vinsauf), it is just as difficult to imagine a medieval theory without the examples that are its practice. Moreover, if I had to point the direction in which medieval theory might make the greatest impact not only on our understanding of medieval literature but on modern thought as well, it would be that of the patristics, which, like the study of the Middle Ages itself, has lately undergone something of a Renaissance.

Recent interest in late Roman and early Christian culture has produced significant changes in our understanding of both the substance and the relevance of patristic thought. Indeed, the writings of the church fathers, once dismissed under the twin paralogisms of theology and Scholasticism, have come increasingly to be seen as essential to our own aesthetic and intellectual sense. This view does not emanate from the current worldwide wallowing in religious fundamentalism, or from the tendency to push the origins of modernism toward an ever more distant past, or even from the impulse toward analogy on the part of those anxious to root contemporary theory in some more subsuming context. The return of the patristics stems from a recognition of the numerous and important similarities between a culture for which speculation about representation (verbal signs in particular) was essential to speculation about the wider universe and our own attempt to rethink the relation of linguistics, isolated since the Renaissance in the solitary of science, to the erotic, to the social, to ontology, and even to metaphysics.

The history of the early church has indeed begun to detach itself, strictly speaking, from the limits of religious doctrine and from narrow intellectual history to become the focus of an anthropology of the formative Christian period. I refer not only to comparative religious studies, as well as to reconsiderations of major figures in the light of psychoanalysis, political theory, and even semiotics, but to a certain turning upon the writings of the church fathers and the institutions mobilized by their writings of questions normally reserved by the sciences of man for non-Western cultures. A good deal of work has been done in the past decades on heresy and reform, sainthood, friendship, poverty, and asceticism alongside the monumental reformulations of the meaning and impact of gnosticism and the Stoics. More important, a wave of fresh scholarly activity has revitalized the ways we have traditionally understood religious ideals and movements by placing them within the broader perspective of social, political, legal, and economic institutions while enriching our knowledge of the everyday life of the Mediterranean world: habits of eating, fasting, and even starvation; modes of makeup, adornment, and dress; medical and sexual practice. In particular, the intense scrutiny accorded Roman and early medieval family structure, not the least of which has come from anthropologists, has tended toward a radical revision of our notion of the relation of kinship to patristic writings on sexuality and gender.

This brings me to a third and final area in which the medieval past corresponds so powerfully with the modern temper as to render its study compelling and urgent: gender. The myriad of books that appear each year on the question of women in the Middle Ages—historical studies, literary studies, studies in the history of religion—leave no doubt that it is one of the most vital aspects of present-day medievalism. With a zeal that must surely resemble that of the nineteenth-century scholars discovering and publishing unknown manuscripts, the most committed scholars of our discipline are writing the hidden history of the medieval period, the history of literature written by women, and, more difficult, the history of women's experience. Such intense

interest in the question of gender signals, of course, a shift in the composition of the scholarly community. In the future, medievalists not only
will adjust to changes in the canon, the recognition of female writers
who have historically been neglected, but will take into account the
determining effect of women scholars upon the redefinition of what
was until relatively recently an almost exclusively male preserve.

Here too lies a bridge between medieval studies and the larger university community, indeed another area in which medievalists might not
only speak to those in other disciplines but take the lead. The conception of gender as we know it in the West came into being in the first centuries of the Christian era and has survived more or less intact to the
present. Contemporary discussions that overlook this fundamental shift
in the cultural expression of the differences between the sexes risk
merely projecting our own views of gender upon the past and, by essen-
tializing, risk being caught in the movement of the very thing that they
seek to undo. What I am suggesting, then, is not so much the dismissal
of patristic views of sexuality as stultifying or archaic, not so much the
positive identification of sources in previous tradition, as an understanding of just how deeply determining the patristic "invention" of sexuality as we know it really was. Such an understanding already manifests
itself in studies of the male and female bodies, homosexuality, trans-
vestism, androgyny, prostitution, impotence and frigidity, contraception
and fertility, abortion, eroticism, intercourse (position-specific), orgasm,
menstruation, and, in particular, the ideal (and the practice) of sexual
renunciation. So great, in fact, is the abundance of work on the theme
of virginity that it alone practically constitutes an independent field.[11]
Here, too, many of the most significant contributions to the current reinterpretation of the patristic period come from women writing from a feminist perspective: studies of feminine piety and the role of women in the
primitive church, of female patronesses, friends, missionaries, prophets,

---

[11] See, for example, Peter Brown, *The Body and Society: Men, Women, and Sexual
Renunciation in Early Christianity* (New York: Columbia University Press, 1988); John
Bugge, *Virginitas: An Essay in the History of a Medieval Ideal* (The Hague: Martinus
Nijhoff, 1975); Elizabeth Castelli, "Virginity and Its Meaning for Women's Sexuality
in Early Christianity," *Journal of Feminist Studies in Religion* 2 (1986): 61–88; Elizabeth
A. Clark, "Ascetic Renunciation and Feminine Advancement: A Paradox of Late
Ancient Christianity," *Anglican Theological Review* 43 (1981): 240–57; Henri Crouzel,
Virginité et mariage selon Origène (Paris: Desclée de Brouwer, 1963); Jo Ann McNamara,

and heroic martyrs; explanations of the tremendous appeal of early Christianity, despite the condemnation of the feminine among the patristics, to
women anxious to escape the patriarchy of the ancient world.[12]

Here, then, is less a program for the future than the identification
of several current trends in medieval studies that seem to me promising for the coming decade.

"Sexual Equality and the Cult of Virginity in Early Christian Thought," *Feminist Studies*
3 (1976): 145–58; Elaine Pagels, *Adam, Eve, and the Serpent* (New York: Random
House, 1988); Aline Rousselle, *Porneia: de la maîtrise du corps à la privation sensorielle,
deuxième–quatrième siècles de l'ère chrétienne* (Paris: Presses Universitaires de France,
1983); Rosemary Ruether, "Misogynism and Virginal Feminism in the Fathers of the
Church," in *Religion and Sexism*, ed. Rosemary Ruether (New York: Simon and Schuster,
1974), 150–83; Jane Tibbetts Schulenberg, "The Heroics of Virginity: Brides of Christ
and Sacrificial Mutilation," in *Women in the Middle Ages and the Renaissance: Literary and
Historical Perspectives*, ed. and intro. Mary Beth Rose (Syracuse, N.Y.: Syracuse University
Press, 1986), 29–72; and Giulia Sissa, *Le Corps virginal: la virginité feminine en Grèce anci-
enne* (Paris: J. Vrin, 1987).

[12] See, for example, Kari Elisabeth Borresen, *Subordination and Equivalence: The
Nature and Role of Women in Augustine and Thomas Aquinas*, trans. Charles H. Talbot
(Washington, D.C.: University Press of America, 1981); Sebastian P. Brock and Susan
Ashbrook Harvey, intro. and trans., *Holy Women of the Syrian Orient* (Berkeley: University
of California Press, 1987); Caroline Walker Bynum, *Jesus as Mother: Studies in the Spiri-
tuality of the High Middle Ages* (Berkeley: University of California Press, 1982); Averil
Cameron and Amélie Kuhrt, eds., *Images of Women in Antiquity* (Detroit: Wayne State
University Press, 1983); Elizabeth A. Clark, *Jerome, Chrysostom, and Friends*, Studies in
Women and Religion, 2 (New York: Edwin Mellen, 1979); Mary Daly, *The Church and
the Second Sex* (Boston: Beacon, 1985); Mary Hayter, *The New Eve in Christ: The Use and
Abuse of the Bible in the Debate about Women in the Church* (Grand Rapids, Mich.: Eerd-
mans, 1987); Rosemary Ruether and Eleanor McLaughlin, eds., *Women of Spirit: Female
Leadership in the Jewish and Christian Traditions* (New York: Simon and Schuster, 1979);
Constance Parvey, "The Theology and Leadership of Women in the New Testament,"
in Ruether, *Religion and Sexism*, 117–49; Rosemary Ruether, "Mothers of the Church:
Ascetic Women in the Late Patristic Age," in Ruether and McLaughlin, 71–98; Elisa-
beth Schüssler Fiorenza, *In Memory of Her: A Feminist Theological Reconstruction of Chris-
tian Origins* (New York: Crossroad, 1983); Phyllis Trible, "Depatriarchalizing in Biblical
Interpretation," *Journal of the American Academy of Religion* 41 (1973): 30–48; Marina
Warner, *Alone of All Her Sex: The Myth and the Cult of the Virgin Mary* (New York: Knopf,
1976); and Anne Yarbrough, "Christianization in the Fourth Century: The Example of
Roman Women," *Church History* 45 (1976): 149–65.

LITERATURE, MEANING, AND THE DISCONTINUITY OF FACT

Jerome J. McGann

Textual studies and editing are two exemplary fields of historical criticism. They are also fundamental, since all literary work is grounded in them. These subdisciplines of historical criticism have been dominated for many years by empirical and even positivist methods and goals, sometimes for good, sometimes for ill. That general context has drawn me, for the past ten years or so, to concentrate much of my work in textual criticism and theory. I have done so with two particular goals in view.

First, I wanted to attack traditional historicism in what has always been regarded as its fastness of strength, its (hitherto) impregnable inner tower: textual studies and editing. Second, I wanted to open a parallel critique of contemporary theory and hermeneutics, which has largely avoided a serious engagement with the problem of facticity and positive knowledge. The unwillingness or inability of most influential literary theoreticians of the past twenty-five years to enter the fields of textual criticism and editing is an eloquent historical fact. Even when theoretically sophisticated critics moved beyond a "hermeneutics of reading" into various kinds of "new historical" and "cultural" studies, they did so typically without having addressed the conflicting claims of fact and idea, writing and reading, history and interpretation.

In textual studies and editing, however, these issues cannot be evaded, because the editor's and textual critic's literary works are always encountered as specific, material historical forms. They have what Paul de Man, speaking for hermeneutics generally, said "literary texts" cannot have: "positive existence."

The condition of positivity led traditional historicists, including textual critics, to conceive their obligation as recuperating phenomena that had slipped into the past. Though the theoretical impossibility of such a goal was always acknowledged, its heuristic operation was pursued. The idea was to try to make as close an approach to the lost phenomena as one could manage. Moreover, the pursuit

> (What mad pursuit? What struggles to escape?
> What pipes and timbrels? What wild ecstasy?)

involved an engagement to recover not so much the lost phenomena as their lost meanings. The works of the past survive in documentary forms. In their historical passage these documents appear to grow . more distant and difficult to understand. The traditional historicist— and here the textual critic stands as the supreme model—works to clear the documents of their accumulated detritus and obscurities, ideally exposing, and explicating, an original and complete truth that lies in the eternity of the past. Strict constructionists of the Constitution express an analogous goal when they speak of adhering to what the Founding Fathers intended.

Without arguing the matter—I have done so often elsewhere—let me say that this is not my view of what either textual criticism in particular or historical criticism generally entails. Historical method is for me strictly a form of comparative study. From that vantage, a historical criticism does not imagine that its object is to recover some lost original text or meaning. Such goals lie within neither its province nor its power. Normative goals of these kinds are hypothesized, as one commonly sees in the case of editing and textual studies. Norms are constructed, however, only to set in motion the special critical dynamic peculiar to every historical procedure: the method of comparative analysis. The basic form of historical method is not positivist—positivism is one of its Kantian "moments"—it is dialogical.

The points of departure for such a dialogue are, in the most general sense, the present and the past. The more deeply the dialogue form is engaged, the more clearly we perceive the multiple possibilities for situating what might be understood as the loci of presentness and pastness. Texts, for example, like the readings of the texts, are invariably multiple. When criticism constructs a "textual history" or a "reception history," the differential of the here and now is forced to confront a host of earlier, analogous differentials. The dialogue of history is endless both *between* the present and the past and *within* the present and the past.

Implicit in any historical criticism of literature is a crucial assumption: that literary works are certain human acts carried out within a larger world of other human acts. In this respect historical criticism distinguishes itself from hermeneutics, which is a method for elucidating symbolic forms. For historical criticism, "in the beginning was the deed"; and if that deed is an act of language—if we could also call it a "word"—it has to be first engaged as a rhetorical event rather than as a symbolic form. Though we may be interested in how a novel or a poem is a "virtual world" calling for an interpretation of its inner structure of relations, we cannot neglect in what ways and to what ends its virtualities have been deployed. A novel is also, necessarily, a certain kind of book (in fact, many kinds of book) written and disseminated in many different kinds of ways. The (formal) category we call "the novel" (as opposed to "the story") presupposes the institution of book production. For the historical critic, meaning(s) that might be educed from "the novel" are subsumed within a larger arena of meaningfulness: the social world of writing and reading books, the institutions for transmitting and retransmitting them.

In an epoch like our own, where the limits of knowledge are mapped onto models of language, the special character of historical criticism (as opposed to literary hermeneutics) may be clarified by asking the following question: must we regard the physical channels of communication as part of the message of the texts we study? Or are the channels to be treated as purely vehicular forms whose ideal condition is to be transparent to the texts they deliver? How important, for the reader of a novel or any other text, are the work's various materials, means, and modes of production? Does a work's bibliographical existence, for example, seriously impinge upon its symbolic form and meaning?

Normally, criticism leaves the documents to the bibliographers and the texts (so called) to the critics. For about ten years I have been arguing against this habit of thought—have been arguing that "reading" must cover the entirety of the literary work, its bibliographical as well as its linguistic codes. A recent essay on James's *Ambassadors* brings an especially clear focus to the issues at stake.[1]

The key fact is that the first English edition and the first American edition, published within a month of each other in 1904, have chapters 28 and 29 in different orders. Until 1949 the two orderings were not noticed, and the novel was read in the order printed in the first American edition (which was canonized in the 1909 New York edition and all subsequent printings to 1949). In 1949, however, critical opinion reversed itself and decided—it was a scandalous moment in American literary studies—that the order in the first American edition was a printer's mistake. Editions after 1949 change the chapter order to the sequence in the first English edition. As it happens, a close critical study of the bibliographical materials reveals no mistake in the first American edition. The scandal turns out to be worse than was imagined in 1949. The scandal is that the novel makes sense no matter which order the two chapters are put in.

What is startling here is that both ways of reading the novel are authorized at the bibliographical level, not at the hermeneutic level. Our imaginations do not impose a meaning upon the work; it imposes meanings upon our imaginations. The originary work seems to have transcended, equally and at once, the law of authorial intention and the law of integral aesthetic form. In its bibliographical doubleness *The Ambassadors* establishes alternative ways of thinking and reading both with and without an order of intentions. James's novel lies open to two linear sequences of text simultaneously, and it has generated them as if by some fate, or deliberation, of its special textual condition.

The situation argues that text may be founded as an order of discontinuous phenomena. The question is, just how deeply are these orders of chaos grounded? Does the case of *The Ambassadors* expose a textual freak, an accident and exception that prove the rule of normal orders of conscious control? Or is it a dramatic instance of just how strongly, and in the end vainly, we resist the presence of aleatory orders?

When we think with a post-Heisenbergian imagination (or, alternatively, with a pre-Socratic one), we have no difficulty grasping the ran-

---

[1] Jerome McGann, "Revision, Rewriting, Rereading; or, 'An Error [not] in *The Ambassadors,*'" *American Literature* 64 (1992): 95–110.

dom order of things. We are not surprised by sin, by the operations of fate, by Lucretian swerves, by Mandelbrot sets. Seen through the text of the Bible, they reveal the necessity of a willful refusal of necessity. Seen through the text of *De rerum natura*, they declare the presence of love— Aphrodite, alma Venus genetrix—at the foundation of the human world. We have also developed distinctive twentieth-century literary and artistic methods for expressing analogous forms of order. (By "we" I mean Euro-Americans.) But in our scholarship and criticism we still behave as if randomness and contradiction were not essential to the order of things. Perhaps we merely execute our habits of contradiction.

However that may be, let me close by returning to the subject of historical criticism. The case of *The Ambassadors* is important because no amount of nonhistoricized analysis could have exposed what is going on in that work. Reciprocally, the historicized analysis shows the objective, the positive, existence of the work's contradictions. Meaning outstares the blindness or insight dialectic of the hermeneutic circle. The analysis exposes (by critical reciprocation) a chaotic originary order in the textual condition. In rough terms, facticity appears logically prior to the concept of facticity. That logical priority assumes a concrete material form. We experience and define it as a historical priority. For all its historical character, the priority is a philosophical condition.

That condition explains why *The Ambassadors* needs to be faced as a complex (and evolving) set of material and sociohistorical events. If it isn't, we shall encounter it at no deeper level than that of its semantics. We will be limited to either structural analysis or thematized reading. While both of these critical procedures are important, they require a historical dialectics to supply them with reflexive power. Criticism needs this vantage because the works it investigates are themselves eventual and interactive.

Eventual: While criticism wants to know what literary works are saying, even more it needs to know what they are doing in saying what they say.

Interactive: Literary work comprises a ceaseless dialogue of many agents. By their fruits we shall know them . . . and they us.

Empiricism
Once More

Marjorie Perloff

[A]ll theory is transient & after the fact of writing
—Steve McCaffery and bpNichol, first manifesto (may 1972) lost[1]

G ary Saul Morson likes to tell the story about the professor who
came up to the podium at the end of a lecture he was giving on
Bakhtin's theory of narrative and said contemptuously, "Oh, you're
only interested in accuracy!" This is by no means an exceptional reaction: *accuracy, facticity, information, induction, empiricism*—these, we
know, are now bad words, implying that it is possible to give causal
explanations of "what happened," to provide linear models of development, to accept the discredited notion that history can somehow
provide the facts that govern interpretation. Lee Patterson describes
the Old History in his excellent summarizing essay for Frank Lentricchia and Thomas McLaughlin's *Critical Terms for Literary Study*:

> The discovery of America, the English Civil War, the French Revolu-
> tion—these were historical events that had a facticity and objectivity, a
> presence in the world, that allowed of precise and accurate description.
> They existed "out there," as part of the historical record, and diligence
> and discipline could reconstruct them accurately. Such a reconstruc-
> tion could in turn govern the interpretation of literary texts by defining
> the parameters of possible significance, showing what texts could and
> could not mean.[2]

---

[1] *Rational Geomancy: The Kids of the Book-Machine: The Collected Research Reports of
the Toronto Research Group, 1973–1982*, ed. Steve McCaffery (Vancouver: Talon
Books, 1992), 23.

[2] Patterson, "Literary History," in *Critical Terms for Literary Study*, ed. Frank Lentricchia and Thomas McLaughlin (Chicago: University of Chicago Press, 1990), 251.

The faith in such historical reconstruction went hand in hand, Patterson points out, with the assumption that a given culture was self-consistent, that it displayed a particular zeitgeist, a "period consciousness that was then read back into the 'literature.' The effect was that 'literature' could never say anything that 'history' had not authorized" (251). Literature, in this nineteenth-century positivistic scheme of things, assumed a secondary status to a history, patriotically conceived on nationalist lines.

Deconstruction and the various Marxisms that have dominated literary study from the late sixties to the present, Patterson observes, have transformed "literary history" in two main ways:

> First, literary critics have come to realize that the distinction between objective and subjective forms of cultural study cannot be sustained, that every historical account is constructed only by recourse to practices that are themselves as thoroughly interpretive as those that characterize literary criticism. And second, the term "literature" has been revealed as functional rather than ontological, as designating a kind of writing whose difference from other kinds is a matter not of its essential being but of its cultural function. In other words, a piece of writing is "literature" not because it possesses certain characteristics that other pieces lack, but because its readers regard it—for a variety of reasons— *as* literature. (256)

I quote this passage at some length because it nicely summarizes what is now official academic dogma. The dominant presence in Patterson's account is of course Foucault, although he is not cited directly, perhaps because his lessons have been so fully absorbed. The corollary theses that go with the twin doctrines of the fictionality of history and the functionality of literature are the following:

1. "What counts as a fact is determined not by its existence in the world but by the discursive practices that make it possible for something in the world to serve as a fact within a certain discourse" (257). Indeed, "history is itself as much the product of interpretive practices as are the literary interpretations it is being used to check."

2. Although we know that there is no such thing as literariness, the term *literature* remains useful because it performs essentially a social function. As Raymond Williams has shown, the crucial moment in the history of the concept "literature" is the late eighteenth century, when,

in Patterson's words, "the idea of the aesthetic established itself as the site where a disinterested concern for formal beauty and emotional authenticity could be protected from the relentless commodifications of consumer capitalism" (258).[3] Once the function of the term *literary* is understood, we must think of it as, so to speak, under erasure. Indeed, "literary writing is best understood not as a diacritical or disengaged activity but instead as one of the main forms of cultural production by which men and women have made their world. Far from being divorced from the world, literary production is itself a form of social practice: texts do not merely reflect social reality but create it" (260).

Authoritative as the latter statement sounds—and one can read similar statements in book after book, article after article, published over the past decade—it raises, at least for me, large questions. Let me pose a few of them here and then turn to some examples:

1. If essentialism is the enemy, if we know that there is no intrinsic or essential property that we can designate as "literary," how is it that we can make essentialist statements about what literature is *not*? How do we know that literature is "*not* a diacritical or disengaged activity"?

2. If "history is itself as much the product of interpretive practices as are the literary interpretations it is being used to check," then Raymond Williams's comment on "the relentless commodifications of consumer capitalism" is itself such a product. To say that "consumer capitalism" entailed "relentless commodifications," from which "beauty" and "emotion" had to be "protected," is certainly an *interpretation* of history, not an assumption that goes without saying.

3. Moreover, if a particular concept (in this case, the idea of the aesthetic) is said to have arisen in response to a particular economic system (in this case, capitalism), doesn't this assertion depend on causal as well as temporal explanations? And when we speak, say, of the literature of early capitalism, aren't we positing a zeitgeist?

4. Given our rejection of nineteenth-century metanarratives of literary evolution, which pinpoint the time when a given genre reached

[3] Williams, *Marxism and Literature* (Oxford: Oxford University Press, 1977), 150–51.

its maturity, and so on, how is it that we implicitly valorize progress models in literary theory, which suggest that theory has come of age, has reached a new level of knowledge and insight, exposing as "old-fashioned" and "naive" the claims of earlier theoretical paradigms? How, for example, can we assert, as do Patterson and his fellow contributors to Lentricchia and McLaughlin's state-of-the-art collection of essays, that Roman Jakobson's famed distinction between ordinary and extraordinary (i.e., literary) language is merely false? And again, if theory is steadily improving—we know more than earlier critics did and hence can correct their mistakes—what is the source (origin) of our greater knowledge?

5. If "literary writing is best understood . . . as one of the main forms of cultural production by which men and women have made their world," as "a form of social practice," the question remains: *whose* cultural production and *which* social practices shall be foregrounded? To put it another way: since the study of literary history, however we define it, operates under particular temporal and practical constraints, which texts command our attention, which are expendable, and which of their features do we privilege?

For me, as a critic of modernist and postmodernist literature, the last area has proved most troubling. It is no coincidence, I suspect, that the New Historicism has been most successful in medieval and Renaissance studies, where the corpus of written texts can be more readily limited and defined, and where much artistic production was anonymous. Carolingian illuminated manuscripts, for example, manifest a verbal-visual practice that can, indeed can only, be studied as a form of cultural production. Or the Gregorian chant. Or thirteenth-century French stained glass. Or the writings of fourteenth-century female mystics. Or the Renaissance "self-fashioning" (in "literary" and "nonliterary" texts) that Stephen Greenblatt has delineated so brilliantly.[4]

But the closer we come to the present, the more difficult it becomes to know whose cultural production is to be regarded as representative or exemplary. Which art forms will be central to histories of postmodern American culture? Hollywood film? Feminist photogra-

---

[4] Greenblatt, *Renaissance Self-Fashioning: From More to Shakespeare* (Chicago: University of Chicago Press, 1980).

phy? Prime-time TV sitcom? The video art of Dara Birnbaum and Bill Viola? Whose fiction as social practice is an index to the experience of African-American women, Toni Morrison's or Terri McMillan's? And whose language exemplifies the aporias of postmodern culture? John Updike's? John Cage's? John Ashbery's? John Ash's? If all of the above, what history (or history of what) can come to terms with so many contradictory materials?

Or take the now-fabled 1950s, the subject of any number of recent literary and cultural "histories." Were the "tranquillized fifties," as Robert Lowell called them, primarily the era of cold war, McCarthyism, and "the bomb"? Or was it the age of Guy DeBord and his situationist aesthetic? Or of the Beats? Or of the beginnings of German neo-expressionism? Or of the British *New Lines* poets? Or of the international concrete poetry movement? And, when we go back to "high modernism" and talk, as so many critics do, of the inherent relationship between modernism and fascism, have we included the Russian avant-garde or, say, the Chilean poet Neruda? If not, is modernism to be equated, as it is in so many of our studies, with Anglo-American modernism? If it is, whatever happened to the decline of nationalism that Patterson talks of?

The Old History would have dealt with these questions by making value judgments. Toni Morrison would be pronounced "better" than Terri McMillan, and hence she would get more space in our history. And so on. But if literature is defined as that which the culture in question takes to be literature, as one among many forms of cultural production, creating rather than reflecting the political unconscious, there is no satisfactory way to resolve these problems.

Consider the analysis of postmodernism in Fredric Jameson's influential *Postmodernism; or, The Cultural Logic of Late Capitalism.* The introduction to this more than four-hundred-page book opens with the sentence, "It is safest to grasp the concept of the postmodern as an attempt to think the present *historically* in an age that has forgotten how to *think historically* in the first place."[5] History, in Jameson's Althusserian scheme of things, is of course economic history: he begins by positing that "postmodernism is the consumption of sheer

---

[5] Jameson, *Postmodernism; or, The Cultural Logic of Late Capitalism* (Durham, N.C.: Duke University Press, 1991), ix; my italics.

commodification as a process. The 'life-style' of the superstate therefore stands in relationship to Marx's 'fetishism' of commodities as the
most advanced monotheisms to primitive animisms or the most rudi-
mentary idol worship" (x). True, "late capitalism," the "cultural half" of
his title, as Jameson calls it, has become somewhat compromised since
he began his project in the early eighties; *late,* he is forced to admit in
the face of the demise of communism in Eastern Europe, no longer
means "about to end"; it conveys no more than "the sense that something has changed, that things are different, that we have gone
through a transformation of the life world which is somehow decisive
but incomparable with the older convulsions of modernization and
industrialization" (xxi). In the chapters that follow, however, as in most
materialist studies of postmodern culture, the decisive role or "cultural
logic" of "late capitalism" is considered as at least as axiomatic as the
role of the Great Chain of Being was in the Renaissance studies of the
fifties or as theories of organicism were in the romanticist studies of
the sixties.

Postmodernism, in any case, refers, according to Jameson's "peri-
odizing hypothesis," to the decades since 1960 or so, when "aesthetic
production . . . has become integrated into commodity production
generally" (4). "One fundamental feature of all the postmodernisms,"
says Jameson, "is the effacement in them of the older (essentially high-
modernist) frontier between high culture and so-called mass or commercial culture" (2), an effacement that goes hand in hand with the
"new depthlessness, which finds its prolongation both in contemporary 'theory' and in a whole new culture of the image or the simulacrum" (6). His Exhibit A of this "depthlessness" is a comparison of
"one of the canonical works of high modernism," Van Gogh's painting
A Pair of Boots, to a work called *Diamond Dust Shoes,* produced by "the
central figure in contemporary visual art," Andy Warhol. The former,
writes Jameson, can be read either as "the willed and violent transformation of a drab peasant object world into the most glorious material-
ization of pure color in oil paint," or, in Heideggerian terms, as the
ability of the artwork to "disclose" what "the equipment . . . *is* in
truth," the humble peasant shoes "slowly re-creat[ing] about themselves the whole missing object world which was once their lived context." In either case, the work of art "is taken as a clue or a symptom for

some vaster reality which replaces it as its ultimate truth" (7–8). Warhol's gelatin print *Diamond Dust Shoes*, by contrast, is nothing more than a "random collection of dead objects hanging together on the canvas like so many turnips, as shorn of their earlier life world as the pile of shoes left over from Auschwitz." They represent "the emergence of a new kind of flatness or depthlessness, a new kind of superficiality in the most literal sense, perhaps the supreme formal feature of all the postmodernisms." Indeed, their "glacéd X-ray elegance mortifies the reified eye of the viewer," thus "inverting Van Gogh's Utopian gesture" (8–9).

However telling Jameson's interpretation of the two paintings may be, as history his account is guilty of what I have elsewhere called the synecdochic fallacy.[6] Jameson is comparing one of the least appreciated and most cruelly marginalized European artists of the late nineteenth century to an American artist who has become an icon of self-promotion, publicity, and commercial success. Is Warhol really Van Gogh's postmodernist counterpart, or should we more accurately compare the former to a salon painter like Bouguereau, who similarly knew how to manipulate the public into making him a star? Or, to take the other side of the parallel, suppose we compare Van Gogh not to Warhol but to Jasper Johns. The "modernist" "disclosure of what the equipment, the pair of peasant shoes, *is* in truth," the emergence of the painted "entity . . . into the unconcealment of its being, by way of the mediation of the work of art," has a perfect counterpart in Johns's paintings of coat hangers and light bulbs, beer cans and paintbrushes, the various *Alphabets* and number series.

A Warhol print cannot, in any case, represent *the* postmodern any more than John Portman's Bonaventure Hotel (another Exhibit A in Jameson's lexicon of postmodernism [38–44]) can represent the "new depthlessness" of architecture over against the international style of Le Corbusier and Gropius. Common sense suggests that whatever the "hyperspace" of the Bonaventure is or isn't, its modernist counterpart is not a Bauhaus monument but, say, New York's art deco Waldorf Astoria, the grand commercial hotel of the thirties and forties, even as the Bonaventure, with its revolving skytop cocktail lounge and "reflec-

---

[6] See my "Postmodernism/Fin de siècle: The Prospects for Openness in a Decade of Closure," *Criticism* 35, no. 2 (March 1993): 161–92.

tive glass skin [that] repels the city outside" (42), is a popular building of our own day.

Van Gogh/Warhol; Le Corbusier/John Portman: these would-be synecdoches, representing the modern and postmodern, respectively, also display a curious way of relating the European to the American. If modernism is regularly considered a European phenomenon, postmodernism is almost by definition "born in the U.S.A." This means that although Van Gogh's most logical postmodernist successor might well be the Belgian Marcel Broodthaers, now recognized as a seminal figure in the development of postconceptual art, pride of place must nevertheless be given to the quintessential American product of late capitalism, Andy Warhol. Note that neither in his discussion of pastiche nor in his differentiation of postmodern from modern architecture does Jameson feel obliged to justify the U.S.-centrism of his position.

Subtle and brilliant as many of its arguments and insights are, then, *Postmodernism; or, The Cultural Logic of Late Capitalism* is not really satisfactory "as an attempt to think the present historically." One wishes that the "facts" to be interpreted were more plentiful and didn't always have to function as examples of a prior theoretical paradigm, which has become all too common in the "new" cultural studies. At a recent conference entitled "From Romanticism to Postmodernism," held at a British university, I heard a paper on John Ashbery as the "poet of empire." Its young author, Stephen Clark, first dismissed the various "formalisms" according to which Ashbery had thus far been read and then announced that his own paper would submit Ashbery's poetry to a more culturally based reading. The logic of his argument went like this: (1) After World War II, the United States became an imperialist, neocolonialist nation in which art, seemingly depoliticized, as Serge Guilbaut has shown in his Marxist history of the abstract expressionist movement,[7] was increasingly co-opted by the dominant culture, whose interests it has unconsciously served. (2) Ashbery was and is a New York poet of this period, and one can find in his work references to expensive paintings, stereos, elegant parties, and various desired exotica, viewed in an "apolitical" context. Therefore, (3) Ashbery must be

---

[7] Guilbaut, *How New York Stole the Idea of Modern Art: Abstract Expressionism, Freedom, and the Cold War*, trans. Arthur Goldhammer (Chicago: University of Chicago Press, 1983).

understood as a "poet of empire." This label then provided Clark with a comparison between the American Ashbery and his young British disciple John Ash, whose absorption into New York culture, formative as it has been since he became an expatriate some years ago, still betrays his less fully commodified, less wealthy and imperialist Manchester roots.

I must confess to squirming in my seat as I heard this earnestly delivered and carefully "researched" paper. Stephen Clark had obviously done his homework, insofar as he had read the major scholarship *on* Ashbery (so as to contest it) and had read his way *through* Ashbery in search of instances that might make his case. Since he knew what he wanted to prove and since Ashbery's disjunctive, fragmented, elusive lyric can yield up any number of conflicting "statements," it wasn't too difficult to find lines that seemed to illustrate his thesis. "The Instruction Manual" of 1956, for example, was criticized for its fond evocation of a prettied-up Guadalajara, depicted as a "City of rose-colored flowers!" where "The band is playing *Scheherazade* by Rimsky-Korsakov" and "Around stand the flower girls handing out rose- and lemon-colored flowers, / Each attractive in her rose-and-blue striped dress (Oh! such shades of rose and blue)."[8] Ashbery, Clark commented, seems to be quite insensitive to the plight of the poor Mexicans; for him, Guadalajara is just a scene in a travel poster, a place where wealthy Americans can vacation.

In order to advance his interpretation, Clark had to ignore the poem's tone altogether, had to ignore the campy humor of passages like "(Oh! such shades of rose and blue)," which mark "The Instruction Manual" as presenting not a serious fantasy about the heavenly city but a parodic rendering of what it means to have such self-indulgent fantasies while one is sitting (as Ashbery was sitting in 1956) at a desk in a dreary office (in Ashbery's case, the offices of McGraw-Hill, near the Port Authority Bus Terminal), trying to hold down a dreary job writing dreary instruction manuals. Whoever was able in 1956 to vacation in Guadalajara, it certainly wasn't the thirty-year-old John Ashbery, a poet still quite unknown in the literary world, who had no

[8] Ashbery, "The Instruction Manual," in *Some Trees* (1956; New York: Corinth Books, 1970), 14.

money, lived, as did his poet friends, in a series of tenements in the Village or on the Lower East Side, and was soon to go to France for a decade, working at various newspaper jobs, because, among other things, he couldn't afford to live in New York. So much for the pleasures of wealth in the great American Empire.

But more to the point: Ashbery's daydream about lovely flower girls and of the beautiful "young boy and girl" who "lurk in the shadows of the bandstand," kissing and whispering, is intentionally presented as a comic travel-book cliché, the poet himself necessarily standing outside the picture, since, being homosexual, he has no place in the world of this village fiesta. Indeed, Ashbery's sexual difference, which in the New York of the fifties could not help but distance him from the dominant imperialist culture, was never so much as alluded to in Clark's talk.

What I am arguing is that even as *in theory* we pay lip service to the principle that "what counts as a fact is determined not by its existence in the world but by the discursive practices that make it possible for something in the world to serve as a fact within a certain discourse," what is really going on in much of our cultural criticism is that the "discursive practices" used to authorize interpretation are all too often reduced to labels—capitalism, imperialism, colonialism, patriarchy—which the individual instance must then somehow fit, however many items that would emerge from a more empirically and more inductively generated picture have to be eliminated. In the case in question, the author chose wholly to ignore not only Ashbery's biography and the chronology of his poems, not only the sociocultural history of the postwar New York art scene, but also the language, rhythms, conventions, allusions, and construction of subjectivity in the poems themselves.

Is such reductionism inherent in the theory that literature is to be understood as one of the main forms of cultural production? Strictly speaking, not at all, but it seems to be a likely trap. Serge Guilbaut, for example, avoids the pitfalls I have just discussed by keeping his focus not on individual painters or paintings but on the gradual depoliticization imposed, whether overtly or not, on figurative painting (if even vaguely construable as socialist realism) in response to the campaign to discredit communism in the postwar era. Even so, Guilbaut's insistence on viewing abstract expressionism as a unitary phenomenon (talk about zeitgeist!) blinds him to certain "facts" that a less partisan discursive practice would have brought into the open: for example, that New York "stole the idea of modern art" from Paris, not only because New York was now an aggressive imperialist power but because many of the great European artists, having converged on New York as refugees, were disseminating European avant-garde theory and practice. Consider Hans Hoffman's classes at the New School or the mediation of the Dutch-born Willem De Kooning. Secondly, in ignoring individual work in favor of the larger "cultural production," Guilbaut misses the important point that, far from being merely co-opted by the dominant cold war ideology, the New York school was the first American school of painters to include a sizable number of Jews as well as women. The movement can, in short, be regarded as an opening of the field rather than as simple co-option.

All these points are, of course, open to debate. As Jerome McGann remarked in the discussion period following Stephen Clark's paper, one *could* make a good case for Ashbery's poems as representations of the imperial America of the postwar decades, but it would have to be made on different and more complex grounds. The first requisite, it seems to me, is to proceed more inductively than we are currently used to doing, to avoid the imposition of a prior set of theory isms on complicated historical data.

"All theory," declare the poets Steve McCaffery and bpNichol in the manifesto that gives me my epigraph, "is transient & after the fact of writing." This proposition is, of course, a witty pun: we can take it to mean that (1) "writing" (i.e., literature) is prior to theory, which is secondary and transient, or, conversely, that (2) theory exists only in the material form of writing, but writing is itself transient. The former is a tenet of the Old History, the latter of the New, and so the sentence makes, as McCaffery says, a nice "testimonial" to the poets' "lasting belief in the provisionality of thoughts inevitably subjected to historical forces, socio-cultural change, and the fluctuating relations of cultural disciplines" (13).

A *lasting* belief in *provisionality*: it might be a good way to maintain the "interest in accuracy" that literary history cannot quite do without.

SOME PROSPECTS
FOR LITERARY HISTORY

David Perkins

There are approximately sixteen thousand professors of English in the United States. Their deans, chairs, colleagues, conscience, and vanity, their needs for tenure, salary, status, and self-respect require that they publish. What the prospects for literary history ought to be, intellectually speaking, may be questioned. In *Is Literary History Possible?* I inquire whether any writing in this genre can fulfill our present criteria of plausibility in historical representation.[1] But in a material sense, the prospects for literary history are of the brightest. To the sixteen thousand professors of English we must, of course, add those of comparative literature, foreign languages, and other academic literary disciplines, professors in other countries, and all the graduate students whose dissertations will further swell the future bibliographies of articles and books. Viewing these impressive numbers, we may know that literary history has a future, like a gold mine, the more so as literary history is not hard to produce. New facts, topics, or angles are readily found and can be written up, usually, without mental overexertion.

This is a sour, cynical note, and apologies are in order, especially as the note will become sourer. Younger colleagues may, if they wish, compare me to old dough, kneaded so often it can no longer rise, or to milk churned too long to yield butter. When I was in graduate school, forty years ago, I was taught and practiced positivist literary history; intellectual history; the history of literature as that of generic con-

---

[1] David Perkins, *Is Literary History Possible?* (Baltimore, Md.: Johns Hopkins University Press, 1992).

ventions; the history of United States literature à la Perry Miller and
F. O. Matthiessen as that of the American "mind"; also, medieval
philology; psychoanalytic (Freudian) criticism; and a humanistic discourse about literature derived from Matthew Arnold and best exemplified, at that time, by Lionel Trilling. I was not taught the so-called
New Criticism, because none of my professors could do or approve of
it, but it was what I wanted to teach myself, and did.

To number the academic critical moons that have since waxed and
waned, myself sometimes riding on their tides, would be especially boring and is anyway the tale of the tribe. But they would include, in no
particular order, archetypal criticism, existentialist criticism, structuralism, reader response analysis, deconstruction, and several more
models of literary history, including Harold Bloom's. An old stager
may, perhaps, be forgiven if he assumes that whatever now holds the
spotlight or waits in the wings will be no more lasting than what went
before. And neither should these critical modes last, for as soon as
their blaze of novelty dims, their limitations stand exposed. In talking
about literature as in writing it, the only secret, as T. S. Eliot once con-
fided, is to be very intelligent, but that is exactly what cannot be
expected of sixteen thousand professors of English. We require a theory, a method, a critical machine that can be driven over one text after
another, even though (to borrow a phrase from Wallace Stevens) the
squirming facts forever exceed the squamous mind that tries to order
them in its grand narratives and systems. We must explain the rotating
critical modes by some principle other than their truth claims.

The engines that propel this rotation have already been indicated
and are anyway well known. Since scholars must publish, and usually
on works that have already been much published on, and since, other
things being equal, scholarship is more valued if it has a certain novelty, there must be, in the profession, a constant provision of new
premises and methods. Secondly, the methods must be such as persons of ordinary intelligence can apply. For, to repeat, not all professors have a special profundity, sensitivity, or inwardness with literature,
but all strive for tenure and promotion. These two conditions do not
explain the concrete succession of academic critical modes. They do
not tell, for example, why cultural criticism may come after deconstruction. One could imagine a quite different successor, and to

explain why it was one rather than another, one must look to the contingencies of the particular case. But unless a critical mode satisfies the general requirements I have mentioned, of novelty, reducibility to method, and availability to the less talented, it cannot come into fashion. Archetypal criticism and New Historicism, for example, are different in almost every conceivable way *except* that both serve the material needs of their practitioners with full efficiency. For their moments of prevalence, such merits are as necessary as their intellectual content. What succeeds in academic literary criticism is what can be imitated, what, in other words, supplies topics for Ph.D. dissertations, articles, and books. Thus we may conclude—it is, sadly, a commonplace—that the purpose of academic literary criticism is to produce more criticism.

How shall we explain the rapidity of the succession at present? It used to be thought that every generation had its set of ideas, formed by its life experience, that lasted and passed with the generation. "But our Idea itself," Valéry cries to his generation, "and our Sovereign Good . . . How can it perish, O comrades?—What is it that has so secretly deformed our certainties, diminished our truth, destroyed our courage? Has the discovery been made that light can grow old?"[2] But in the present world of academic criticism, light grows old almost before it shines. If we consider how many persons are jostling for "visibility," we can understand why a dominant theory quickly attracts challengers. One looms more visibly if one stands against the light, a point that is also not lost on modern poets and painters. Yet while one wants to be visible, one wants also to have the protection and power of comrades, and so, typically, the newer thought does not "whisper results to its neighbour," in Keats's phrase,[3] but organizes itself politically for attack and defense, becoming the newer school in the offing. It is not surprising if, while satisfying our career necessities, our literary criticism rarely satisfies the ordinary, unprofessional needs people have for it.

Resuming the apologia for sourness, I should explain that since puberty I have been a lover of poetry. I once asked Alfred Harbage, a

[2] Valéry, *The Art of Poetry*, trans. Denise Folliot (New York: Pantheon, 1958), 45.
[3] Keats, *Letters*, ed. Hyder Edward Rollins, vol. 1 (Cambridge, Mass.: Harvard University Press, 1958), 232.

great editor of Shakespeare, how much all Shakespeare's editors together had contributed to the sum total of a reader's enjoyment of the plays. So little that it was scarcely reckonable, was Harbage's estimate, and for the enjoyment of poetry (for I assume enjoyment is the purpose), I fear that the same meager harvest of added pleasure has been yielded, in my case, by most of the critical and scholarly books I have read. This statement demands explanations and qualifications, of course, but they would make a very long excursus. So I'll simply report that the criticism that has most helped me comes, generally, when people tell me, in a direct, personal way, what they see in a poem, what seems to them moving or admirable. The criticism of poetry must be appreciative—let us not shrink from the old-fashioned word—for otherwise it is inert. "What we have loved," as Wordsworth puts it at the end of *The Prelude*, "others will love, and we will teach them how" (14.446–47). This is the best purpose of criticism. But to love one must perceive with imagination, and to teach one must write with sensitivity. Not everyone can produce criticism of this sort, and the rest must follow a method or theory, or write about method or theory.

In all modes of literary history, old-fashioned or new, the method is to set works in contexts. For this reason, literary history is a self-contradictory project. A basic premise of contextualism is that the event (work) is shaped by its *whole* context. But the whole cannot be reconstructed by a historian. Therefore, a more limited context is constructed by a selective use of information. We must then ask whether this selectivity distorts more than it reveals, and whether this matters. Whatever construction we produce can always be deconstructed by citing different information. With different premises, different areas of context become important. What counts as a historical "cause" for one person does not for another. In literary histories the contexts may be other literary works, other discourses, sociological circumstances, political events, and so forth, but whatever they are, Dilthey's criticism applies:

> The true way in which we handle the historical conditions is . . . [that] we leave the greater part of them entirely out of account, and without further consideration treat a limited set, that we select from them, as the totality. If, then, we claim to represent the historical conditions in

our analysis, our claim, already on this ground, can only be approximately correct.[4]

If, for example, the text to be interpreted or explained is Thomas Hardy's "Darkling Thrush," which was written on 31 December 1900, the literary historian may relate the depressed mood of the poem to Victorian religious discourse, to Hardy's philosophical readings, to his class position as a member of a weakening bourgeoisie, to poetic convention, to Hardy's belatedness in the romantic tradition of poetry, or to general fears of political exhaustion as the nineteenth-century ended, one year before Queen Victoria's death. A biographer might also think of Hardy's wounded feelings at the reception of *Jude the Obscure* and of his unhappy domestic situation. The creation of a context is, then, inherently selective and disputable. We see in this why, as a resource for professional careers, literary history is inexhaustible. Even if its methods and premises were not constantly changing, it would still enable endless more writing on the same texts.

Contextualism necessitates that only a single feature of the work, or a selected set of features, be noticed. For most of the historical essay must be devoted to constructing contexts. In other words, in literary histories the movement of attention is from some feature of the work into its context, where attention lingers, and there is not space to do this with every feature of the work, especially as one might have to construct different, relatively unrelated contexts for each feature. If the mood of "The Darkling Thrush" were explained out of Victorian religious and philosophical writings, its stanzaic structure, if discussed at all, would presumably send the historian into a different context. Traditionally, this point has been expressed as a complaint that literary history cannot present (describe, explain, interpret) works as such, but can only write about parts or aspects. In a more radical, though no less traditional, phrasing of this complaint, literary history has no power to express the actual experience of readers.

Whatever is said against literary history is said against my own work also, for I dabbled in literary history for twenty years. Moreover, though I convinced myself of its limitations, I am still content to par-

---

[4] Dilthey, *Das Erlebnis und die Dichtung*, 12th ed. (Göttingen: Vandenhoeck und Ruprecht, 1921), 171. My translation.

ticipate in the gold rush in one way. The complaints voiced above apply to the history of reception, but with a diminished force. Reception history can attempt to tell how a poem actually was read, was experienced, in a given time and place, by persons of a certain class, gender, age, education, and so forth. To the extent that a historian succeeded in this ultimately impossible project, he would be reporting a "reading"—not his own, but someone's. To me this would be interesting only if the reading reconstructed were that of a literatus, a good reader, for the reactions of hoi polloi are unlikely, I think, to enhance one's experience of a poem. Reception history on its sociological side has little interest for the literary intelligence. But if one could reconstruct how Milton may have read a poem, or Coleridge, or Henry James, this would be valuable, not out of antiquarian curiosity but because it might directly enrich one's own reading. For example, in *Imagination and Fancy* Leigh Hunt makes an excellent comment on lines 69–70 of Keats's "Ode to a Nightingale": "Charm'd magic casements, opening on the foam / Of perilous seas, in faery lands forlorn." "You do not know," says Hunt,

> what the house is, or where, nor who the bird. Perhaps a king himself. But you see the window, open on the perilous seas, and hear the voice from out the trees in which it is nested, sending its warble over the foam. The whole is at once vague and particular, full of mysterious life. You see nobody, though something is heard; and you know not what of beauty or wickedness is to come over the sea. Perhaps it was suggested by some fairy tale.[5]

This romantic type of reading was later called impressionistic. Amalgamating Keats's words with his own associative creativity, Hunt produces a new poem in prose. Moreover, his creativity, again typically for his age, tends in a certain direction. He does not interpret the open casements and perilous seas as symbols, as bearing overtones of unconscious or transcendent meaning, as might have been done by a later reader. He does not supplement the images psychoanalytically, archetypally, intertextually, or by semiotic *différance*, as we might at present. The creativity of his reading, which is certainly not less than that

---

[5] Hunt, *Imagination and Fancy: Selections from the English Poets* (New York: Wiley and Putnam, 1845), 254.

of present-day critics, works instead toward picturing and narrativizing the images, toward completing them visually and placing them in a story.

Hunt's comments are interestingly similar, in some ways, to the response to the Grecian urn enacted in Keats's famous ode. Hunt dwells on the particulars that are represented, the window, the sea, the voice, just as Keats's speaker does on the figures ornamenting the urn. Hunt notes, as Keats's speaker does (what "leaf-fring'd legend"? what "men or gods are these"?), that the story behind the images cannot be known, and yet seeks to guess it. In the same way, no doubt, Hunt would feel that the "emperor and clown," earlier in the same stanza, allude to a story, and when Keats's ode mentions the biblical tale of Ruth, Hunt as a reader would develop its pathos. The king Hunt imagines is not as distant an import into the text as is Keats's little town into the ornamentation of the urn, most especially since Hunt doubtless produces the king by association with the emperor in Keats's ode, and Keats's "faery" evokes Hunt's fairy tale, in which the bird might be a king in metamorphosis.

Hunt's romantic, narrativizing impulse, his questions of what, where, and who, his intuition that something "is to come over the sea," bring what we would not get from reading these lines only as we read poetry now, however that may be. The sense that there is a story there adds to the fascination of the images; the impossibility of knowing the story enhances, irrationally, the remoteness of the scene; the feeling of expectancy, of something about to happen, which Hunt's reading introduces, works powerfully though vaguely on the imagination and makes this spellbound moment, which the lines describe, one that will soon be shattered. Thus it makes the lines proleptic of the different breaking of the spell that takes place in the ode in the movement of the speaker's thought, as he is called back from the land of fairy to his sole self. Precisely its difference from our own makes Hunt's reading valuable to us. To recover it and to understand it are acts of literary history, though our personal use of it is not. A reception history focused on good readings, good in the opinion of their time, is directly valuable to our own reading.

Literature in History

PUBLIC MEMORY AND ITS DISCONTENTS

Geoffrey H. Hartman

I want to raise the issue of how to focus public memory on traumatic experiences like war, the Holocaust, or massive violations of human rights. You might think that it is not an issue at all; that we are, in fact, too absorbed in such painful matters. I have often heard objections that the study of the Holocaust, in particular, is displacing among Jews a learning tradition two thousand years old. There may be some truth to the charge; it is easy to become fascinated with cruelty and violence, with the mystery of such extreme inhumanity. But we cannot turn away from the world in which it happened; and the question of what impedes our focus is complicated by the very efficiency, the realism and representational scope, of modern media.

The substantial effects of film and telecommunications are having their impact. An "information sickness," caused by the speed and quantity of what impinges on us, and abetted by machines we have invented that generate endless arrays, threatens to overwhelm personal memory. The individual, we complain, cannot "process" all this information, this flak: public and personal experience are being moved not closer together but farther apart. The arts, it used to be said, aspire to the condition of music; now the "total flow" of video seems to dominate. Can public memory still be called memory, when it is increasingly alienated from personal and active recall?

Among the symptoms of this malady of our age are philosophical discussions about the existence or nonexistence of a "posthumanist subject," a conference on "the uses of oblivion," and the fear, openly expressed, that "our past will have no future in our future" (David

Rieff). Even as our senses are routinely besieged, the imagination, traditionally defined as a power that restores a kind of presence to absent things, has its work taken away and is in danger of imitating media sensationalism. It becomes, as Wallace Stevens said, a violence from within pressing against the violence from outside. In the midst of an unprecedented realism in fiction and the public media, there is reason to worry about a desensitizing trend, one that keeps raising the threshold at which we begin to respond.

How do we keep our sensitivity alive, when such vivid and painful events become our daily fare? How do we prevent denial or indifference? At least since the Book of Job was written, we have known that there is great, unjustifiable suffering in the world. But from the time of Job's so-called friends to that of the Holocaust negationists, we have also known that it is explained or rationalized against all odds.

Today we are learning a new truth about human indifference. Until recently, perhaps until news from Bosnia reached the screen, we clutched at the hope that if the indifferent masses in Germany and America had known what was going on in the concentration camps, known with the same graphic detail communicated today by TV, the atrocities could not have continued. There would have been an outcry of the popular conscience and so much protest that the Holocaust would have had to stop. Yet now, as the media make us bystanders of every act of violence and violation, we glimpse and even find reasons for a terrible inertia in ourselves. No event is reported without a spin, without an explanatory or talky context that buffers the raw images; pictures on TV remain pictures; a sort of antibody builds up in our response system and prevents total mental disturbance. Even while deploring and condemning the events, we experience what John Keats called "the feel of not to feel it" as we continue with everyday life.[1]

My intent is not to add to our already considerable sense of guilt or powerlessness but to point out that the media place an insatiable demand on us. Paradoxically, their extended eyes and ears, so impor-

[1] The shock factor seemed greater during the Vietnam War, the Biafra famine, and even occasionally before that. Filmed Japanese atrocities in China in 1941 and pictures of southern brutality against blacks during the civil rights movement caught the attention of the American public.

tant to informed action, also distance the reality of what is perceived. Terrible things, shown repeatedly, begin to appear matter-of-fact, natural rather than man-made. Zygmunt Bauman has labeled this effect the "production of moral indifference."[2] For our compassion is not superhuman; it is finite. Sooner or later coldness sets in, whether we admit to it or not. We remain deeply engaged, however, because official morality does not cultivate that coldness. It is an important difference between our situation and that of Germans under the Nazi regime: viewer reaction splits schizophrenically into passionate response to and exhausted self-distancing from images of global misery, which for all their immediacy become too often electronic phantoms.[3]

Such desensitization—Robert Lifton calls it "psychic numbing"— was noticed by Wordsworth near the beginning of the industrial revolution. He complained in 1800 that a "degrading thirst after outrageous stimulation" was blunting "the discriminating powers of the mind" and reducing it to "a state of almost savage torpor." People were losing their ability to be moved by ordinary sights and events, by "common life," because of "the great national events which are daily taking place, and the increasing accumulation of men in cities, where the uniformity of their occupations produces a craving for extraordinary incident which the rapid communication of intelligence hourly gratifies." Wordsworth created, in response, a minimalist poetry, a "lyrical" ballad that reduced the narrative or romance interest to near zero, and urged the reader to "find a tale in everything."[4]

---

[2] See Bauman, *Modernity and the Holocaust* (Ithaca, N.Y.: Cornell University Press, 1989). The context of his discussion is Nazi bureaucracy and Hannah Arendt's thesis on the banality of evil. Concerning immediate media coverage of the Bosnian conflict, Slavenka Drakulic asks: "Here they are, generations who have learned at school about concentration camps and factories of death; generations whose parents swear it could never happen again, at least not in Europe, precisely because of the living memory of the recent past. What, then, has all the documentation changed? And what is being changed now by what seems to be the conscious, precise bookkeeping of death?" (*New Republic*, 21 June 1993, 12).

[3] No wonder many in the younger generation, who are the most susceptible, are drawn to the unreality of fiction, to horror movies and other artificial plots, ever more crude, gothic, and violent: one can pretend that they, at least, are mere fantasy.

[4] Wordsworth, preface to *Lyrical Ballads*. Compare Goethe's notation circa 8 August 1797 in his *Reise in die Schweiz*: "Sehr merkwürdig ist mir aufgefallen, wie es eigentlich mit dem Publikum einer großen Stadt beschaffen ist; es lebt in einem

Since Wordsworth's time, psychic numbing has made considerable progress. The contemporary problem is not Bovarysm or Quixotism—seeing the real world (defensively) with an imagination steeped in romance—but looking at whatever is on the screen as if it were unreal, an interesting construct or simulation. Actuality is distanced by larger-than-life violence and retreats behind special effects. While Adorno discerns an "obscene merger of aesthetics and reality," it is not surprising that Robert Rosenblum, the art historian, should defend Warhol's "deadpan" by claiming that it reflects a "state of moral and emotional anaesthesia which, like it or not, probably tells us more truth about the realities of the modern world than do the rhetorical passions of *Guernica.*"[5]

But if the present now has less of a hold on us, if abstractness and psychic numbing have indeed infected us, how can we remain sensitive to the reality of the past? Spielberg's *Schindler's List* won acclaim in part by getting through to us, albeit by spectacular means.

Consider a related problem intensified by the media: whether we can trust appearances. Because our technical power of simulation has

---

beständigen *Tummel von Erwerben und Verzehren.*" He goes on to mention, in particular, theater and the inclination of the reading public to novels and newspapers as their major distractions. These early symptoms of a consumer culture show that, from the outset, sensations are among the commodities produced and consumed.

   [5] Rosenblum, "Warhol as Art History," in *New Art—An International Survey*, ed. Andreas Papadakis, Clare Farrow, and Nicola Hodges (New York: Rizzoli, 1991). Henri Lefebvre's theory of "everydayness" diagnoses a "generalized passivity" that accompanies the increasing uniformity of daily life (itself a functionalist result of the industrial and electronic revolutions), often beneath a surface of modernity: "News stories and the turbulent affectations of art, fashion and event veil without ever eradicating the everyday blahs. Images, the cinema and television divert the everyday by at times offering up to it its own spectacle, or sometimes the spectacle of the distinctly noneveryday, violence, death, catastrophe, the lives of kings and stars—those who we are led to believe defy everydayness" (*Yale French Studies* 73 [1987]: 7–11). Gianni Vattimo characterizes a "growing psychological dullness": "Technical reproduction seems to work in exactly the opposite sense to *shock.* In the age of reproduction [the reference is to Walter Benjamin's essay of 1936], both the great art of the past and new media products reproducible from their inception, such as cinema, tend to become common objects and consequently less and less well defined against the background of intensified communication" (*The Transparent Society*, trans. David Webb [Baltimore, Md.: Johns Hopkins University Press, 1992], 47–48).

increased but our forgetfulness has not decreased—the speed with
which events fall into "the dark backward and abysm of time" has, if
anything, accelerated—the greatest danger to public memory is *official
history*. Even the dead, as Walter Benjamin declared, are not safe from
the victors, who consider public memory part of the spoils and do not
hesitate to rewrite history. Or reimage it: In the opening episode of
The Book of Laughter and Forgetting, Milan Kundera recalls how a discredited Communist leader was airbrushed out of a famous historical
photo. So readily is history falsified and the public deceived.

In Puenzo's film *The Official Story*, set in Argentina under the military dictatorship—it could also have been set in Eastern Europe under
Soviet domination—a mother learns that her adopted child was stolen
from a "disappeared" woman. At first she does not suspect the truth,
but from the moment a small doubt punctures her trust in the system,
her search for answers grows until, as also in *Oedipus the King*, a hidden
past is revealed. Tragically, the mother's resolute pursuit of the truth
breaks up the family and endangers the child. The plot is close to universal, as old as the historical record itself. What is the difference, then,
between past and present? The contemporary difference can be
summed up in a famous phrase of Emerson: "We suspect our instruments." The very means of exposing untruth are tainted with suspicion. All verbal, photographic, and filmic evidence meets with demystifying discourse or charges of manipulation. The intelligent scrutiny
to which we habitually submit appearances becomes a crisis of trust, a
lack of confidence in what we are told or shown, a fear that the world
of appearances and the world of propaganda have merged through
the power of the media. To break the spell and gain true knowledge is
trickier than in gnosticism, which distrusted nature and tried to gain
knowledge of the true god behind the god of nature.

Thus there is a link between epistemology and morality: between
how we get to know what we know (through various, including electronic, media) and the moral life we aspire to lead. My rather pessimistic account implies that the gap between knowledge and ethical
action has not grown less wide for us. The pressures to be politically
correct, to say and do the right thing, have increased, but neither our
thinking nor our actions have adjusted to the challenge so clearly
stated by Terrence Des Pres, who claimed that, after the Holocaust, "a

new shape of knowing invades the mind" and opens our eyes, beyond the Holocaust, to the *global extent* of political misery.[6] In a democracy during the electronic age, moreover, this greater realism comes with a liability: a gnawing distrust of public policy and official memory. The free speech that is one of the foundations of truth in the democratic "marketplace of ideas" leads to continual probing, testing, and even muckraking, which has an unexpected effect on the integrity of the public life it was intended to assure.

Indeed, the more official history is disputed by scholarship or media journalism, the more an insidious and queasy feeling of unreality grows in us. What are we to do, for example, with all the speculations about John Kennedy's assassination that parade as investigative journalism or docudrama? It is as if the political realm, and possibly all of public life, were inauthentic—a mask, a Machiavellian web of deception.[7] This negative insight undermines the specific gravity, the uniqueness, of lived events and encourages a deep skepticism about the world—or a relentless, compensatory belief in something fundamental and unfalsifiable, often voiced in nationalistic or religious fanaticism.

My aim in addressing the relation of morality to knowledge in a democratic and electronic age is, frankly, moralistic. I seek to draw some conclusions, not only to describe as clearly as possible a contemporary dilemma framed by Terrence Des Pres, again, with the precision of a proverb: "Thanks to the technological expansion of consciousness, we cannot not know the extent of political torment; and in truth it may be said that *what others suffer, we behold*" (prologue; my emphasis).[8] The triumph of technology has created two classes: those who suffer, and those who observe them. This fact cannot be touted as moral progress, but there is one gain from it. Given our new eyes for the pain of others, and given that "we cannot not know," all monopolistic claims about suffering no longer make sense.

[6] Des Pres, prologue to *Praises and Dispraises: Poetry and Politics, the Twentieth Century* (New York: Penguin, 1989).

[7] The result can also be comic: think of the energy some expend to prove that Shakespeare was really Francis Bacon or the Earl of Essex, or consider that even children's literature has begun to exploit revisionism, as in *The True Story of the Three Little Pigs*, by Alexander T. Wolf.

[8] That which "we cannot not know" is "the real," according to Henry James.

"What others suffer, we behold" is like a second fall from innocence, a second bite of the fatal apple. It removes every excuse by taking away our ignorance, without at the same time granting us the power to do something decisive. Often, therefore, we fall back on a religious feeling, as President Reagan did at Bitburg, though in his case it served the bottom line of NATO policy. Mr. Reagan's reconciling memorial perspective equated fallen German soldiers, including Waffen-SS, with the civilians they killed, many of them Jewish. This "dead" perspective short-circuits reflection on a torment Des Pres called political because of its manmade rather than inevitable nature.

Even when the politics are not so obvious, skeptical contemporary thought sees them everywhere: in religion, in memory, in art. But that insight, too, has no activist or redemptive value. It simply confirms Des Pres's hellish vision of universal political torment. When we ask, haunted like Tolstoy by such suffering, "What is to be done?" no course of action proposes itself as entirely credible. Rather, the ethical impasse breeds, I have suggested, desperate and Manichaean solutions, post-Tolstoy fundamentalisms, whether religious or political.[9]

A related reaction is cultural revolution and its instrument, the politicized memory. In flight from human and hermeneutic complexities, cultural politics saturates everything with ideological content and claims redemptive power for a purified vision of the past. I have already mentioned the role of official history, promoted by the apparatus of state. It manipulates memory like news. It is true that a war is always going on to modify memory, and we all wage it in ourselves first: who does not remember moments of altering (or rationalizing or shad-

---

[9] Such as blaming the "white devil" or the Jew for the world's suffering, or the notion of an evil empire. In one of the few treatises to take up the possibility of ethics in a technological age, Hans Jonas argues that our sense of technological power has led to utopian expectations: it is all too easy to conceive of action on the pattern of technical progress, and we need, therefore, a new "modesty" as the basis of moral activism: "In view of the quasi-eschatological potential of our technical processes, ignorance about ultimate consequences becomes itself a ground for responsible hesitation—a second-best quality, should wisdom be lacking" (*Das Prinzip Verantwortung* [Frankfurt am Main: Insel, 1979]). In America, televangelism spawns its own sublime simplicity: the sinful past can be overcome by turning to a savior figure. The sense of universal suffering conveyed (painfully) by the media is relieved (painlessly) by the media.

ing) experiences painful to self-esteem? When waged publicly, however, such warfare leads to an institutionalized, bogus recollection, a churlish denial of the history of others (for instance, covering up the Jewish identity of most of the victims at Theresienstadt and Auschwitz) or an artificially inseminated perspective. A single authorized narrative then simplifies not just history but the only *active* communal memory we have, made of such traditional materials as legends, poetry, dances, songs, festivals, and recitations, the sum of which helps define a "culture" when combined with various interpretive traditions.

Art as a performative medium—art not reduced to official meaning or information—has a chance to transmit *this* inheritance most fully. When art remains accessible, it provides a counterforce to manufactured and monolithic memory. Indeed, despite its imaginative license, art is often more effective in "embodying" historically specific ideas than the history writing on which it may draw. Scientific historical research, however essential it is for its negative virtues of rectifying error and denouncing falsification, has no positive resource to lessen grief, endow calamity with meaning, foster a vision of the world, or legitimate new groups.[10] But art remains in touch with or revives traditional materials that satisfy our need for community without repressing individualist performance.

---

[10] Indeed, Jean-François Lyotard defines our "postmodern" condition as "incredulity toward metanarratives" produced by progress in the sciences. There is often a rupture, then, between the increasingly scientific history of the historians and the culture of the community, that is, collective practices structured by group memory. In Judaism the separation from communal ways of remembering becomes painfully clear after the Holocaust. The command *zakhor,* "Remember!" which resounds throughout the Bible and Jewish tradition, used to refer to observances that stressed, in Yosef Yerushalmi's words, "not the historicity of the past, but its eternal contemporaneity" (*Zakhor: Jewish History and Jewish Memory* [Seattle: University of Washington Press, 1982]). Today the same "Remember!" documents in volume upon volume a genocide that has weakened Jewish continuity. A form of memorizing rather than remembrance, and information- rather than performance-oriented, it is very different from the liturgical memory, the collectively recited lamentations, petitions, and hymns, or the scripture study by which Jews as a community healed or at least integrated the catastrophes in their past. Amos Funkenstein reintroduces the notion of "historical consciousness" to show that the split between historical and liturgical memory is not, today or in earlier times, as absolute as Yerushalmi represents it ("Collective Memory and Historical Consciousness," *History and Memory* 1 [1989]: 5–27).

We start indeed with a cultural inheritance, yet it cannot be fixed as immutably as doctrine is in theology. Memorial narratives asserting the identity of nation or group are usually modern constructs, a form of antimemory limiting the subversive or heterogeneous facts. Invented to nationalize consensus by suggesting a uniform and heroic past ("O say, can you see . . ."), they convert "great memories" into political theology. Cults and myths do not go away in modernity; on the contrary, revolution, national rebirth, and the drive for political legitimation make blatant ideological use of paradigms from the past. So Marx objected in *The Eighteenth Brumaire* to the French Revolution's historical masquerade: its archaic revival of symbols from the Republican phase of the Roman Empire.[11] This tendency, taken to its extreme, views the culture of a community not as its "nonhereditary memory" but as a pristine essence to be repristinated, a foundation with biological or mystical force that determines history.

What is viable in the notion of collective memory tends therefore to be artistic rather than nationalistic; and unless we keep in mind the link between art and memory—recognized when the Greeks made Mnemosyne mother of the Muses—national or ethnic politics will reduce culture to a tyrannous and frozen difference, a heroic narrative demanding consent.

---

[11] Two more contemporary examples: (1) East Germany's foundational cult centered on the prewar Communist leader Thälmann. Thälmann may have been brought to Buchenwald and executed there toward the end of the war. To magnify Buchenwald as the symbol of German resistance to fascism, the East German government identified the cell where he was killed, made it a cavernous shrine, and used it to initiate young devotees of the youth movement. The Thälmann cult excluded all perspectives on the Nazi era except that of heroic Communist revolt and became for East Germany a sterile and self-exculpatory "god-term" that allowed its inhabitants to transfer guilt for fascism and war crimes exclusively to the citizens of the *other* (West) Germany. (2) The rebirth of Israel, as Saul Friedlander and Alan Mintz (among others) have shown, activated the retrieval of a paradigm that had long ago linked catastrophe and redemption. ("The national historian," Funkenstein writes, "who in the nineteenth century enjoyed the status of a priest of culture, and whose work, even professional, was still read by a wide stratum of the educated public . . . even created some of [the symbols], some almost from nothing, such as the legend of Hermann, the victorious Cheruskian hero of early Roman-Germanic encounter" [21].)

A sense of the nation as vital to cultural memory arose in romanticism. Throughout Europe artists and scholars tried to free literature from the yoke of "foreign" classics by retrieving (and counterfeiting, if necessary!) a native tradition. Their literary nationalism was often a reconstruction, motivated by visionary nostalgia. "A people who lose their nationality create a legend to take its place," Edwin Muir wrote about Walter Scott's attempt to carry on a tradition that had lost its continuity. The ideal culture, according to romantic historicism, was produced by the spirit embodied in a people (*Volksgeist*), which expressed the true, distinctive voice of each nation among the nations. Collectors and antiquarians hunted for old stories, songs, and ballads: relics of a past now disappearing too quickly, and to which popular or archaic strength was imputed. A lively interest arose for anything regional rather than cosmopolitan: the buzzwords were *local attachment, local romance,* even *local superstition.* Hence Wordsworth's "Hart-Leap Well," a self-consciously re-created ballad, typical of a return to stories represented as emanations of particular places impressed on the collective memory and still part of the imaginative life of ordinary people.[12]

Legends about place stretch back to the Bible and seem to reflect traces of a popular memory. Being topocentric—subordinating time to place—they also lessen our anxiety that the ancient rapport between singer and audience, or artist and community, has broken down. "We have no institutions," Alasdair MacIntyre declares, "through which shared stories can be told dramatically or otherwise to the entire political community, assembled together as an audience, no dramatists or other story tellers able to address such an audience. . . . Our audiences are privatized and dispersed, watching television in homes or motel rooms."[13] His panicky view shows how deep the nostalgia for a collective memory runs. Since it is indeed difficult to humanize modern urban spaces, to invest them with a historically charged sense of place, the picture arises of a storyless modern imagination moving

[12] The stories often crystallize or cluster around proper names, especially place-names (Hart-Leap Well; Beth-El; Wessex; Balbec; Paris, Texas; Ole Kentucky; Chelm; Homewood). Some are fictional places, but such is the power of art that names outlive in our imagination referents they may never have had.

[13] MacIntyre, *After Virtue: A Study in Moral Theory* (Notre Dame, Ind.: Notre Dame University Press, 1984).

from nonplace to nonplace, even enjoying the anonymity of highways, airports, large hotels, and shopping malls. Each sacred memory-place (*lieu de mémoire*) is emptied out to become what Marc Augé defines as a nowhere-place (*non-lieu*).[14] Yet the old myths die hard: Michael Kammen notices "the remarkable way in which local events can be conceptualized to conform to paradigms of religious tradition or to the totally secular needs of a modern state struggling for existence."[15]

Before I discuss three recent literary ventures that respond to the challenge of reattaching imagination to the collective memory, or creating a communal story under the modern conditions described in the introductory part of my essay, I wish to add a few words to define contemporary *public* memory in its difference from the traditional *collective* memory.

Maurice Halbwachs, killed at Buchenwald, viewed the collective memory as a "living deposit" preserved outside academic or written history. "In general," he writes in his posthumous book, "history begins only at the point where tradition ends, at a moment where social memory is extinguished or decomposes. . . . the need to write the history of a period, a society, even of an individual does not arise until they are already too far removed in the past" for us to find many living witnesses.[16]

Although these lines were probably composed in the 1930s, they

[14] Pierre Nora, *Les Lieux de mémoire* (Paris: Gallimard, 1984–); and Augé, *Non-Lieux: Introduction à une anthropologie de la surmodernité* (Paris: Seuil, 1992). The conception of *non-lieu* plays with the legal term by which courts refuse to receive a complaint or nullify its basis in law. Cf. Claude Lanzmann, "Le Lieu et la parole," *Les Cahiers du cinéma* 37 (1985). Lanzmann describes how he developed a technique to overcome the "non-lieu de la mémoire."

[15] Kammen, *Mystic Chords of Memory: The Transformation of Tradition in American Culture* (New York: Knopf, 1991).

[16] Halbwachs, *Mémoire collective*, 2d ed. (Paris: Presses Universitaires de France, 1968), 68–69; my translation. This "collective memory" is a broader concept than "communal memory": memory, according to Halbwachs (in the wake of Durkheim and Marc Bloch), is never purely individual but always depends on an "affective community" (which need not be religious or ritual). Edward Shils makes the case that there is a sense of the past that is inculcated early and is important as a general "sensibility to past things" as well as for its specific contents (*Tradition* [Chicago: University of Chicago Press, 1981]).

already seem dated, for today we feel a need to record everything, even
as the event is occurring; and the media not only make it possible but
encourage it. This nervous effervescence marks modern experience
and the rise of public memory in distinction from collective memory.
The loss or subsumption of the past in the present, a present with very
little presence beyond the spotlight moment of its occurrence, a present that wearies itself out of the mind by its violence or is almost
immediately displaced by another such moment, sound bite, instantly
fading image—this self-consuming present, both real and specious,
vivid and always already a trace, is curiously like the collective memory
in that it has, to quote the historian Yosef Yerushalmi, "not the historicity of the past but its eternal contemporaneity." (Yerushalmi offers
the example that in Jewish liturgy the destruction of the First and Second Temples is conflated, as if it were the same *hurban*; and the Holocaust is often assimilated as the third *hurban*.) Of course, public memory is also utterly different; it strikes us as a simulacrum that, unlike the
older type of communal or collective memory, has no stability or *durée*,
only a jittery, mobile, perpetually changing yet permanently inscribed
status.[17] Hence my opening question of what *could* focus public memory on the traumatic events it busily recordis.

Halbwachs's observation that we are motivated to write things
down only when they are in danger of fading entirely can be made relevant to his own project. Today the collective memory is doubly endan-
gered, because public memory, with its frantic and uncertain agency, is
taking its place and because a politicized collective memory, claiming a
biological or mystical permanence, tries to usurp the living tie between
generations.[18]

[17] "Commentators on American culture note that a sense of historicity is shifting
away from singular stories that are forever true—away from story-lines that are hero-
oriented and confrontational. There are fewer authentic moments of 'catastrophe
time'" (Don Handelman, on "media events," *Models and Mirrors: Toward an Anthropology of Public Events* [Cambridge: Cambridge University Press, 1990], 266–67).

[18] Jacques Le Goff, describing the work of Pierre Nora on memory-places and a
new history "which seeks to create a scientific history on the basis of collective memory," does not entirely confront this difference between public and collective memory in his rather optimistic assessment: "The whole evolution of the contemporary
world, under the impact of an *immediate history* for the most part fabricated on the
spot by the media, is headed toward the production of an increased number of collective memories, and history is written, much more than in earlier days, under the

With this remark I return to literature. One reason literature remains important is that it counteracts, on the one hand, the impersonality and instability of public memory and, on the other, the determinism and fundamentalism of a collective memory based on identity politics.[19] Literature creates an institution of its own, more personal and focused than public memory yet less monologic than the memorializing fables common to ethnic or nationalist affirmation. At the same time, because today the tie between generations—the "living deposit" or "passé vécu," as Halbwachs calls it—is jeopardized, creative activity is often carried on under the negative sign of an "absent memory" (Ellen Fine) or *mémoire trouée* (Henri Raczymow).[20] A missed encounter is evoked through a strenuous, even cerebral exercise of the imagination, as if the link between memory and imagination had been lost.

I turn first to Toni Morrison's *Beloved*. Its epigraphs suggest not only a comparison between the political suffering of blacks and Jews but also the passing of the pathos and the covenant to the former. One epigraph is a dedication: "Sixty million and more." The other alludes through a New Testament quotation to the concept of the chosen people: "I will call them my people, which were not my people; and her beloved, which was not beloved" (Rom. 9.25).[21]

It is no exaggeration to call *Beloved* that people's *zakhor* ("Remember!"). Where in black history is there something comparable to a

---

influence of these collective memories" (*History and Memory*, trans. Steven Rendall and Elizabeth Claman [New York: Columbia University Press, 1992], 95).

[19] Cf. the description of what Jan Assmann names "das kulturelle Gedächtnis," which seeks a stability beyond the *saeculum* of oral history and the span of Halbwachs's collective memory ("Kollektives Gedächtnis und kulturelle Identität," in *Kultur und Gedächtnis*, ed. Jan Assmann and Tonio Hölscher [Frankfurt am Main: Suhrkamp, 1988]). For Funkenstein the difference emerging in the historical consciousness is between a purely liturgical memory and a more dynamic, heuristic collective memory that appears in the *hidushim* (new insights) of *halakhic* (rabbinic) law finding as well as in literature. But he does not provide us with a conceptualized understanding of the difference between "the liturgical incantations of a dynasty of tribal leaders" and "the poetry of Homer or the Book of Judges."

[20] On post-Holocaust Jewish writers (especially the children of survivors) see Fine, "The Absent Memory," in *Writing and the Holocaust*, ed. Berel Lang (New York: Holmes and Meyer, 1988); and Nadine Fresco, "Remembering the Unknown," *International Review of Psycho-Analysis* 11 (1984): 417–27.

[21] Morrison, *Beloved* (New York: Knopf, 1987).

genealogy of begats or the millennia of myths, chronicles, scriptures, and scriptural interpretations that characterize the collective memory of the Jews? (Concerning the begats, Julius Lester reminds us on the dedication page of *To Be a Slave* that "the ancestry of any black American can be traced to a bill of sale and no further. In many instances even that cannot be done"; John Edgar Wideman prefaces *Damballah* with "A Begat Chart" and a "Family Tree.")[22] African American memory remains to be recovered. But more important still, where is the conviction of being loved that makes memory possible? What kind of story could have been passed on, or who stayed alive long enough to remember a suffering that destroyed those who might have been tradents, a suffering that allowed no development of person, family, or ethnic group? "Anyone Baby Suggs knew, let alone loved, who hadn't run off or been hanged, got rented out, loaned out, bought up, brought back, stored up, mortgaged, won, stolen or seized."

Between Baby Suggs—or Grandma Baby, as she is also called—and Beloved, the little girl killed by her mother, there is no growth or normal history or significant genealogy. The child whose life was aborted after less than two years and who preternaturally reenters the mother's house as a young woman (now able to talk and carry on conversations of the most affectionate kind) is a ghost from folklore who expresses hauntingly the unlived life, and a love that never could come to fulfillment except in this fantasy form. Morrison's startling use of the *revenant*, the spirit figure that returns in many a romantic ballad (a genre that itself needed "revival"), challenges us to suspend not so much our disbelief affecting the preternatural return of Beloved—for that partly pagan, partly Christian myth has "a foundation in humanity," as Wordsworth would have said—as our disbelief of the atrocities suffered by black Americans, *that* ghost which we have not entirely faced.

African American history discloses, then, in a novel like Morrison's, a special difficulty concerning its absent memory. The black community is so scattered by suffering, so "disremembered and unaccounted for," that the story to be passed on "is not a story to pass on," and Morrison can represent it only by a ghostly "devil-child," a fantasy-

[22] Lester, comp., *To Be a Slave* (New York: Dial, 1968); and Wideman, *Damballah* (New York: Avon, 1981).

memory of the love or election this people has not known. In search of
that reversal of fate, *Beloved* becomes a Song of Songs, the Shulam-
mite's scripture.

My second example of absent memory is very different. For the
postmodern work of art, to which I now turn, cultivates it and does
not seek to recover even the possibility of memory—of "rememory," as
Morrison names it. Raymond Federman, for example, tries to do without resonant names and local romance in *To Whom It May Concern*,
though he too subverts an unfeeling realism. He uses gimmicks (as he
admits) to fight "the imposture of realism, that ugly beast that stands at
bay ready to leap in the moment you begin scribbling your fiction." He
renounces realism even in a novel that recalls the great roundup and
deportation of Jews from Paris in July 1942 and its impact on two children who escaped. His self-defeating venture takes courage from
experiments starting with Sterne and Diderot, which portray life as an
infinite detour rather than a punctual drama or epiphany: as something less than heroic, composed of accidents, small gestures, and simple, even insignificant words. Thus the *non-lieu* gains a sort of authenticity. "The grim story of Sarah and her cousin should be told without
any mention of time and place. It should happen on a timeless vacant
stage without scenery. No names of places. No decor. Nothing. It simply happened, sometime and somewhere."[23]

Federman is indebted to the new novel that evolved in postwar
France and to such films as *Last Year at Marienbad*. They depict memory
as a mode of seduction, as a narrative of past encounter suggesting
that the human condition is so empty or forgetful, so deprived of
sacred space (*lieu de mémoire*) and therefore so needy, that it cannot be
redeemed except by the construction and imposition of an imaginary
history. This deliberate recourse to a perhaps fictional past returns us,
of course, to the province of the collective memory, except that *Marienbad* seeks to erode the latter's historical and nationalist pretensions
(the Versailles-like decor in the film is meant to be only that, decor) in
favor of the private, imaginative needs of one man and one woman.
Federman, like Resnais or Robbe-Grillet, refuses to give his characters

[23] Federman, *To Whom It May Concern* (Boulder, Colo.: Fiction Collective Two,
1990).

more memory than they have. The wound of an absence remains. In this he speaks for an entire postwar generation that lost parents or relatives, while they themselves missed the brunt of the war. "They suffered from not suffering enough," he writes of his escaped children.

My last example is a genre that, in documentaries like *Eyes on the Prize* or Lanzmann's *Shoah* or the witness accounts in Yale's Video Archive for Holocaust Testimonies, is also oriented toward an absent memory. Personal testimony, long a significant part of both religious and secular literature, is usually considered a type of autobiography. Videotaped oral testimony, however, is partly a creation of modern technology and so has a chance of influencing that environment. As history it seeks to convey information, but as oral witness it is an act of remembrance. As a spoken and more spontaneous mode, which can be recorded without being written down, it contributes to a group biography through highly individual yet convergent stories. The collective memory thus becomes a collected memory (James Young), at once a private and a public legacy, and through video itself counters video's dispersive flow.

Each testimony is potentially an act of rescue, as the Israeli poet Haim Gouri observed when covering the Eichmann trial: a rescue "from the danger of [survivors] being perceived as all alike, all shrouded in the same immense anonymity." Moreover, by recording an experience collectively endured, by allowing anyone in the community a voice—that is, by not focusing on an elite—a vernacular and many-voiced dimension is caught.[24] Memory collected in this way is too plural and diverse to be politicized or sacralized. But I can best characterize the genre of these testimonies, and the Archive of Conscience they are building, by saying that they accept the *presence* of memory, however painful, rather than its absence.[25]

The amnesia that invades characters in postmodernist fiction

[24] Videotape adds to that dimension by allowing the recording of "stylistic" and "prosodic" features, such as gestures and visually accented pauses. As in photography generally, more detail previously thought of as incidental or accidental is included, which increases oral history's movement away from *histoire événementielle*.

[25] Claude Lanzmann goes so far as to say that his film seeks an "incarnation": "Le souvenir me fait horreur: le souvenir est faible. Le film est l'abolition de toute distance entre le passé et le présent."

(think of the difference between Beckett and Proust), creating a limbo in which the tape of memory starts and crashes again and again, may reflect a public memory that has become primarily space instead of place, anonymous and occupied by impersonal networks of information. As memory, then, it is purely virtual if not absent. In oral testimonies, however, a burdened recollection asserts itself and fashions a complex relation to the rupture between the positivism of historical experience and the symbolic stores of collective memory. Not only do memory's informative and performative (or ritual) functions try to unite again, but time present, in these testimonies, becomes more than a site of loss or nostalgic recuperation, more than the place that reveals that our capacity to experience has diminished, or that the past must be forgotten to be survived.[26]

Even if memory, as Rimbaud said of love, has always to be reinvented, the truth remains that some kinds of memory are better than others. Though Plato suggested that writing would be harmful to recollection, it proved essential for transmitting thought, both in manuscript and in print. Writing a thing down meant passing it on, for a communal or generational recipient. But who is the addressee of the new electronic writing, with its capacity for near-instantaneous reception and transmission? Every TV program is implicitly addressed "to whom it may concern," which begs the question of who *must* be concerned.

Videotaped oral history is an important compromise, because it comes on the cusp between generations and addresses those still grow-

[26] I must leave aside the more general issue of the revival, through history or art, of memory-places. For the sensibility, for example, that joins Wordsworth to Milton in understanding memory-place, see *Paradise Lost* 9.320–29. In terms of academic transmission, the *lieu de mémoire* becomes a "topos"; but the boundary between discourse, on the one hand, and poetry and even living performance, on the other, is quite porous, as was shown by E. R. Curtius's magisterial book on the way the classical tradition reaches modern European literature, and by the famous research of Parry and Lord on the formulaic compositional methods of Yugoslav bards. See also Halbwachs's interesting treatment of "religious space" (145–46, 160–65). Monuments, too, are *lieux de mémoire*, because like stories they involve real or legendary places. The German filmmaker Alexander Kluge comes to terms with the pressure of the past by incorporating images of ruined or deserted Nazi architecture, negative *lieux de mémoire*, once glorified in Nazi films, that serve as reminders of the "eternity of yesterday."

ing up, at a time when the collective memory is fading into the quasi-timeless, panoramic simultaneity of public memory. From Abel Gance and Walter Benjamin to Jean Baudrillard, this impact of technology on memory institutions such as art and history has been a subject of intense reflection. I have emphasized the difficulty, moral as well as cognitive, of responding to the images before our eyes in a critical or affective manner when the audiovisual mode becomes ineluctable and bypasses or floods timebound channels of personal memory.[27]

I have also suggested that there is such a thing as memory envy. It shows itself in writers who seek to recover an image of their community's past, deliberately destroyed by others or not allowed to form itself into a heritage. Memory envy also touches a generation that feels belated: the "generation after," which did not participate directly in a great event that determined their parents' and perhaps grandparents' life. Memory is lacking in both cases as a basis for the integrity of person or group. At the level of the collective, moreover, memory envy can take the form of foundation narratives, myths of origin that fortify group identity. Some of these decisive but also imposed identity fictions must be labeled false memories.

Increasingly, politicized and simplified aspects of the collective memory take over from an actual artistic heritage. We still have the arts, and literature in particular, to recall that each of us is a being made of many beings, and that the heritage of the past is pluralistic and diverse. But as the collective memory weakens, political religions (Eric Voegelin's name for totalitarian regimes) falsify the complexity of the past and cultivate an official story that seeks to reawaken ancient

---

[27] For Hegel it would have needed the entire history of the world, together with an intellectual odyssey of millennia, before mind was mind, free of its *subservience* to sense perception and able to retrieve all its memory stages in the activity of thought. Meanwhile (i.e., in everyday rather than visionary temporality), interesting makeshift solutions are found. I have mentioned Alexander Kluge; Claude Chabrol's recent *L'Oeil de Vichy* (1993) raises the spectator's consciousness of visual dependence by creating a film purely out of archival propaganda images, countered only by a dry historical commentary that places them in context. And Wilfried Schoeller has written: "Every museum, every monument, every memorial site recalling the Nazi era should reserve a moment of discretion, should leave something open and perhaps even claim the status of ruin or artifact, so that the imagination can still be active toward something in it."

hatreds. This falsified memory, with its foundation myths or funda-
mentalist notions of national destiny and ethnic purity, is the enemy.
We cannot allow it to masquerade as history, as is happening with the
Pamyat movement in Russia, with the attempt to rehabilitate Tiso in
Slovakia, and with nationalistic nostalgia, whether in Bosnia or in the
Middle East. The outbreak of unreal memory can be fought, but only
if younger bystanders, whether artists or scholars, bring testimony of
their own, ballads of their own, before our eyes; and only if, like the
Caribbean poet Derek Walcott, they accept the scarred rather than
sacred, the fragmented rather than holistic, nature of what he names
"epic memory," which has to be recomposed—performed—again and
again. For oral tradition, however monumental its aspiration, remains
an art of assemblage. To reconstruct "this shipwreck of fragments,
these echoes, these shards of a huge tribal vocabulary, these partially
remembered customs" needs a special love. "Nothing can be sole or
whole / That has not been rent," Yeats's Crazy Jane tells the Bishop.
"Break a vase," says Walcott, "and the love that reassembles the fragments is stronger than the love that took its symmetry for granted
when it was whole."[28]

[28] Walcott, "The Antilles: Fragments of Epic Memory" (Nobel lecture), *New
Republic*, 28 December 1992, 27. In emphasizing the performative dimension, however, we need to distinguish between an opportunistic recomposing of the collective
memory, motivated by identity politics, and the creative-heuristic use of its traditions
in art. Such notions as Schiller's "aesthetic education" may provide a beginning for
theorizing that difference. The formalist's deinstrumentalizing emphasis on what is
distinctively literary also responds to the need for critical theory.

Understanding the Living and Talking to the Dead: The Historicity of Psychoanalysis

Meredith Anne Skura

Misunderstanding of the present is the inevitable consequence of ignorance of the past. But a man may wear himself out just as fruitlessly in seeking to understand the past, if he is totally ignorant of the present. . . . This faculty of understanding the living is, in very truth, the master quality of the historian.—Marc Bloch[1]

The literary critics' return to history, one sign of which is this new phase of *Modern Language Quarterly*, has been salutary for everyone interested in the relation between psychoanalysis and Renaissance literature. It has generated questions, for example, about the historical specificity of psychoanalysis and has reminded us that the analyst, already alert to transference—to individual bias in personal perceptions of the analysand—has much to learn about the ways in which even "impersonal" psychoanalytic theory is shaped by the age that produced it. But the real question for me is not whether Freud's (or Klein's or Lacan's or my) psychoanalysis is the product of a historically determined culture (they all are) but whether psychoanalysis, having grown into a loose baggy monster over the years as it spread across national borders and mutated during political infighting, might nonetheless be useful in talking about early modern texts and subjects. To a degree, the uncertainty rests on the difficulty of analyzing anyone outside a clinic, even now. No form of indirect analysis is as useful as the results of prolonged clinical exchanges. Yet, since even in the clinic

I want to thank Martin Wiener for his advice and suggestions about the material in this essay.

[1] Bloch, *The Historian's Craft*, trans. Peter Putnam (New York: Knopf, 1953), 43.

there are no raw data except the analysand's talk (no privileged information about childhood or even about unconscious fantasies), applied
analysis of contemporary subjects is reasonable outside the clinic, too,
wherever there is some kind of "talk," so long as we remember that
interpretation must be especially tentative when the analysand can't
talk back.[2] But most historians of the early modern period, even were
they to accept contemporary analysis outside the clinic, would probably agree with Lawrence Stone's reservations about historical analysis.
Stone, working in the psychoanalytic backyard of family history,
nonetheless argues that Freud's theories about childhood ("Oral, anal,
and sexual experiences of infancy and very early childhood are *decisive*
in moulding character, which, once set, can only with greatest difficulty be modified later on") and about sexuality ("Sex—the id—is the
most powerful of all drives, and has *not changed* over the ages") have
"hamstrung" historians, because they stand "outside history and [are]
unaffected by it."[3]

On the contrary, I want to argue two points here. To begin with,
psychoanalysis is not the rigid doctrine Stone describes; it is rather a
set of assumptions about what is important (or interesting) in the historical record—just like any other assumptions. Let me state a working
version of them. The first is simply that historians should pay attention
to inner reality, to the feelings and fantasies that distort judgment and
perception, and to the irrational motives that complicate our expectation that people act out of rational self-interest. Inner reality includes,
but is not restricted to, one's consciousness of oneself as subject. More
important, it is confounded by the unconscious nature of much of its
contents; the history of subjectivity is not a "history of consciousness"
only or even of self-consciousness only. The relation between inner

---

[2] John Putnam Demos, discussion of "Psychoanalytic Theory and History:
Groups and Events," by Bruce Mazlish, *Annual of Psychoanalysis* 6 (1978): 57–64.

[3] Stone, *The Family, Sex, and Marriage in England, 1500–1800* (New York: Harper
and Row, 1977), 15; italics added. Jack N. Rakove, expressing a similar complaint
about psychohistory, asks why "weaning at age two mattered more than a not unrea-
sonable fear that Satan was running amok"—why an unconscious memory of childhood experience mattered *more than* a conscious, adult, socially supported belief
("Witching Time," review of *Entertaining Satan: Witchcraft and the Culture of Early New
England,* by John Putnam Demos, *New York Times Book Review,* 19 September 1982,
14–15, 30).

and outer, conscious and unconscious, varies widely over time and across cultures, but it needs to be taken into account. The second assumption is that inner reality is shaped, though of course not determined, both by earliest infancy and by later developmental pressure points like adolescence. Childhood experience of one's body (in classical Freudian analysis) and earliest caretakers (in object relations analysis) affects adult life; therefore the study of adult life and behavior in any culture—the study of morality and power relations as well as of sexual identity—will be linked to particular family structures and child-rearing patterns.[4] Third, the inner world of historical subjects is best accessed through one or more (admittedly inadequate) replacements for free associations: oral or written texts; Lacanians would say that there *is* no inner world apart from the texts. Fourth, the texts need to be placed in context ("Who is saying this to whom and why?"), and they need to be heard with an analyst's third ear listening for the speaker's contradictory meanings and motives as well as for its own.

My second point is that psychoanalysis can be useful in understanding historical subjects, provided not only that it is psychoanalytic enough (in the way in which I have countered Stone's psychoanalysis) but also that it is historical enough. The trick, as usual, lies in the details. Even today analysis depends on unrestricted access to the cultural details analyst shares with analysand, for example, to the assumption that in contemporary middle-class families (as opposed to early modern families) parents and children sleep in different bedrooms. To psychoanalyze James I or the author of *Macbeth* (Macbeth himself, of course, presents additional problems), we would have to come as close as possible to that shared world; we would need the broadest and thickest descriptions of cultural context. Here we can learn from the New Historicists, who have known for some time that history matters

---

[4] A number of reductionist efforts to explain a group's collective behavior by its child-rearing practices (as if the group were simply one large individual) have, not surprisingly, failed. (See, e.g., Miles F. Shore's criticism of such efforts in "Biography in the 1980s," *Journal of Interdisciplinary History* 12 [1981]: 89–113, esp. 112.) But the possibility for more flexible and inclusive study of the effects of child rearing remains open. For recent efforts in this direction, see Barry Richards, ed., *Capitalism and Infancy: Essays on Psychoanalysis and Politics* (London: Free Association Books; New Jersey: Humanities Press, 1984), esp. Margaret Rustin and Michael Rustin, "Relational Preconditions of Socialism," 207–25.

and have interpreted literary texts against the "text" of history. But we need to go even farther.[5] The claim that "history is a text" needs to be amended to "history is texts"—many texts, of different kinds, nonnarrative floor plans along with narrative histories, and nondiscursive practices along with discursive materials.

Attempts even to become familiar with so many texts, let alone to integrate them, meet formidable obstacles that are not to be overcome, as David Sacks warns, by dipping here and there into secondary sources to support one's claims.[6] But as more and more historians supplement the study of Great Men with that of popular culture, families, and women, and the study of politics with that of mentalities, sensibilities, and the history of emotions, the relevant secondary sources multiply.[7] (So do the possibilities for collaboration—which may be the most promising strategy for literary criticism in the current interdisciplinary climate.) There is enough information about the discursive context that Janet Adelman, for example, can begin her study of "suffocating mothers" not with a recipe for universal fantasies but with the suggestion that "the infantile fantasies that Shakespeare invokes to

---

culture or otherwise unrepresentative) see, for example, Carolyn Porter, "Are We Being Historical Yet?" *South Atlantic Quarterly* 87 (1988): 743–86; Joseph Kelly and Timothy Kelly, "Searching the Dark Alley: New Historicism and Social History," *Journal of Social History* 25 (1991–92): 677–94; and Robert D. Hume, "Texts within Contexts: Notes towards a Historical Method," *Philological Quarterly* 71 (1992): 69–100, esp. 71.

[6] Sacks, "Searching for Culture in the English Renaissance," *Shakespeare Quarterly* 39 (1988): 474. In a similar argument, David Simpson suggests that the information overload has "some frightening implications for the [literary critical] 'profession,' not the least of which is that if we [literary critics] are going to become historians we are going to have to do more research and publish less" ("Literary Criticism and the Return to 'History,'" *Critical Inquiry* 14 [1988]: 747).

[7] David Garland distinguishes between "those phenomena of cognition known as 'mentalities' and those of affect or emotion usually termed 'sensibilities'" and argues that when we talk about "culture," we are talking about both (*Punishment in Modern Society: A Study in Social Theory* [Chicago: University of Chicago Press, 1990], 193–99). See also Peter N. Stearns and Carol Z. Stearns, "Emotionology: Clarifying the History of Emotions and Emotional Standards," *American Historical Review* 90 (1985): 813–36, rpt. in *Psycho-History: Readings in the Method of Psychology, Psychoanalysis, and History*, ed. Geoffrey Cocks and Travis L. Crosby (New Haven, Conn.: Yale University Press, 1987), 284–309. For recent commentary on and examples of the growing number of secondary studies, see Lynn Hunt, ed., *The New Cultural History* (Berkeley: University of California Press, 1989).

empower his fictions would themselves have been shaped by the actual conditions of infancy and reformulated in adulthood according to the terms provided by his culture. . . . fantasy of suffocation in the womb is no more than scientific fact: . . . the most popular mid-wifery of the day sounds remarkably like [*Richard III*] when it attrib-utes spontaneous abortion to the mother's 'excesse feeding and sur-fetting, by the which the byrth is suffocate and strangled in the belly' (*The birth of mankinde* [1598])."[8] Still more important for thickening the cultural context for interpretation, historians have given us entrée to early modern dreams and fantasies, like Simon Forman's ambiva-lent dream about Elizabeth I, which Louis Adrian Montrose can use as subjective evidence to round out his analysis of politically produced misogyny in Shakespeare's *Midsummer Night's Dream*.[9] Recent studies like Michael MacDonald's *Mystical Bedlam* have allowed us to glimpse even the dreams and delusions of ordinary men, and women.[10] A growing number of studies of women's attitudes and sensibilities dur-ing pregnancy or toward eldest sons, for example, now supplement evidence from male discourse and can help us build a fuller aware-ness of historically specific family relationships in which to locate early modern subjects.[11]

As the details accumulate, it becomes apparent that historians have

[8] Adelman, *Suffocating Mothers: Fantasies of Maternal Origin in Shakespeare's Plays, "Hamlet" to "The Tempest"* (New York: Routledge, 1992), 4–6. B. M. Berry suggests that the theories about infancy formulated by Tudor pediatricians could have been influenced by their own infantile experience ("The First English Pediatricians and Tudor Attitudes towards Childhood," *Journal of the History of Ideas* 35 [1974]: 561–77).

[9] Montrose, "'Shaping Fantasies': Figurations of Gender and Power in Eliza-bethan Culture," *Representations* 2 (1983): 61–94.

[10] MacDonald, *Mystical Bedlam: Madness, Anxiety, and Healing in Seventeenth-Cen-tury England* (Cambridge: Cambridge University Press, 1981).

[11] See, for example, Patricia Crawford, "The Construction and Experience of Maternity in Seventeenth-Century England"; Linda A. Pollock, "Embarking on a Rough Passage: The Experience of Pregnancy in Early-Modern Society"; and other essays in *Women as Mothers in Pre-Industrial England: Essays in Memory of Dorothy McLaren*, ed. Valerie Fildes (London: Routledge, 1990); Crawford, "'The Sucking Child': Adult Attitudes to Child Care in the First Year of Life in Seventeenth-Century England," *Continuity and Change* 1 (1986): 23–52; and Barbara Harris, "Property, Power, and Personal Relations: Elite Mothers and Sons in Yorkist and Early Tudor England," *Signs* 15 (1990): 606–32.

found less change than they expected.[12] Stone's own thesis that sixteenth-century parents were not as attached to their children as nineteenth-century parents were brought on a notorious rush of counterar-
guments. Indeed, Linda Pollock suggests that instead of emphasizing
difference, "historians would do well to ponder why parental care is a
variable so curiously resistant to change."[13] I am trying, not to advance
a New Universalism, but to recommend that we look for something like
variable variability in history: some things change rapidly; others don't.
We can't predict the variability, but we can identify psychoanalytic parameters, along with more traditional ones, to help locate and understand it. We can't talk about unchanging human nature, but we can
talk about what Peter Gay has called the vicissitudes of "human nature
in history."[14] Similar ideas have reformulated the old debate between
Jones and Malinowski about the universality of the Oedipus complex,
which emerges from recent discussions not as a master plot but as a

---

[12] Alan Macfarlane has made the most energetic case for continuity. He argues
that, while most historians and social theorists trace the origins of individualism to
the Renaissance, Reformation, and Enlightenment, "individualism, however defined,
predates sixteenth-century changes and can be said to shape them all" (*The Origins of
English Individualism: The Family, Property, and Social Transition* [New York: Cambridge
University Press, 1979], 196). For a recent review of the debate over Macfarlane's
tendency to discount cultural change in English history, see K. D. M. Snell, "English
Historical Continuity and the Culture of Capitalism: The Work of Alan Macfarlane,"
History Workshop Journal, no. 27 (1989): 154–63. For a balanced presentation of
recent work on the history of the family and the related issues of individualism and
parental attachment, see Patrick Collinson, *The Birthpangs of Protestant England: Religious and Cultural Change in the Sixteenth and Seventeenth Centuries* (London: Macmillan, 1988), esp. 81–90.

[13] Pollock, *Forgotten Children: Parent-Child Relations from 1500 to 1900* (Cambridge: Cambridge University Press, 1983), 271. Cf. Collinson: "As for the children
of [fifteenth-century] marriage, they were emotionally valued, enjoyed, loved, and
probably always had been" (89).

[14] Gay, *Freud for Historians* (New York: Oxford University Press, 1986), 78–115;
italics added. Elsewhere Gay offers a rebuttal of Stone (22–33). Sally Alexander
argues—from a different psychoanalytic camp—that, while Lacanian psychoanalysis
does not imply a monolithic "universal human nature, it suggests that some forms of
mental functioning—the unconscious, phantasy, memory, etc.—seem to be so"
("Women, Class, and Sexual Differences in the 1830s and 1840s: Some Reflections
on the Writing of a Feminist History," *History Workshop Journal*, no. 17 [1984]: 134).
Alexander, along with other works cited here, is discussed in T. G. Ashplant's excellent survey of the issues ("Psychoanalysis and Historical Writing," *History Workshop
Journal*, no. 26 [1988]: 102–19).

force field; though a universal potential, it is continually modified by particular historical and cultural conditions.[15] Such formulations still leave problems, but they are productive problems, opening rather than closing off discussion about which parameters matter and how.

The biggest difficulty in transposing psychoanalysis through time, in fact, is not so much the historicity of its assumptions about the individual as its failure to theorize the individual's relation to his or her culture in any period, including our own. Part of Stone's objection to psychoanalysis is that its assumptions are always inadequate, because they always emphasize the individual's irrational inner world and its childhood origins and neglect social reality and rational adult life. And if historians like Stone want to protect the social surface of history from Freud's archaeology of mind, a more radical critique of psychoanalysis has come from social theorists who are proponents of competing, and also potentially "ahistorical," archaeologies: whether from Marxists interested in an economic base or from Foucauldians interested in their very different archaeology of the surface. Even if psychoanalysis can be historicized, can it be reconciled with social analysis? Certainly the sequence of past efforts to reduce Freud to Marx or Marx to Freud has failed. Freudians have no way of talking about how culture affects the psyche except as superego and have no theory of group structure except as a projection of individual psychology.[16] On the other hand, although Marxists such as Althusser, Macherey, and Jameson have drawn on the psychoanalytic terminology of "overdetermination," socially produced "desire," and "the [political] unconscious," Marxism has no theory of the subject, except as a product of ideology.[17]

[15] Melford E. Spiro reopened the debate in *Oedipus in the Trobriands* (Chicago: University of Chicago Press, 1982); his work has in turn been the subject of a panel entitled "Psychoanalysis and Cultural Relativism," *Psychoanalysis: The Vital Issues* 1 (1984): 165–212.

[16] Freud notes that the individual superego subsumes not only the personal qualities of one's parents "but also everything that had a determining effect on them themselves, the tastes and social standards of the social class in which they lived. . . . the super-ego represents more than anything the cultural past" ("An Outline of Psychoanalysis," in *The Standard Edition of the Complete Psychological Works of Sigmund Freud*, ed. James Strachey, vol. 23 [London: Hogarth, 1953–74], 206).

[17] Assuming homologies between psyche and society, both sides have in the past offered similarly hydraulic visions of subjects as "repressed" or "socially controlled" energies.

But politics can be shaped by individual psyches without being reduced to family drama, and the notion of the unconscious can be culture-specific without being reduced to a political unconscious. And psychoanalysis does not need to posit an asocial autonomous subject just because it explores interiority. Neither Marx's nor Foucault's assumptions about social forces are incompatible with psychoanalytic assumptions about psychological forces, and literary critics can now look to a growing number of scholars who are making room for multiple determinants in their analyses. Norbert Elias's study of the civilizing process looked at both state power and individual psyche and has influenced exciting new literary studies like Gail Paster's work on shame and the body.[18] John Putnam Demos's study of witchcraft in early New England, a model of balanced interdisciplinary research, gives equal attention to demography, (psychoanalytic) psychology, sociology, and history and makes it possible to watch the interaction of independent forces, none of which can be reduced to any other.[19] Anthony Easthope has suggested a similarly inclusive approach to the interpretation of literary texts: "Although the conceptual frameworks of historical materialism and psychoanalysis will remain distinct, resisting a synthesis we have no right to demand, *the literary text always produces ideological and phantasy meanings in a simultaneity* and both must be considered together as social phantasy: *nec tecum nec sine te* (neither with you nor without you). Any attempt to discuss a poetic text only with attention to one side is reductive and inadequate."[20] The socially and psychologically produced readings resist the "synthesis we have no right to demand," and their relationship will vary from text to text, let alone from period to period. But we can learn from the variability.

More than anything, at least for the present, we need to collect specific examples, like the famous case of the two Martin Guerres, reexamined in Natalie Zemon Davis's study, which Stephen Greenblatt uses to discredit psychoanalysis as a tool for understanding Renais-

[18] Paster, *The Body Embarrassed: Drama and the Disciplines of Shame in Early Modern England* (Ithaca, N.Y.: Cornell University Press, forthcoming).

[19] Demos, *Entertaining Satan: Witchcraft and the Culture of Early New England* (New York: Oxford University Press, 1982).

[20] Easthope, *Poetry and Phantasy* (Cambridge: Cambridge University Press, 1989), 43.

sance culture.[21] Greenblatt's work has been widely accepted by literary critics who agree that early modern characters, onstage or off, cannot be suitable subjects for psychoanalysis.[22] But Davis, who has suggested that Greenblatt may exaggerate the difference between Guerre's subjectivity and ours, provides an alternative, more textual approach that not only makes new psychological material available but also theorizes it in ways that psychoanalysis can learn from and extend.[23] The case is fascinating: Martin Guerre was a sixteenth-century Basque peasant who left his family after quarreling with his father and disappeared into Spain, apparently with no intention of returning. Eight years later a man claiming to be the long-lost Guerre turned up and took his place in his village, in his extended family, and in his wife's bed—until Guerre's uncle had him arrested for stealing family property. The case might have been unremarkable, except that neither judges, nor jury, nor family could agree to oust the impostor until Guerre himself reappeared during the trial, minus a leg; even then the judges had a hard time deciding.

The story, Greenblatt says, "seems to solicit psychoanalytic interpretation. . . . Martin's [earlier] impotence, oedipal transgression and flight [are] the classic materials of Freudian speculation" (133). But Greenblatt's point is that such speculation—along with all psychoanalytic assumptions about the importance of body experience and the past in establishing Martin's unique identity—not only would "have seemed almost comically beside the point" (136) to the participants in the trial but would have been beside the point. "At issue was

[21] Davis, *The Return of Martin Guerre* (Cambridge, Mass.: Harvard University Press, 1983).

[22] Greenblatt, "Psychoanalysis and Renaissance Culture," in *Literary Theory/Renaissance Texts*, ed. Patricia Parker and David Quint (Baltimore, Md.: Johns Hopkins University Press, 1986), 210–24, rpt. in *Learning to Curse: Essays in Early Modern Culture* (New York: Routledge, 1990). Fredric Jameson expresses some general doubts about Greenblatt's collection of essays but singles this one out as "superb" ("The Historian as Body-snatcher," review of *Learning to Curse, Times Literary Supplement*, 18 January 1991, 7); Joan Lord Hall cites Greenblatt's earlier but similar point in *Renaissance Self-Fashioning* (Chicago: University of Chicago Press, 1980) in support of her assumption that characters in Renaissance drama, like the people in the audience who went to watch them onstage, cannot be psychoanalyzed (*The Dynamics of Role-Playing in Jacobean Tragedy* [New York: St. Martin's, 1991], 9).

[23] Davis, "On the Lame," *American Historical Review* 93 (1988): 602.

not Martin Guerre as subject but Martin Guerre as object, the place-holder in a complex system of possessions, kinship bonds, contractual relationships, customary rights, and ethical obligations" (136–37). What mattered was not a subject's sense of himself but communal judgment secured by legal authority (136). Subjectivity is only produced (à la Foucault) through such institutions as "the judicial murder of the impostor" (139), and especially (à la Marx) through the "community secured property rights in a name" (141). More to the point for literary criticism, Greenblatt argues that similar questions of property dominate the many examples of fictional impostors that were circulating at the time. Psychoanalysis is not a key for understanding these stories but is itself a belated product of the culture that created trials, stories, and the notion of a subject in the first place. Psychoanalysis is "baffled" and (more than the one-legged Guerre?) is left "crippled" by the trial (131, 137).

Perhaps what baffles psychoanalysis, however, is not Guerre's subjectivity but the questions put to it. Couched in reified twentieth-century terms and either-or form, questions about Guerre's status ("Was Guerre a Subject or not?") run the same danger as old-fashioned psychoanalytic pathography ("Did Guerre have an Oedipus Complex or not?"). Davis asks different questions: What might subjectivity have meant to Martin (or to his wife, Bertrande)? *Was* it incompatible with being a "placeholder" in the communal kinship system? Placing Guerre in the mental and material world of sixteenth-century French village life, she tries to recapture "the interplay between the socially determined and the chosen."[24] In particular, Davis asks what Martin and the others were thinking and how they experienced themselves as selves. When she is finished, we see that of course "communal judgment" was at stake, but only because the occasion was a public trial. Like us, the villagers seemed able to distinguish between legal proceedings and other ways of talking about people; and even in the trial more than communal judgment was at stake. Witnesses claimed to be reliable because, for example, "they had seen and been often with

---

[24] Coras's annotation 68, cited by Davis, "On the Lame," 576. Davis is responding to Robert Finlay's critique of her efforts to locate "the chosen" ("The Refashioning of Martin Guerre," *American Historical Review* 93 [1988]: 553–71).

[Guerre] since his childhood" or "had known [the impostor] from the cradle," that is, had come closest to knowing him as only he knew himself.[25] Part of why Guerre's story has been so compelling, then and now, is that communal judgment was *not* enough. It was starkly in conflict with subjective judgment; indeed, Davis suggests that the impostor's confession, finally given after the trial, provided his contemporaries with the closure they had missed in the legal proceedings.[26] Under Davis's scrutiny, evidence mounts for a sixteenth-century subjectivity not unlike our own; she writes primarily about its conscious adult dimension, but, like an analyst, she asks how childhood experience shapes consciousness,[27] and she allows for speculation about unconscious components as well.

From a psychoanalytic point of view, the most important aspect of Davis's approach is that, while Greenblatt focuses on the duplication of Guerres, the bizarre phenomenon that provides the narrative core of the case, she pays as much attention to Jean de Coras, the judge who presided over the trial and decided to tell the story. Unlike Guerre himself, Coras left a text, the "talk" we can analyze. It is clear that the question for him was, as it would be for us, not whether Martin had an individual identity but what it was. When the judges thought that they couldn't tell, they were not only baffled ("in great perplexity," Coras said) but quite troubled by the confusion.[28] At first Coras even invoked magic to explain the impostor's success—precisely the sort of power, I

[25] Davis, *Return*, 67; quotations from Jean de Coras's report of the trial, "A Memorable Decision of the High Court of Toulouse . . ." (1570), trans. Jeannette K. Ringold, *Triquarterly* 55 (1982): 91.

[26] "On the Lame," 597 n. 96. Davis refers in *The Return of Martin Guerre* to some of those who have written about the story over the years and cites a number of others in "On the Lame" (572 n. 1). Fictional versions of identical twins or impostors have of course been popular throughout Western European literary history; they seem always to have been as uncanny as Freud found the phenomenon of doubling in the nineteenth century. See the issues raised, for example, in Robert B. Heilman, "Farce Transformed: Plautus, Shakespeare, and Unamuno," *Comparative Literature* 31 (1979): 113–23.

[27] For example, Martin, seemingly so unprepared for marriage and family responsibility, grew up fatherless in a family of sisters; by contrast, the easygoing impostor had a group of brothers with whom he got along well (*Return*, 36).

[28] Davis discusses Coras's "mixed feelings" at length (*Return*, 91, 94–113; "On the Lame," 592–97).

might note, that Martin had invoked to explain his earlier sexual impotence. In Davis's reading of Coras's omissions and contradictions, the judge is ambivalent toward the impostor, as if he identified with even though he condemned the wily trickster, who was good with words and knew how to work an audience—just as Coras, a famous lecturer, did.[29] Coras's emotional investment in the case seems produced not only by legal systems, state power, and property rights but also by the rest of his own "talk" (legal reports, letters) and his unique history, stretching back to childhood (on record elsewhere). It invites us to refer to what we might call Coras the subject, not Coras the object. We might add that, however necessary he may have found communal judgment in Martin's trial, there is no indication that Coras experienced himself as an object, a placeholder, or that he would have wanted communal judgment to help him decide who *he* was if a Coras impostor turned up.[30] Indeed, in one letter to his wife he measured the extremity of his passion by the fact (apparently amazing to him) that "without you I don't exist!" (Davis, *Return*, 98). Not only did he find it odd to be so dependent on her for his own sense of identity, but he also knew very well what that identity was.

Greenblatt begs the question by making psychoanalytic subjectivity equivalent to interiority and a continuous sense of self, but then ignoring Coras's sense of self and the texts where it might be found; instead, he asks only what produced it or how it was seen from the outside. Certainly, we cannot assume a modern bourgeois subject (however we wish to define that creature) "behind" the contradictions in Coras's text. But neither can we go to the opposite extreme and assume that

[29] Perhaps too energetically, and perhaps for his own reasons. Davis cites a letter from Coras to his wife in which he tells of "a strange dream that I had yesterday that before my eyes you were remarried to another, and when I reproached you for the wrong you were doing me, you responded by turning your back" (*Return*, 112).

[30] Unless it observes the distinction between attitudes toward the self and attitudes toward other selves, any study of historical mentalities provides only unreliable evidence about subjectivity. From the representation of "tamed death" in medieval chivalric romance, Philippe Ariès generalized that most people of that period thought of their own death with resignation; others, however, have argued that tamed death "primarily refers to the experience with the death of others" and that medieval subjects didn't like to think about dying any more than we do (Peter Spierenburg, *The Broken Spell: A Cultural and Anthropological History of Preindustrial Europe* [New Brunswick, N.J.: Rutgers University Press, 1991], 131).

there was no subjectivity to psychoanalyze and that, unlike us, Coras was only an object. The psychoanalyst's question, like the historian's, is precisely what past subjects were like. The way to collect material for an answer is not simply to look at everything that helped produce them—individual childhood experience along with pervasive social constructions—but to listen to patterns of repetition and inconsistency in their talk, in the texts that will "solicit psychoanalytic interpretation" even more strongly than the facts we know about Guerre. For sixteenth-century subjects, no less than for ours or for Freud's, the royal road to subjectivity in any context is texts. The analyst may differ from the historian in assuming what produced a historical text or how to read it, but historicity itself is not the problem.

FIGURES OF THE FEMININE: AN AMAZONIAN REVOLUTION IN FEMINIST LITERARY HISTORY?

Donna Landry

Feminist literary history recovers figures from the archives—historical figures who were women, and sometimes men, but also figures of femininity and masculinity as they structure textual systems. The best sort of feminist literary history situates individual texts by reading them in the context of the available documentary evidence of sexual and social practices. Tracing the operations of gender through the documents of the past reveals some surprising disjunctures between how we, as late-twentieth-century scholars, may think about gender and sexuality now and what seems in fact to have been the case in past centuries. Yet a question presses. Scholarship, however scrupulously fair-minded, is always selective to some degree. Concerning feminist work in eighteenth-century studies in the U.S. academy, we might well inquire which eighteenth-century figures are being retrieved, or rather, whose.

The question is an important one, for figurations of gendered subjects powerfully help construct people's subjectivities, even map the destinies of real historical persons. In this essay I shall argue for the importance of reading against the grain of much late-eighteenth-century English discourse on womanhood and of many current Anglo-U. S. academic accounts of that discourse. Both kinds of writing have invested heavily in the notion of femininity as domesticity. And on the borders of these late-eighteenth-century texts, specifically those of the 1790s, we can glimpse certain profoundly shared Anglo-U.S. anxieties regarding heroic masculine identity, the military enforcement of colonial commerce troped as a global civilizing mission, and the fear of revolutionary uprisings both from without and within the English polis. These anxieties cohere around the figure of the Amazon, particularly when she is seen in contrast to her psychic and social alternative, the domestic woman.

The turn toward the modern that many scholars have marked in the unfolding of the long eighteenth century, from 1660 to 1800, has usually pointed to the consolidation of a hegemonic heterosexuality and a binary gender system, from which gay male and lesbian identities diverge in a binary way. It is the eighteenth century of the emergent bourgeois domestic woman reading and writing herself into social power through the respectable pen. A long downhill run away from early modern complexity, queerness, perversity, and agency, this eighteenth century looks awfully bleak from a feminist perspective. When one argues from a materialist feminist perspective that questions of race, nation, and empire are finally inseparable from a proper consideration of gender, the century looks even bleaker. Nancy Armstrong's *Desire and Domestic Fiction* may argue that women had social power, indeed that they were the prototypes of bourgeois subjects to such an extent that we should read Robinson Crusoe as a woman when he drones on about his stewardship of the island as a series of perpetual domestic economies. But at what cost, in the form of a repressive apparatus or machine of gender, so often crucial in the service of imperial domination, is this wielding of feminine social and moral authority achieved?[1]

Other feminist scholars, notably Mary Poovey, Felicity Nussbaum, and Ellen Pollak, have found the eighteenth century to tighten the stays on women, increasingly constricting female possibilities into strictly gendered codes.[2] But the straitjacket or tight-corset-of-gender approach, though descriptive of much eighteenth-century discourse

[1] The phrase "turn toward the modern" is Michael McKeon's. See Armstrong, *Desire and Domestic Fiction: A Political History of the Novel* (New York: Oxford University Press, 1987), 16. In *Materialist Feminisms* (Oxford: Blackwell, 1993), with Gerald MacLean, I explore these issues at greater length.

[2] See Poovey, *The Proper Lady and the Woman Writer: Ideology as Style in the Works of Mary Wollstonecraft, Mary Shelley, and Jane Austen* (Chicago: University of Chicago Press, 1984), 3–47; Nussbaum, *The Autobiographical Subject: Gender and Ideology in Eighteenth-Century England* (Baltimore, Md.: Johns Hopkins University Press, 1989), 127–53, 201–24; and Pollak, *The Poetics of Sexual Myth: Gender and Ideology in the Verse of Swift and Pope* (Chicago: University of Chicago Press, 1985), 22–76.

in its prescriptive and didactic modes, has also begun to prove unsatis-fying. More recent work by Nussbaum, for example, as well as the work of Laura Brown, Kristina Straub, and Lisa Moore, explores some of the excesses uncontainable by a modern binary gendering of the eigh-teenth-century archive. Reviewing Nussbaum's *Autobiographical Subject*, Lisa Moore finds that feminists working in eighteenth-century studies have both "a rich opportunity" and "a pressing obligation" to "expose the straining seams by which gender and sexuality are sewn together in representations of women."[3] Not only the join of those categories strains at the seams; the seams are bursting where nationality and race are stitched together *with* gender and sexuality to constitute eigh-teenth-century representations of women. Laura Brown's new book is particularly relevant to my discussion here because she traces in the first half of the eighteenth century some convergences similar to the ones I have found between the figures of the Amazon and the native or colonized other. For Brown, reading Defoe, "as a figure for the other, the image of the Amazon includes and thus conjoins both women and natives."[4] Clearly, many eighteenth-century texts are haunted by the phantasmagoric other of the proper domestic woman. By the 1790s, the decade of revolutionary Frenchness and the celebration of patri-otic motherhood in its service, the specter of feminine otherness has infected English sensibilities to the point of frenzy.

[3] Moore, " 'She Was Too Fond of Her Mistaken Bargain': The Scandalous Rela-tions of Gender and Sexuality in Feminist Theory," *Diacritics* 21, nos. 2–3 (1991): 100. See also Straub, *Sexual Suspects: Eighteenth-Century Players and Sexual Ideology* (Princeton, N.J.: Princeton University Press, 1992), and my comments on Straub and Moore in *Criticism* 36 (1994): 143–47; and Nussbaum, " 'Savage' Mothers: Narratives of Maternity in the Mid–Eighteenth Century," *Cultural Critique* 20 (1991–92): 123–51, and *Torrid Zones* (Baltimore, Md.: Johns Hopkins University Press, forth-coming).

[4] Brown, *Ends of Empire: Women and Ideology in Early Eighteenth-Century English Lit-erature* (Ithaca, N.Y.: Cornell University Press, 1993), 167. She also argues that "the Amazon, by occupying the positions of the native other and of the female other and by functioning in both to expose the violence and self-interest concealed behind the humanist claims of imperialist ideology, might mark an instance of joint disruption, a point of articulation where a common system of oppression encounters a common resistance" (168–69). Brown's book is notable for its articulation of feminist critique with antiracist and anti-imperialist critiques. Her conclusion encapsulates her case for a radical political criticism: "Let's say that the end of empire is only truly possible when we see the extent to which we have been serving the ends of empire" (200).

What would feminist literary and social historians do without the 1790s, that volatile moment during which political emancipation and radical social transformation seemed almost possible? Since 1989, both metaphorically and historically, the Bastille has been stormed, and the marketwomen have marched on Versailles, again and again. The 1990s seem to demand further reflection upon the 1790s. Within the scholarly community, however, this bicentenary attention marks only an intensification of the continued preoccupation with the decade 1789–99 exhibited in recent historiographical practice, in Britain and the U.S. as well as in France. Of course, such specific pre-occupations with previous historical moments are nothing new. As Bridget Hill has remarked, "Many revolutionaries in the 1790s concerned with the legitimacy of removing, and possibly executing, a king looked back to seventeenth-century England."[5] Like the 1640s and 1650s, the 1790s in their turn often serve historians, such as Barbara Taylor and Gareth Stedman Jones, as a touchstone in the recovery of Britain's radical past.[6] For Ernesto Laclau and Chantal Mouffe, seeking to propose a new socialist strategy for our times, the 1790s figure importantly as the moment when feminism, represented by Mary Wollstonecraft's *Vindication of the Rights of Woman*, is inspired by the democratic discourse of the French Revolution.[7] Functioning as a narrative

[5] Hill, *The Republican Virago: The Life and Times of Catharine Macaulay, Historian* (Oxford: Clarendon, 1992), 51.

[6] For Taylor, tracing the intertwined histories of early feminism and socialism, the 1790s constitute a point of departure for the articulation of feminist and democratic principles (*Eve and the New Jerusalem: Socialism and Feminism in the Nineteenth Century* [New York: Pantheon, 1983]). Similarly, for Stedman Jones the artisanal radicalism of the 1790s represents working-class political engagement before the advent of a strictly class-conscious social critique. Paineite attacks on old corruption provide a political language useful for the working class, and the 1790s help the social historian bridge what might otherwise seem like a gap between older forms of popular radicalism and Chartism (*Languages of Class: Studies in English Working Class History, 1832–1982* [Cambridge: Cambridge University Press, 1983]).

[7] Laclau and Mouffe, *Hegemony and Socialist Strategy: Towards a Radical Democratic Politics*, trans. Winston Moore and Paul Cammack (London: Verso, 1985), 154: "In the case of women we may cite as an example the role played in England by Mary Wollstonecraft, whose book *Vindication of the Rights of Women* [sic], published in 1792, determined the birth of feminism through the use made in it of the democratic discourse, which was thus displaced from the field of political equality between citizens to the field of equality between the sexes."

origin, however provisional or merely convenient, the 1790s have inspired a certain discursive domain we might usefully call "post-1790s historiography": all things one needs to know originate there, and earlier social movements or social movements outside the European democratic tradition are thereby displaced. The repetition of "the French Revolution" or "the Jacobin imaginary" can thus be seen to constitute a sufficiently historicizing gesture, and such repetition precludes certain kinds of analysis.

Thinking deconstructively, however, we know very well that there can be no repetition without a difference. If we read the 1790s as a text in which, for example, feminism does or does not figure, what do we find? Reading British texts of the 1790s reveals that reading "the 1790s" as a text produces many empty spaces in the historiographical territory. One such absence may be indicated by the contemporary connection sometimes hysterically made by British male writers between British women writers, widespread female sympathy with the French Revolution, and militant feminism. Was there indeed significant coincidence between women's literary production and a radical politics in the 1790s? What does it mean to find British male writers claiming that "the most sensible women . . . are more uniformly on the side of Liberty, than the other sex—witness a Macaulay, a Wollstonecraft, a Barbauld, a Jebb, a Williams, a Smith"?[8] For another Englishman, the spectacle of events in France was not nearly so worrying as the specter of British women's increasing politicization: "Our unsex'd female writers now instruct, or confuse, us and themselves, in the labyrinth of politics, or turn us wild with Gallic frenzy."[9] What became of their revolutionary energy? The relative absence of this British female or feminist revolution from the literary or historical record suggests the importance of seeking out in such anxious claims the operation of significant discursive displacements.

[8] [Richard Polwhele], *The Unsex'd Females: A Poem, Addressed to the Author of "The Pursuits of Literature"* (London: Cadell and Davies, 1798), 16–17n.

[9] Polwhele takes as his epigraph this sentence from T. J. Mathias's poem *The Pursuits of Literature*, which he claims has stabilized readers' principles in favor of religious authority, monarchy, and the suppression of the French Revolution: "For I can assert, on the best authorities, that many in this country, whose politics and even religion have been long wavering, are now fixed in their principles by 'the Pursuits of Literature'" (3n).

By reading some of the British literature of the French Revolution as "Amazonian," and some of the literature against the Revolution as an attack on the perceived Amazonian qualities of events in France, I do not mean to suggest that an "Amazonian Revolution" actually occurred between 1789 and 1798. My subtitle is what Gayatri Spivak might call a catachresis, a signifier for which there is no literal referent.[10] By invoking this catachresis, *Amazonian Revolution*, then, I am gesturing as much toward what is *not* there, in the historical or the literary record, as toward what is. This essay constitutes a speculative effort toward an understanding of why such absences and displacements might summon, as they often seem to do, considerable rhetorical and political power.

The catachrestical narrative of Amazonian Revolution I wish to examine seems to be a story about xenophobic fears compounding male anxieties. Some of the chief actors in the historiographical drama are an Anglican clergyman, Richard Polwhele, author of *The Unsex'd Females*, a poem published in 1798; John Robison, author of a piece of conspiracy literature against the French Revolution published in 1797; Mary Wollstonecraft, feminist, radical, and supporter of the Revolution; Hannah More, cryptofeminist, moral reformer, and anti-Jacobin polemicist; Ann Yearsley, plebeian poet and figure of the laboring-class woman, the precise meaning of whose politics seems at stake in this period on both sides of the Channel; and the Amazon herself.

A few years ago this investigation might have had a purely antiquarian interest. Now, however, at least a provisional feminist countercanon has been established, featuring Wollstonecraft's *Vindication of the Rights of Woman* as *the* eighteenth-century, and indeed *the* 1790s, text. A section from Polwhele's attack is included in the second Norton Critical Edition of *A Vindication*, so that this previously little-known

---

[10] In a sense, of course, all language is catachrestical; no referent is adequate to the excess of signification generated by the play of the signifying chain. Or, as the character Robyn Penrose in David Lodge's novel *Nice Work* might say, there is a perpetual sliding of the signified under the signifier. But the catachresis in Spivak's sense is a particularly clear case of sliding, which frequently marks productive sites for deconstructive investigation (see, for example, "The New Historicism: Political Commitment and the Postmodern Critic," in *The New Historicism*, ed. H. Aram Veeser [New York: Routledge, 1989], 277–92).

poem has itself become marginally canonical because partially teach-
able.[11] Polwhele's Wollstonecraft prophesies from the grave that by
"unsexing" themselves, or divesting themselves of a highly constructed
femininity, the women of Britain will exchange feminine influence for
rights and public political participation, an unappealing prospect to
this Anglican clergyman, against which he musters the weapon of condescending satire.

So it is the shade of Wollstonecraft, dead after giving birth to her
daughter (the Mary who later wrote *Frankenstein*), who speaks in the
poem. Wollstonecraft's ghost rallies her British sisters to the Amazonian cause, advocating physical training, intellectual application, and
frank acknowledgment of female desire. A curriculum that some of us
might applaud, Polwhele scorns, though it has clearly aroused considerable anxiety in male middle-class intellectuals like himself:

> . . . Soon shall the sex disdain the illusive sway,
> And wield the sceptre in yon blaze of day;
> Ere long, each little artifice discard,
> No more by weakness winning fond regard;
> Nor eyes, that sparkle from their blushes, roll,
> Nor catch the languors of the sick'ning soul,
> Nor the quick flutter, nor the coy reserve,
> But nobly boast the firm gymnastic nerve;
> Nor more affect with Delicacy's fan
> To hide the emotion from congenial man;
> To the bold heights where glory beams, aspire,
> Blend mental energy with Passion's fire,
> Surpass their rivals in the powers of mind
> And vindicate *the Rights of womankind.*
>   (ll. 77–90)

This projected future Polwhele represents as Amazonian, attributing it
to the "Amazonian band—the female Quixotes of the new philosophy" (6n). From his negative recitation, it is clear that the Amazon
embodies those characteristics most vilified in antirevolutionary, anti-
Jacobin discourse: female obstreperousness, political agency, and sexual agency and the severing of family ties. If such scholars as Mitzi

[11] See Carol H. Poston, ed., "*A Vindication of the Rights of Woman*": An Authoritative Text, Backgrounds, the Wollstonecraft Debate, Criticism, 2d ed. (New York: Norton,
1988), 235–37.

Myers and Kathryn Shevelow, as well as Nancy Armstrong, Mary Poovey, Felicity Nussbaum, and Ellen Pollak, have chronicled the rise of the domestic woman in the later eighteenth century, the Amazon is her terrifying other.[12]

This mythical warrior tribe of women, said to be rulers of Asia Minor and thus figuratively both proto-Turks and Eastern exotics, mated once a year with the men of their choice, keeping the daughters and maiming the sons or giving them back to their fathers. Samuel Johnson writes: "The Amazons were a race of women famous for their valour; so called from cutting off their breasts. A virago. *Shakespeare.*" Lemprière locates the Amazons "near the river Thermodon in Cappadocia," commenting, "Themyscyra was the most important of their towns; and Smyrna, Magnesia, Thyatira, and Ephesus, according to some authors, were built by them." He also speculates on a race of African Amazons "more ancient than those of Asia."[13]

If, as Ludmilla Jordanova claims, the language of gender in the late eighteenth century increasingly conflates the private, the familial, the feminine, and the maternal, the Amazon transgresses these boundaries. If the ideology of bourgeois republican virtue converges with the demand for women to retire from public political participation to maternal domesticity during the French Revolution, as Mary Jacobus has argued, then in the advocacy of maternal breast-feeding, the Amazon counters this definition of femininity.[14] Bare-breasted for fighting, not for nursing, and traditionally one-breasted, having burned away the right breast for greater freedom in combat, the Amazon potentially withholds the maternal breast, the fountain of repub-

[12] See Myers, "Reform or Ruin: 'A Revolution in Female Manners,'" in *Studies in Eighteenth-Century Culture,* 11, ed. Harry C. Payne (Madison: University of Wisconsin Press, 1982), 199–216; and Shevelow, *Women and Print Culture: The Construction of Femininity in the Early Periodical* (London: Routledge, 1989).

[13] Johnson, *A Dictionary of the English Language,* 4th ed., 2 vols. (London: Strahan et al., 1770); and *Lemprière's Classical Dictionary of Proper Names Mentioned in Ancient Authors,* ed. F. A. Wright (1788; London: Routledge and Kegan Paul, 1972), 36–37.

[14] Jordanova, "Naturalizing the Family: Literature and the Bio-Medical Sciences in the Late Eighteenth Century," in *Languages of Nature: Critical Essays on Science and Literature,* ed. L. J. Jordanova (London: Free Association, 1986), 86–116; and Jacobus, "Incorruptible Milk: Breast-Feeding and the French Revolution," in *Rebel Daughters: Women and the French Revolution,* ed. Sara E. Melzer and Leslie W. Rabine (New York: Oxford University Press, 1992), 54–75.

lican virtue, thereby challenging the ties of family and patriarchal nation-state.

So from the outset, the importance of gender in the signifying chain is clear. What is most fundamentally terrifying to British observers in the spectacle of French revolutionary action is female agency, or at least the specularization of female agency represented by such symbols of the Revolution as the feminine figure of Liberty, known as Marianne, and by such reports of women's uprisings as made 5 October 1789 famous as "the day of the marketwomen" and caused Hannah More to write that "the throne of the grand monarque ha[s] been overturned by fisherwomen!" Delacroix's *Liberty on the Barricades* (1831), her full right breast exposed in republican-nurturing, or Jacobin-Amazonian, fashion, could serve as a visual culmination of the accumulated symbols of revolutionary female agency analyzed by Maurice Agulhon and Lynn Hunt.[15] Whether the Amazon in question was the classically republican figure of French liberty or such real historical figures as the French feminists Olympe de Gouges and Théroigne de Méricourt, or such collectives in political struggle as the French marketwomen, or the British women writers who were inspired by French examples in their arguments for feminism and democracy,[16] the figure of Amazonian militancy was always threatening.

The Amazon thus represents an "unsexing" of that carefully gendered construction, the domestic woman of late-eighteenth-century culture. Let us return to Polwhele's denunciation of the "unsexed female": "Our unsex'd female writers now instruct, or confuse, us and themselves, in the labyrinth of politics, or turn us wild with Gallic frenzy." Thus are female liberties and revolutionary liberty deliberately confused in moralistic anti-Jacobin rhetoric. In *The Unsex'd Females* it sometimes seems that what is most objectionable about events in France is precisely the notoriety attached to women of questionable,

---

[15] William Roberts, *Memoirs of the Life and Correspondence of Mrs. Hannah More*, 4 vols. (London: Seeley and Burnside, 1834), 2:189; Agulhon, *Marianne into Battle: Republican Imagery and Symbolism in France, 1789–1880*, trans. Janet Lloyd (Cambridge: Cambridge University Press, 1981); and Hunt, *Politics, Culture, and Class in the French Revolution* (Berkeley: University of California Press, 1984).

[16] For a recent take on this popular topic see Anne K. Mellor, "English Women Writers and the French Revolution," in Melzer and Rabine, *Rebel Daughters*, 255–72.

meaning sexual, virtue, who continue to play an important role in politics long after the defeat of certain feminist proposals made early in the revolutionary debate.

Setting against the late Mary Wollstonecraft his anti-Jacobin heroine Hannah More, founder of Sunday schools and author of the Cheap Repository tracts (penny pamphlets advising the lower classes about household and political economies in a popular style), Polwhele conflates fashion and political principles so that the new revolutionary simplicity in dress, both leveling in class terms and newly revealing of sexual difference, becomes a sign of female emancipation as sexual license:

> I shudder at the new unpictur'd scene,
> Where unsex'd woman vaunts the imperious mien;
> Where girls, affecting to dismiss the heart,
> Invoke the Proteus of petrific art;
> With equal ease, in body or in mind,
> To Gallic freaks or Gallic faith resign'd,
> The crane-like neck, as Fashion bids, lay bare,
> Or frizzle, bold in front, their borrow'd hair;
> Scarce by a gossamery film carest,
> Sport, in full view, the meretricious breast
>   (ll. 15–24)

To the "meretricious breast," object of desire and loathing, sign of the harlot, the time-serving woman for hire, Polwhele attaches a telling footnote, inexplicably absent from Carol Poston's reprinting of this section of the poem in her second edition of *A Vindication.* Could it be that a certain dehistoricizing of what Poston terms "the Wollstonecraft debate" is occurring in this very edition, whose explicit purpose is to provide a thicker contextualization for Wollstonecraft's feminism?[17] It would seem that emphasizing feminism in editing *A Vindication* also

[17] In the "Preface to the Second Edition," Poston writes: "Finally, a new section has been added: The Wollstonecraft Debate. Modern students want to be apprised of the history of the whole feminist struggle. The Debate is a gathering of materials that show how Mary Wollstonecraft's reputation has veered over the years alongside the fortunes of the women's movement. It is a way to chart what has happened in each generation to the 'woman question.' It is a chance to look at one feminist's history, how her stock rose and fell in the idea market because she wrote about the rights of women and lived them" (vii).

means cutting out "extraneous" matters, such as Frenchness and revolutionary sympathies, which, I would argue, are inextricable from both Wollstonecraft's feminism and Polwhele's abhorrence of it.

Polwhele footnotes the "meretricious breast," so exposed by Jacobin fashion, so contested as a site of Amazonian militancy or republican motherhood, as follows: "The fashions of France, which have been always imitated by the English, were, heretofore, unexceptionable in a moral point of view; since, however ridiculous or absurd, they were innocent. But they have now their source among prostitutes—among women of the most abandoned character" (7–8n). Polwhele would seem to be well aware of the etymological origins of *meretricious*, "showily attractive," making a false display (*OED*), in the supposed practices of the meretrix. And one might think from reading him that prostitutes were at the forefront of political upheaval in the new revolutionary regime. As a gloss on this concatenation of Frenchness, fashionably bared breasts, and female militancy, Polwhele now quotes from John Robison's *Proofs of a Conspiracy*: "See Madam Tallien come into the theatre, and other beautiful women, laying aside all modesty, and presenting themselves to the public view, with bared limbs, à la sauvage, as the alluring objects of desire" (8n). If we consider such a text as Robison's, the precise psychic and social stakes of Polwhele's repudiation of the Amazon may be clarified. Robison writes:

> Are not the accursed fruits of Illumination to be seen in the present humiliating condition of woman in France? pampered in every thing that can reduce them to the mere instrument of animal pleasure. . . . I am fully persuaded that it was the enthusiastic admiration of Grecian democracy that recommended to the French nation the dress *à la Grecque*, which exhibits, not the elegant, ornamented beauty, but the beautiful female, fully as well as Madame Talien's dress *à la Sauvage*. It was no doubt with the same adherence to *serious principle*, that Mademoiselle Therouanne was most beautifully dressed *à l'Amazonne* on the 5th of October 1789, when she turned the heads of so many young officers of the regiments at Versailles. . . . But see how all this will terminate, when we shall have brought the sex so low, and will not even wait for a Mahometan paradise. What can we expect but such a dissoluteness of manners, that the endearing ties of relation and family, and mutual confidence within doors, will be slighted, and will cease; and every man must stand up for himself, single and alone, in perfect

equality, and full liberty to do whatever his own arm (but that alone) is able to accomplish.[18]

Robison thus characterizes Amazonian fashion as a product of insurgent licentiousness rather than revolutionary militancy or a desire to throw off the symbols of the old regime, one of which was the corruption brought about by female political influence, best embodied in Marie-Antoinette herself.[19] As Dorinda Outram argues, "Boudoir politics, the exchange of political gifts for sexual favours, were seen both as a cause of the weaknesses of the old regime, and as a justification for the Revolution itself" (125). Olympe de Gouges protested, "Women are now respected and excluded; under the old regime they were despised and powerful."[20] Hence, says Outram,

> to the degree that power in the old regime was ascribed to women, the Revolution was committed to an anti-feminine rhetoric, which posed great problems for any women seeking public authority. . . . Thus, in the rhetoric of the Revolution, the entire struggle for the achievement of legitimacy, for the creation of a new legitimate public embodiment by the Revolutionary governing class, was predicated not on an inclusion of the female, but on its exclusion. (125–26)

But to the spectacle of which women do Robison and Polwhele object? They cite Thérèse Tallien, daughter of the banker to the king of Spain, whose salons and self-display earned her the name "Queen of Paris," and who represents that collusion of revolutionary will to power, elite but anti-Royalist sentiment, and international capital characterized so vividly by Marx in *The Eighteenth Brumaire* as eventually determining the failure of the Revolution. Tallien, described by one recent feminist

[18] Robison, *Proofs of a Conspiracy against all the Religions and Governments of Europe, carried on in the secret meetings of Free Masons, Illuminati, and Reading Societies* (Edinburgh: William Creech; London: Cadell and Davies, 1797), 251–54.

[19] See, for example, Dorinda Outram, *The Body and the French Revolution: Sex, Class, and Political Culture* (New Haven, Conn.: Yale University Press, 1989); and Joan Wallach Scott, "French Feminists and the Rights of 'Man': Olympe de Gouges's Declarations," and Elizabeth Colwill, "Just Another *Citoyenne?* Marie-Antoinette on Trial, 1790–1793," *History Workshop: A Journal of Socialist and Feminist Historians* 28 (1989): 1–21, 63–87.

[20] Gouges, *Les Droits de la femme* (Paris, 1791), quoted in Darline Gay Levy, Harriet Branson Applewhite, and Mary Durham Johnson, eds., *Women in Revolutionary Paris, 1789–1795* (Urbana: University of Illinois Press, 1979), 93.

commentator as the "beautiful face" of the Directory, "a courtesan of the Thermidor period who served as a symbol both of the defeat of the Terror and of the recovery of pleasure," exhibits her beautiful bare limbs in the style of the noble savage.[21] The Amazon, however, is Théroigne de Méricourt, of a different social provenance altogether, who may be the prostitute Polwhele has chiefly in mind, especially since she had traveled briefly in England.

Théroigne, who began life as Anne-Josèphe Terwagne, the daughter of a well-to-do peasant family from the village of Marcourt, in the Ardennes, had an unhappy childhood after her mother's death and, leaving home as a young girl, worked as a maid, a cowherd, and a governess before being befriended by a Madame Colbert, who taught her to write and sing. At twenty she entered the demimonde, fell in love with an unscrupulous English infantry officer, and traveled in France, England, and Italy, failing in her career as a singer, sometimes serving as the mistress of a rich man, but forever doomed in love and cheated by male patrons. She suffered from venereal disease and was treated for melancholy but then was fired by revolutionary fervor in the summer of 1789 and became a feminist and Girondist activist. In 1794 she was arrested and thereafter interned in a series of madhouses, culminating in the asylum of La Salpétrière, where she spent the last ten years of her life. Here the myth of Théroigne de Méricourt began to overtake her participation in historical events. The Royalist press contrived the name, a Frenchified version of her surname combined with a corruption of the name of her birthplace; she never acknowledged it.[22]

As Elisabeth Roudinesco has been at some pains to point out, such was the effect of Théroigne's appearance on the revolutionary stage that, although she was merely an observer at the October 1789

[21] Elisabeth Roudinesco, *Théroigne de Méricourt: A Melancholic Woman during the French Revolution*, trans. Martin Thom (London: Verso, 1991), 18.

[22] See Roudinesco, 4–13, 7. Roudinesco, a member of Jacques Lacan's Ecole freudienne de Paris from 1969 to 1980, usefully attempts to separate popular misconceptions and historiographical tropes from the archival evidence while mounting a particular kind of psychoanalytic case. For a sketch that recycles some of the myth along with some of the facts see Jennifer S. Uglow and Frances Hinton, eds., *The International Dictionary of Women's Biography* (New York: Continuum, 1982), 137. See also Joan B. Landes, *Women and the Public Sphere in the Age of the French Revolution* (Ithaca, N.Y.: Cornell University Press, 1988), 110, 233–34 n. 19.

Figure 1

march of the marketwomen on Versailles, the legend of her dramatic participation in it persists in contemporary historiography and in documents like Robison's, fueled by supposed eyewitness reports. Since Théroigne did later organize women's clubs in the faubourg Saint-Antoine and speak passionately on behalf of women's rights, including the right to take up arms in the war effort as a "legion of amazons," the phantasmic projection of her should not be surprising. Representing what Roudinesco calls "warrior feminism," the second stage of French revolutionary feminism, Théroigne herself, at her most Amazonian, was not above invoking the October days, subtly implying that she had indeed been a heroic participant among the women of the people, just as the Royalist press claimed (97). The anonymous drawing after which Charles Dewritz engraved the portrait that appears in Michelet's *Femmes de la Révolution* figures Théroigne in this way, and as a bare-breasted Amazon (Roudinesco, 205–6; see fig. 1).

Far from displaying herself bare-limbed or bare-breasted, however, Théroigne chose for her Amazonian costume a riding habit and a round hat, worn sometimes with a saber and a brace of pistols, as in the painting by Auguste Raffet, engraved by Bosselman for Lamartine's *Histoire des Girondins* (Roudinesco, 206). She attended the king's receiving of the tricolor cockade at the Hôtel de Ville on 17 July, in the wake of the fall of the Bastille, in this costume; thereafter, "in order to seem to be a man, and thereby avoid the humiliation of being a woman,'" she never abandoned it (Roudinesco, 6, 26, 98). So striking a figure did she present in public that many assumed, or imagined, that she had ridden dashingly alongside the marketwomen at Versailles. Here, in Robison's invocation of the "Amazonne" Théroigne de Méricourt, we read revolutionary Frenchness as a spectacle of both female and feminist agency, in cross-dressed, pistol-brandishing style, coupled with lower-class origins and public acknowledgment of the oldest female profession.

It is thus hardly surprising that Ann Yearsley, the laboring-class woman poet from Bristol who was represented in the frontispiece of her 1796 volume of verse *The Rural Lyre* as "British Liberty" in the potentially Amazonian mode, should need to distinguish her investments in revolutionary liberty from both sexual licentiousness and the

Figure 2

figure of Amazon militancy.[23] As "British Liberty," Yearsley's right breast is bared, her neoclassical gown is fashionably draped, and her hair is curled in fashionably long locks, but her face is not militant with anger or political challenge. It is, rather, a feminine face sorrowfully imploring (see fig. 2).

In her poem on what we could reasonably term a Jacobin scheme for social change, through a domestic revolution in maternal breast-feeding and the emancipatory education of children, Yearsley therefore explicitly rejects the epithet "Amazon," as if it might automatically spring to mind when a woman dared to philosophize about the transformation of civil society. Written during the war with France, "To Mira, on the Care of Her Infant" opposes male militancy to a female world of education and nurturance.[24] The poem opens with a startling paradox and a very peculiar image of female nurturing "warmth." The times are hostile ones in which "war, destruction, crimes that fiends delight" flourish (l. 1). These clashes of will so prodigal of life could be avoided if men turned the other cheek or spread pacifism by example (ll. 7–8), but as it is, women are left to themselves, to care for the next generation, a more blessed occupation:

> Let us, whose sweet employ the Gods admire,
> Serenely blest, to softer joys retire!
> Spite of those wars, we will mild pleasure know—
> Pleasure, that, long as woman lives, shall flow!
> We are not made for Mars; we ne'er could bear
> His pond'rous helmet and his burning spear;
> . . . .
> I am no Amazon; nor would I give
> One silver groat by iron laws to live.
> Nay, if, like hers, my heart were iron-bound,
> My warmth would melt the fetters to the ground.
>   (ll. 9–22)

As a woman writer with limited social power who had to pose the mildest radical sentiments with caution, Yearsley would have wished to be associated neither with French licentiousness nor with Jacobin mil-

[23] Yearsley, *The Rural Lyre; A Volume of Poems: Dedicated to the Right Honourable the Earl of Bristol, Lord Bishop of Derry* (London: G. G. and J. Robinson, 1796).
[24] The poem is signed "Bristol Wells, September 16, 1795"; *The Rural Lyre*, 124.

itancy. The Jacobin imaginary is too dangerous a spectacle for her to invoke, even obliquely through the possibility of Amazonian self-representation. So intense is female "warmth," and so inextricable from the desire for unbounded liberty, that the poet claims that she would *melt* herself free from armor and arms, physical signs of the iron discipline of combat. In the domestic sphere, therefore, women can undermine martial prowess with the power of reproduction, transforming subsequent generations through Enlightenment pedagogy and the theorization of child rearing so as to produce revolutionary subjects.

Ironically, the transposition of Amazonian militancy into patriotic domesticity exactly parallels the course of the debate over women's rights during the French Revolution itself. By 30 October 1793 the women's societies had been banned. That autumn the Convention adopted a negative attitude toward women's emancipation and postponed any resolution of their demands; Marie-Antoinette, Olympe de Gouges, and Madame Roland, three women representing three very different sorts of female or feminist political agency, were guillotined; and all women were exhorted to resume caring for their families as their proper contribution to the French republic (see Roudinesco, 140–42).

And so the Jacobin imaginary, banished as public spectacle, returns as a domestic project under the sign of women's culture: revolutionary breast-feeding; women as the mothers of the republic; the distinctively bourgeois contours of separate-sphere ideology that Yearsley, in other, clearly political texts, explicitly sought to challenge.[25] This very caution seems to have saved Yearsley from Polwhele's harshest criticism; she figures in *The Unsex'd Females* as recuperable, for Polwhele writes that his "business" with her "is to recall her, if possible, from her Gallic wanderings—if an appeal to native ingenuousness be not too late; if the fatal example of the Arch-priestess of female Libertinism, have any influence on a mind once stored with the finest moral sentiment" (20 n).

What phantasmagoric figures lurk in the displacements of this dis-

---

[25] For an analysis of the politics of other poems see my chapter on Yearsley in *The Muses of Resistance: Laboring-Class Women's Poetry in Britain, 1739–1796* (Cambridge: Cambridge University Press, 1990), 120–85.

course of the Amazon?[26] For the Englishmen Polwhele and Robison, the Amazon is a Jacobin. For the Englishwoman Yearsley, the Jacobin is a domestic woman, breast-feeding new post-Rousseauesque citizens. The Amazon of these Englishmen's fantasies is a figure for English anxiety over the possibility of domestic disruption in some sense consequent upon events in France, but not reducible to them. The Englishmen's trope of French Amazons covers and displaces the glaring contradictions posed by class and gender conflict within the Revolution itself: the differences between revolutionary marketwomen and Marie-Antoinette, between the figure of Marianne in combat and the republican mother with a child at her breast.

Robison's concatenation of the savage and the Amazon, however, suggests a further displacement. Englishmen's feared domestic revolution at home is represented by the colonialist trope of native warrior women, the foils to English femininity, whether they are native to the New World or to the ancient world of the East. But for Robison, the East is now safe from Amazonian incursions, as a "Mahometan paradise" of male prerogative and female sensuality, to be repudiated on religious, moral, and xenophobic grounds, but no longer to be feared.

Wollstonecraft, too, employs the tropes of Mahometanism inculcating female enslavement and of Turkishness as a sign of corrupt sensuality. What Polwhele scandalously labels the "libertinism" of *A Vindication* might best be found in its attacks on old corruption, aristocratic sensuality, and male prerogative, frequently couched in the xenophobic orientalist language paradigmatically analyzed by Edward Said and, from a feminist perspective, by Rana Kabbani.[27] Wollstonecraft figures contemporary England as, indeed, already a Mahometan paradise in need of some Amazonian-Jacobin emancipation. "Liberty," she writes, "is the mother of virtue, and if women be, by their very constitution, slaves, and not allowed to breathe the sharp invigorating air of freedom, they must ever languish like exotics, and be reckoned beautiful

---

[26] Not exactly Neil Hertz's Medusa's head, with its specter of castration, or the market economy gone haywire identified by Catherine Gallagher in her exchange with Hertz. See Hertz, "Medusa's Head: Male Hysteria under Political Pressure," and Gallagher, "More about 'Medusa's Head,'" *Representations* 4 (1983): 27–54, 55–57.

[27] Said, *Orientalism* (New York: Vintage, 1979); and Kabbani, *Europe's Myths of Orient* (Bloomington: Indiana University Press, 1986).

Figure 3

flaws in nature" (Poston, 37). To languish like an exotic is to submit to one's status as a female commodity, and as a colonial commodity at that, a luxury item in need of expensive conservation, whose languishing indicates debility as much as overwhelming desire.

The figure of the Amazon thus registers obliquely what imagining the East as a consumer's paradise elides: the possibility of colonial revolt elsewhere in the empire, in the wake of 1776 and 1789. With her threat of militant female self-sufficiency, the Amazon simultaneously invokes and displaces the threat of "native" female resistance, both in the colonies and in Britain. So profoundly internalized is this threat that even in sentimental antislavery discourse of the 1790s there appears a tendency to render African slave women or native American women as Amazonian in comparison with their European counterparts. In John Gabriel Stedman's *Narrative of a Five Years' Expedition against the Revolted Negroes of Surinam* (1796), the devotion of Joanna, a mulatto slave who repeatedly nurses Stedman back to health and bears him a son, and whom the Englishman marries but leaves behind when he returns to Europe, is coded as exemplary in terms of English domesticity. And yet the text's illustration of Joanna, an engraving based upon Stedman's own drawing of her, represents her single bared breast in subliminally Amazonian fashion, nearly figuring it as an armored weapon (see fig. 3). Stedman insists that it is solely Joanna's wish not to accompany him to Holland or England, because, as she predicted when they first met, he has not been able to afford to purchase her freedom, and she will not go with him while still a slave. Yet, regardless of whose agency is most at stake, the crucial textual and material consequence is that Joanna remains forever confined to the colonial periphery and never enters upon the European stage, to which the *Narrative*, like Stedman himself, inevitably returns.[28]

Some Englishmen saw Englishwomen of the 1790s as threatening

[28] Mary Louise Pratt observes that Joanna's rejection of the possibility of European assimilation is the new element in Stedman's account; her wish to remain in Surinam signals the inauguration of "a new postcolonial elite" (*Imperial Eyes: Travel Writing and Transculturation* [London: Routledge, 1992], 101, 90–102). The only edition I have been able to consult so far is Christopher Bryant, *Expedition to Surinam, being the narrative of a five years expedition against the revolted negroes of Surinam in Guiana on the wild coast of South America from the year 1772 to 1777 elucidating that country and describing its productions with an account of Indians of Guiana and negroes of Guiana by*

"natives" to be domesticated just as native peoples were to be. But the native woman herself is not figured in this discourse except through her European simulacrum, in the context of which *à la Sauvage* and *à l'Amazonne* function equally phantasmagorically as fashion statements. Toiling in the archives, feminist literary historians would do well to remember not only the nothing that is not there but the nothing that is, the phantasmagoric as well as the strictly, concretely "historically present." Although we might now regret that no Amazonian blast of revolutionary fervor turned the world upside down around Polwhele, Robison, and other Englishmen like them, despite their fears and anxieties that such a revolution was imminent, their crisis of masculinity undoubtedly is itself deserving of meticulous historical analysis. Let the Amazon spectrally haunting the figure of the domestic woman stand as provisional shorthand for the beginning of such an analysis.

Captain John Stedman (London: Folio Society, 1963). For Joanna see esp. 33–34, 39–42, 120, 166–69, 207, 216–17, 232–34, 238. My thanks to Charlotte Sussman for bringing Joanna's portrait to my attention.

Editing as Cultural Formation: The Sexing of Shakespeare's Sonnets

Peter Stallybrass

For the past two years, I have been trying to understand the work of bibliographers and editors. I undertook this "retraining" for two contradictory but related reasons. The first is that as I became increasingly engaged in the teaching and organization of cultural studies courses, I began to wonder what the strengths of specific disciplinary trainings might be. That is, one of the obvious dangers of interdisciplinary work is that one ends up doing history, anthropology, economics—badly. It is hard to gather the technical skills of another discipline on the side: the historical skills, for instance, of finding sources, let alone knowing how to read them. I began to wonder what exactly the technical skills of someone teaching in a department of English might be. Whatever they were, I didn't seem to know about them or have them. (By contrast, I did have at least the rudiments of a historical training through having worked with various historians in England.) I found that the librarians at the University of Pennsylvania had an extraordinary range of skills that, as someone who worked on and with books, I felt I should know. The second reason for my turn to editing and bibliography is that I came to believe that the material culture of books was central to any cultural analysis of "literature" and therefore to one aspect of cultural studies.[1] Ques-

[1] Formative work in this field has been done by Roger Chartier, Jerome J. McGann, and Donald F. McKenzie. See, for instance, Chartier, *The Cultural Uses of Print in Early Modern France*, trans. Lydia G. Cochrane (Princeton, N.J.: Princeton University Press, 1987); Chartier, ed., *The Culture of Print: Power and the Uses of Print in Early Modern Europe*, trans. Lydia G. Cochrane (Princeton, N.J.: Princeton University Press, 1989); McGann, *A Critique of Modern Textual Criticism* (Chicago: University of

tions of, say, the formation of nationalism (and national languages), the construction of the individual, and the making of genders and sexualities are materially embedded in the historical production and reproduction of texts.

A further reason to shift interests has been to interrogate a notion of historicity that emphasizes the *punctual* emergence of its objects of study. That is, a course on the seventeenth century would be about writers who wrote ("on time") in the period one was studying (Milton, Donne, Behn). In such a course, one might incorporate "precursors" or earlier writing as "background," but that only reproduces the notion of a series of punctual moments that can be related chronologically through their dates of origination. Margreta de Grazia powerfully challenges this view in *Shakespeare Verbatim*.[2] She contends that the Shakespeare we still study is the construction of the late eighteenth century and, above all, of the editorial labors of Malone. In other words, "our" Shakespeare is (or until recently was) the contemporary of the French Revolution rather than of the Armada. What I attempt to do here is to give a working example of the implications of such a proposition. I argue that in an important sense, if we take seriously the labor of production (editorial work, theatrical stagings, critical commentary, the global production and distribution of books, the incorporation of texts into the educational apparatus), Shakespeare is a central nineteenth-century author. But what is being authored remains a question. In the case of the *Sonnets*, which I shall examine, we can read the inscription of a new history of sexuality and "character." But that new history emerges unpunctually, dislocated by its need to write itself over the culturally valued but culturally disturbing body of the *Sonnets*.[3]

Chicago Press, 1983); *The Textual Condition* (Princeton, N.J.: Princeton University Press, 1991); and McKenzie, *Bibliography and the Sociology of Texts* (London: British Library, 1986).

[2] De Grazia, *Shakespeare Verbatim: The Reproduction of Authenticity and the 1790 Apparatus* (Oxford: Clarendon, 1991).

[3] For other work on the *Sonnets* to which I am indebted, see Gregory W. Bredbeck, *Sodomy and Interpretation: Marlowe to Milton* (Ithaca, N.Y.: Cornell University Press, 1991), 167–80; Bruce R. Smith, *Homosexual Desire in Shakespeare's England: A Cultural Poetics* (Chicago: University of Chicago Press, 1991), 228–70; and de Grazia, "The Scandal of Shakespeare's Sonnets," *Shakespeare Survey*, forthcoming.

Until Edmond Malone's 1780 edition, the history of the publication of the *Sonnets* was that of the reproduction of John Benson's edition of 1640, in which Benson had radically reordered the sonnets, given titles to individual sonnets, conflated sonnets to create longer poems, changed at least some pronouns so as to render the beloved female rather than male, and added many other poems that modern editors do not regard as Shakespearean (de Grazia, *Shakespeare Verbatim*, 132–76). In returning to the 1609 quarto of the *Sonnets*, Malone was intent upon rescripting Shakespeare's poems to show the contours of the man behind them. That is, he was inventing the character Shakespeare as he is still visible to us. Above all he turned, as de Grazia has argued, to the *Sonnets*, which he believed gave a crucial key to Shakespeare's inner life;[4] now, much to Malone's credit, the "boy," the "friend," "he" appear as central figures. But they do so as the site of moral panic. Once created, the "authentic" character of Shakespeare steps into the spotlight as a potential sodomite.

The 1821 edition of Malone prints the sonnets together with the remarks of John Boswell Jr., who presents the characters of the new edition (Shakespeare, the young man, the rival poet, the dark lady) *and* the panic that attends their presentation. Boswell seems appalled at the prospect of what the reader will make of Malone's Shakespeare: the Bard has been given a rich interiority, but at the cost of impugned reputation. In the final page of his remarks Boswell dedicates himself to proving that Shakespeare was not a pederast. In the process, as hysterical symptom, he draws the lines of defense that have governed nearly all subsequent readings of the *Sonnets*: (1) In the Renaissance, male-male friendship was expressed through the rhetoric of amorous love. (2) Shakespeare didn't love the young man anyway, because he was his patron, and the poems are therefore written in pursuit of patronage. (3) The poems are not really about love or friendship, because sonnets are conventional. They are, then, less about a young man or a dark lady than about Petrarch, Ronsard, Sidney, and the like (a boy's club, but not *that* kind of boy's club). (4) Malone was wrong,

---

4 Malone, *Supplement to the Edition of Shakespeare's Plays Published in 1778 by Samuel Johnson and George Steevens* (London: Bathurst, 1780); and John Benson, *Poems: Written by Wil Shake-speare. Gent.* (London, 1640).

and the sonnets are, after all, a miscellany. They "had neither the poet himself nor any individual in view; but were merely the effusions of his fancy, written upon various topicks for the amusement of a private circle."[5]

Now there is nothing necessarily wrong with any of these readings. I'm not concerned here with their truth or their scholarly credentials but with their emergence as attempted solutions to a crisis. As these readings get established, the crisis that produced them gets progressively buried, only to reemerge at junctures like the trial of Oscar Wilde in the 1890s.

At the moment of the formation of "Shakespeare" through a reading of the *Sonnets* in the 1780s and 1790s, it is striking how nakedly the issues are presented. Malone prints his commentary at the bottom of the page, but his own remarks are frequently framed as a response to the criticisms of George Steevens, who thought that the *Sonnets* should not be published at all. Malone's footnote to sonnet 20, for instance, reads as follows:

> —the MASTER-MISTRESS of my passion;] It is impossible to read this fulsome panegyrick, addressed to a male object, without an equal mixture of disgust and indignation. We may remark also, that the same phrase employed by Shakespeare to denote the height of encomium, is used by Dryden to express the extreme of reproach:
>> "That woman, but more daub'd; or, if a man,
>> "Corrupted to a woman; thy *man-mistress*."
>>> *Don Sebastian.*
>
> Let me be just, however, to our author, who has made a proper use of the term *male varlet*, in Troilus and Cressida. See that play, Act V. Sc. I. STEEVENS.
>
> Some part of this indignation might perhaps have been abated, if it had been considered that such addresses to men, however indelicate, were customary in our author's time, and neither imported criminality, nor were esteemed indecorous. See a note on the words—"thy deceased *lover*," in the 32d Sonnet. To regulate our judgement of Shakespeare's poems by the modes of modern times, is surely as unreasonable as to try his plays by the rules of Aristotle.

[5] Boswell, "Preliminary Remarks," in *The Plays and Poems of William Shakspeare*, ed. Edmond Malone (London, 1821), 20:220.

> *Master-mistress* does not perhaps mean *man*-mistress, but *sovereign* mistress. See Mr. Tyrwhitt's note on the 165th verse of the Canterbury Tales, vol. iv. p. 197. MALONE. (20:241)

In the most literal sense, character assassination precedes the construction of character: Malone's justification of Shakespeare comes after (both temporally and upon the printed page) Steevens's assault.

Nor did Malone's response satisfy Steevens, who, in his 1793 edition of Shakespeare, wrote: "We have not reprinted the Sonnets etc. of Shakespeare, because the strongest act of Parliament that could be framed, would fail to compel readers into their service; notwithstanding these miscellaneous Poems have derived every possible advantage from the literature and judgement of their only intelligent editor, Mr. Malone, whose implements of criticism, like the ivory rake and golden spade in Prudentius, are on this occasion disgraced by the objects of their culture."[6] The passage is a paradoxical mixture of the direct and indirect: the word *sodomy* nowhere appears, and yet everywhere it underpins the argument in a curiously inverted form. The acts of Parliament by which sodomites were persecuted and punished are here magically displaced by imaginary decrees that, however strong, will have no force to make the reader turn to Shakespeare's *Sonnets*. Readers cannot be "compel[led]" to the "service" of these poems; that is, they will refuse to be seduced, corrupted, sodomized. A familiar scenario, in which the state apparatus contrives to represent its victims as the agents of oppression, has been invoked.[7] But Steevens limits the danger of those demonic agents by transforming them into the objects of "culture," by which he surely means the excrement that contaminates even that distinguished "culture-critic," Edmond Malone, despite the long handles of his ivory rake and golden spade.

Culture as contamination. The gentle Shakespeare as contaminator and corrupter of youth. But if this character is reiterated throughout the nineteenth century, it is above all as a character denied. Critics,

---

6 Steevens, "Advertisement," in *Plays*, by William Shakespeare, ed. Samuel Johnson and George Steevens (London, 1793), 1:vii–viii.

7 See Jonathan Dollimore, "Transgression and Surveillance in *Measure for Measure*," in *Political Shakespeare: New Essays in Cultural Materialism*, ed. Jonathan Dollimore and Alan Sinfield (Manchester: Manchester University Press, 1985), 72–87.

in other words, worked *from* what they imagined as character assassination (e.g., Shakespeare as pederast) *to* character. But how many character assassinators are there to be reproduced and ritually denounced? In the nineteenth century, as for Malone at the end of the eighteenth, Steevens is virtually alone as the assassinator who must be endlessly named, denounced, put straight. From this distance, the repeated act of putting straight appears as a form of cultural hysteria, but its excesses inscribe a crisis in the attempt to form a normative character and sexuality through Malone's Shakespeare.

One of the most drastic responses to Malone's edition of the *Sonnets* was William Henry Ireland's forgery of a letter purporting to be from Elizabeth I to Shakespeare, thanking him for his sonnets.[8] The *Sonnets*, in other words, were addressed neither to a male beloved nor to a common woman but to the monarch herself. The forgery was only one of several by Ireland, so what is perhaps more remarkable is that the supposition that Shakespeare's beloved was Elizabeth I was justified at great length (and with considerable learning) in two books by George Chalmers.[9] In the latter, *A Supplemental Apology*, Chalmers marvels at the assumption of Steevens and Malone that "Shakespeare, a husband, a father, a moral man, addressed a hundred and twenty six *Amorous* Sonnets to a *male* object!" (55). Chalmers, rightly noting that Malone was the first editor to posit a male beloved, sets out to erase that defamation: "Every fair construction ought to be made, rather than consider Shakespeare as a miscreant, who could address amatory Verses to a man, with a romantic *platonism of affection*. But I have freed him, I trust, from that stain, in opposition to his commentators, by shewing, distinctly, his real object. This object, being once known, darkness brightens into light, order springs out of confusion, and contradiction settles into sense" (73–74).

If Chalmers's position gained little support, the structure of his argument was endlessly repeatable. First, the claim that Shakespeare is heterosexual is always supplementary. Indeed, heterosexuality is itself

---

[8] *Miscellaneous Papers and Legal Instruments under the hand and seal of William Shakespeare* (London: Egerton, 1796), 30.

[9] Chalmers, *An Apology for the Believers in the Shakespeare Papers* (London: Egerton, 1797); and *A Supplemental Apology* (London: Egerton, 1799).

constructed as a back-formation from the prior imagination of pederasty and sodomy. Secondly, it is simply assumed that the taint of
male-male love will destroy the character of the national bard. So just
as heterosexuality is the belated defense against sodomy, so "character"
is the belated defense against an imagined character assassination that
has preceded it. The *Sonnets* thus produce in the nineteenth century a
formidable apparatus to invent a new self: the interiorized heterosexual, projected back onto (or formed in opposition to) Shakespeare.

That apparatus can be seen at its most spectacularly troubled in
the writing of Coleridge. On "Wed. morning, half past three, Nov. 2,
1803," Coleridge picked up a volume of Wordsworth's set of Anderson's *British Poets,* which contained Shakespeare's *Sonnets.* In the margin he found a pencil note by Wordsworth, objecting to the later sonnets (that is, to the sonnets addressed, according to Malone, to the
dark lady and thus "heterosexual"). Coleridge wrote: "I can by no
means subscribe to the above pencil mark of W. Wordsworth; which,
however, it is my wish should never be erased. It is *his*: and grievously
am I mistaken, and deplorably will Englishmen have degenerated if
the being *his* will not in time give it a value, as of a little reverential relic
—the rude mark of his hand left by the sweat of haste in a St. Veronica
handkerchief."[10] Wordsworth is wrong about Shakespeare; but his
error is encoded in the enduring, sexualized mark of his hand, which
Coleridge reveres as a "relic" of his friend (the paper on which he has
written becomes the handkerchief that, like St. Veronica's, immortal-
izes his physical being). Writing as masturbation with eternal effects. In
response to Wordsworth's comments on the later sonnets, then,
Coleridge fetishizes the material trace that homoerotically binds him
to his friend.

But at this point Coleridge seems to forget that Wordsworth is writing about the *later* poems, as if what names his relation to Wordsworth
were the name that Steevens silently attributes to the *earlier* sonnets and
to the relationship between Shakespeare and the young man. Abruptly,
Coleridge veers from his meditations upon his friend to an apostrophe
to his own infant son, Hartley, who is being christened that very day:

[10] *Coleridge's Miscellaneous Criticism,* ed. T. M. Raysor (Cambridge, Mass.: Harvard University Press, 1936), 454.

These sonnets thou, I trust, if God preserve thy life, Hartley! thou wilt read with a deep interest. . . . To thee, I trust, they will help to explain the mind of Shakespeare, and if thou wouldst understand these sonnets, thou must read the chapter in Potter's *Antiquities* on the Greek lovers—of whom were that Theban band of brothers over whom Philip, their victor, stood weeping; and surveying their dead bodies, each with his shield over the body of his friend, all dead in the place where they fought, solemnly cursed those whose base, fleshly, and most calumnious fancies had suspected their love of desire against nature. This pure love Shakespeare appears to have felt—to have been in no way ashamed of it—or even to have suspected that others could have suspected it. Yet at the same time he knew that so strong a love would have been more completely a thing of permanence and reality, and have been more blessed by nature and taken under her more especial protection, if this object of his love had been at the same time a possible object of desire—for nature is not soul only. In this feeling he must have written the twentieth sonnet; but its possibility seems never to have entered even his imagination. . . . O my son! I pray that thou may'st know inwardly how impossible it was for a Shakespeare not to have been in his heart's heart chaste. (*Miscellaneous Criticism*, 455)

Wordsworth writes about the late sonnets; Coleridge responds by writing about the early sonnets as they had been read by Steevens and Malone. And Coleridge's reading is a tortuous and tortured reading of the possibility or impossibility of a sexual relation between men. But every move by which he attempts to erase the specter of sodomy conjures it up. To set one's mind at rest, one needs, of all things, to read a commentary on the Greeks (by no less a person than the archbishop of Canterbury, despite Coleridge's denunciation of christening in the same note as "unchristian . . . foolery"), as if the "purity" of the Greeks were sufficiently secure to secure the "purity" of Shakespeare. Even more strange is Coleridge's attempts to deny the function of the "imagination" to the poet to whom he attributed it in the highest degree. The possibility of sodomy "seems never to have entered even his imagination"; he could not "have suspected that others could have suspected" his love.

Which makes it the more remarkable that later, in a note of 14 May 1833, Coleridge decided not only that all the sonnets were written to a woman but also (more remarkably still) that Shakespeare inserted the twentieth sonnet to *obscure* his heterosexuality (and thus to raise, seemingly unnecessarily, the thought of pederasty, which before he could not "have suspected that others could have suspected"). Again, the movement of Coleridge's thinking is revealing. His note in 1833 begins with the reflection that "it is possible that a man may under certain states of the moral feeling, entertain something deserving the name of love towards a male object—an affection beyond friendship and wholly aloof from appetite."[11] When he turns to the friendship between Musidorus and Pyrocles in Sidney's *Arcadia*, it looks as if he is preparing his way for a restatement of Malone's position on the sonnets. "In Elizabeth's and James's time," Coleridge remarks, "it seems to have been almost fashionable to cherish such a feeling" (*Table Talk*, 178). But Malone's "defense" of Shakespeare is no longer adequate as a defense for Coleridge. Shakespeare must be purified even of the "rhetorical" male-male love that is said to characterize his age. To the extent that his sonnets are "sincere," they must be heterosexual: "It seems to me that the sonnets could only have come from a man deeply in love, and in love with a woman; and there is one sonnet which from its incongruity, I take to be a purposed blind" (*Table Talk*, 180–81). Shakespeare, in other words, disguises himself as a pederast to avoid detection as a man "deeply in love" with a woman.

If Coleridge's later interpretation of the *Sonnets* seems incredible, it testifies to the great *obstacle* that they formed in the smooth reproduction of the national bard. That there should be such a smooth reproduction was, of course, increasingly important as Shakespeare was inscribed within a national and colonial pedagogy. If strategies as desperate as Coleridge's could not command assent, what could one do with the sonnets? Steevens had a rare follower. Henry Hallam, in his *Introduction to the Literature of Europe*, describes Coleridge's "heterosexualizing" of the sonnets as "absolutely untenable."[12] But Hallam, like Steevens, consequently finds the "frequent beauties" of the sonnets "greatly diminished" by the supposed "circumstances" of their production. "It is impossible," Hallam concludes, "not to wish that Shakespeare had never written them" (264).

[11] Coleridge, *Table Talk* (London: Murray, 1835), 2:178.
[12] Hallam, *Introduction to the Literature of Europe in the Fifteenth, Sixteenth, and Seventeenth Centuries*, 263n.

What Hallam and other nineteenth-century critics wanted to
unwrite was the primal scene in the modern production of Shakespeare: the scene conjured up by Steevens's denunciation. Strangely,
although Steevens had taken aim at the Quarto and at Malone's edition, his polemic came to color even Benson's, which continued to be
reprinted in the early nineteenth century. In 1808 there appeared an
edition of love poems by "William Shakspeare" (the spelling of the
author's name itself testified to the influence of Malone).[13] The second volume included Benson's edition of the sonnets, but many of
Steevens's and Malone's notes were incongruously affixed to these significantly different poems. Even stranger perhaps is the case of Dr.
Sherwin of Bath, who sometime after 1818 wrote a series of marginal
comments in his 1774 copy of the *Poems* (i.e., the sonnets in their pre-
Malone, Benson form).[14] Sherwin, in other words, was reading an edition of the sonnets from which it would have been *impossible* to abstract
the story of Shakespeare, the young man, the rival poet, and the dark
lady, since the sonnets had been totally reordered, sometimes run
together so that two or more sonnets were made into a single poem,
and given titles that pointed in quite other directions, as well as occasionally having their pronouns changed. Moreover, the poems Sherwin read in his copy were entitled "Poems *on Several Occasions.*"

Yet what Sherwin responded to was not the text before him but the
mode of interpretation that Steevens and Malone had instituted and "the
unaccountable Prejudices of the late Mr. Steevens": "When Mr. Steevens
compliments his Brother-Commentator [Malone] at the Expence of the
Poet, when he tells us, that his Implements of Criticism are on *this Occasion disgraced by the objects of their Culture,* who can avoid a mingled Emotion
of Wonder and Disgust? Who can, in short forbear a Smile of Derision
and Contempt at the folly of such a declaration?" (2: flyleaf). Steevens
and Malone between them had constructed and passed down an impossible legacy: a legacy from Malone of the *Sonnets* as crucial documents of
the interior life of the national bard; a legacy from Steevens of that interior life as one that would destroy the life of the nation.

---

[13] Shakspeare, *Love Poems* (London: Cundee, 1808).

[14] Shakespeare, *Poems* (London: Etherington, 1774). Sherwin's copy, with his
marginalia, is in the Folger Shakespeare Library.

The effects of this impossible legacy were complex. David Lester Richardson, for instance, blamed the "flippant insolence of Steevens" for the neglect of the *Sonnets* (which Richardson still referred to as "a volume of Miscellaneous Poems").[15] Yet even as he promoted them, he was embarrassed by them. A registering of their beauty is, he writes, "accompanied by [a] disagreeable feeling, bordering on disgust" at the "indelicate" expressions of love between man and man (26). Sonnet 20 is "one of the most painful and perplexing I ever read. It is a truly disagreeable enigma. If I have caught any glimpse of the real meaning, I could heartily wish that Shakespeare had never written it" (38). A hundred years later the same sonnet, according to Walter Thomson, "threatened to mislead us and sent us searching for almost twelve months," until he could reassure himself that the word *passion* in the sonnet meant "emotional poem" rather than "amorous desire": "'Passion' is the crucial word, the foundation whereon the fantastic edifice is built in which it is alleged that Shakespeare was perverse in his morals. No more subversive mis-statement could be disseminated about any author or man, and not its least pernicious feature is that it places in the minds and mouths of the perverse a defence of their perversities. . . . We have it from a doctor of wide experience that it is no uncommon thing for perverse persons to cite Shakespeare as their exemplar."[16]

Thomson's last claim is not as wild as it may first appear. For as Alan Sinfield has argued, one of the effects of the Oscar Wilde trial was to help constitute a gay subculture with its own privileged texts and modes of reading.[17]

What particularly frightens Thomson is the connection between that new subculture and the uses of Shakespeare as a colonial text. In Calcutta in 1840 Richardson could write of the *Sonnets* as an unread text (1), but the educational apparatus of imperialism transformed that. The *Sonnets* by the late nineteenth century were being reproduced in school editions that quoted Dowden as saying that "in the Renas-

[15] Richardson, *Literary Leaves* (Calcutta: Thacker, 1840), 1, 3.

[16] Thomson, *The Sonnets of William Shakespeare and Henry Wriothesley* (Oxford: Blackwell, 1938), 2–3.

[17] Sinfield, lecture delivered at Georgetown University, 23 April 1992. For related considerations, see his *Faultlines: Cultural Materialism and the Politics of Dissident Reading* (Berkeley: University of California Press, 1992), 290–302.

cence epoch, among natural products of a time when life ran swift and free, touching with its current high and difficult places, the ardent friendship of man with man was one."[18] Thomson found just such an interpretation unacceptable. "We have information," he complains, "which justifies the statement that about 40 per cent. of the people who buy and read Shakespeare entertain the belief that he was a moral pervert" (9). "The supreme literary ornament of our race" (12) had become a contaminated source that subverted the colonial project: "What, for instance, of the many tens of thousands of students who, since Lord Macaulay's day, have come to our universities from India? They are frequently of literary bent and Shakespeare strongly attracts them. How many of them must return to India with these fallacies planted in their minds?" (7). But it is, of course, the "fallacy" of "perversity" that drives the writing of Thomson (as of Malone and Chalmers before him). The justification of Shakespeare is always subsequent to the charge of deviation—just as the concept of the "heterosexual" is a belated response to the *prior* concept of the "homosexual."

The *Sonnets*, I believe, played a central role in the constitution of a new "history of sexuality." Since Foucault, we have been accustomed to trace such a history through religious confessions, through medical discourse, through architecture. But one primary site in the formation of sexualities was the post-Enlightenment formation of "literature." If the *Sonnets* were crucial to it, then in their post–Steevens-Malone variant they lent themselves to intense critical and editorial labors that brought forth narratives of "normal" and "deviant" sexualities. The two great spurs to such narratives were the Steevens-Malone debate (and the Malone edition) at the end of the eighteenth century and Oscar Wilde's "Portrait of Mr. W. H." and trial at the end of the nineteenth century. Wilde published the piece in *Blackwood's* in 1889 after Frank Harris's *Fortnightly Review* had rejected it. As Harris notes in his biography of Wilde: "'The Portrait of Mr. W. H.' did Oscar incalculable injury. It gave his enemies *for the first time* the very weapon they wanted, and they used it unscrupulously and untiringly with the fierce delight of hatred."[19] Bal-

[18] W. J. Rolfe, ed., *Shakespeare's Sonnets* (New York: Harper, 1883), 15–16.
[19] Frank Harris, *Oscar Wilde* (East Lansing: Michigan State University Press, 1959), 69.

four and Asquith, to whom Wilde sent the story, advised against publication on the grounds that it would corrupt English homes.[20] Wilde created a specter that produced, by reactionary back-formation, not only the "normal" Shakespeare but "normality" itself.

That "normality," I have been arguing, was a hysterical symptom that accompanied Malone's construction of a unified character attributable to Shakespeare (and to the "characters" in his writing). But the narrative of characterological unity that Malone assembled was ideologically fruitful. That is, it did not merely erase the prior text of the *Sonnets* but prepared the site of a new kind of struggle. For the drive toward unity of character (Shakespeare's character, the characters of the *Sonnets*) led to more and more dramatic consequences at the level of sexual identity. The *Sonnets*, previously a marginal aspect of Shakespeare's corpus, became the ground on which "sexual identity" was invented and contested. If we need now to reconstruct the cultural history of Shakespeare, it is to understand how the imaginary terrain of our own bodies came into being.

---

[20] Richard Ellmann, *Oscar Wilde* (New York: Knopf, 1988), 298.

TEXTUAL POLITICS/
SEXUAL POLITICS

Richard Dellamora

When an author decides that a text will not be published until after his death, what is implied? I raise this question in connection with the posthumous publication of Thomas Hardy and E. M. Forster. In the case of Hardy, the text is a sentence that appears in no published text of *Jude the Obscure* but is included in the holograph manuscript that Hardy presented to the Fitzwilliam Museum at Cambridge University in 1911. In Forster's case, several texts are involved, including the novel *Maurice* and a collection of gay short stories that remained unpublished until after his death in 1970. Both writers address their texts to readers who will live after their own lives end. What demands do such appeals make? And what responsibilities do they entail for a historical understanding of texts?

In the passage from Hardy, Jude, looking back on his own defeats, comments to the Widow Edlin:

> When men of a later age look back upon the barbarism, cruelty & superstition of the times in which we have the unhappiness to live, it will appear more clearly to them than it does to us that the irksomeness of life is less owing to its natural conditions, though they are bad enough, than to those artificial conditions arranged for our well being, which have no root in the nature of things.[1]

Thanks to Eduardo Cadava and Richard Kaye, whose contributions to a discussion of this essay at Princeton University enabled me to pursue its arguments farther. I also thank Andrew Hewitt and the editor of *MLQ*, who read the essay in its short version.

[1] Quoted in Patricia Ingham, "The Evolution of *Jude the Obscure*," *Review of English Studies*, n.s., 27 (1976): 37.

Address in the quotation proleptically convenes a set of readers who will have overcome the moral outlook and philistine taste of hegemonic culture in the 1890s. Given the date of publication of *Jude* in book form, a few months after the Wilde trials, the "men of a later age" are a group reconstituted after men will have surmounted the division, suppression, and silencing of those who had questioned norms of gender and sexuality in the first half of the decade. The absence of women from this group, which is motivated for *Jude* by the collapse of Sue Bridehead into a perverse embrace of conventional morality, can also be read as a general challenge posed to women to confront the conditions that led to her defeat. The passage asks later readers to take into account both the narrowing limits of public expression in 1895 and the prophecy of a future more in sympathy with Jude's aspirations and beliefs. In both ways, the address cannot be received apart from the reader's sexual politics. Such temporal and ideological uncertainties problematize the assumption, stated in the passage, that proper knowledge will confirm the distinction to be drawn between natural and artificial conditions.

Hardy's sentence includes a double temporal anticipation. It addresses—in the present tense—the men of the future; but Hardy then places his prophecy under the mark of erasure. When he does so, he anticipates that this act will be reversed. He anticipates the restitution of the sentence. In other words, the sentence means: "A time will come when this sentence will be read/restituted." Hardy's double action permits him to hedge his bet. For his opinion to become true, the sentence must be restituted by future readers. But if he is wrong, he will not be *proved* wrong, because the sentence (and the prediction) will not appear. Moreover, the temporality is that of a past anterior: Hardy "will have been proved" right. He points not at the future but at the men (and women) who will point back at him. Yet the situation is more complex, since he can retain the potential to act only by placing his wager *within* institutions—the museum, the discipline of textual scholarship—that are antiquarian or monumental.[2] For this reason, he anticipates a third possibility: that the passage will be restituted in a way that ensures that it will come back—as a mummy.

---

[2] The terms are Friedrich Nietzsche's. See Nietzsche, *The Use and Abuse of History*, trans. Adrian Collins (Indianapolis, Ind.: Bobbs-Merrill, 1957), 12.

Patricia Ingham, who published the quotation in 1976, effaces Hardy's address in the name of textual scholarship as it came to define English studies in the same years in which Hardy wrote and disposed of the manuscript.[3] Since he was well aware of these circumstances, he in effect entrusted the text to a receiver beyond the limits within which its preservation was possible. Ingham attempts to locate the passage in relation to the "authentic" text of the novel (37). But since the serial version, the first book edition, and the holograph manuscript all differ, the search for a singular text proves impossible. Nonetheless, Ingham fails to infer that it might be more productive to take into account the conditions of production that affect the meaning of each state of the text.

Instead, the commitment to authenticity enables Ingham to make otherwise gratuitous comments about Hardy's intentions. The leap from expertise about textual truth to knowledge of the consciousness of the author is an assumption basic to the discipline of romantic philology, from which modern textual scholarship derives. If one can specify and define the actual language of a text, one can experience unmediated access to the consciousness that produced that text. Although the development of scientific philology during the nineteenth century put this assumption in doubt, it persisted within nascent English studies. In the early twentieth century, experts continued to uphold the belief, expressed by Coleridge, in a *lingua communis* based on shared understanding of a national literary canon. In this light, English studies took part in the work that Coleridge entrusted to the "clerisy," that " 'permanent, nationalized, learned order,' one part of which was to 'remain at the fountain heads of the humanities, in cultivating and enlarging the knowledge already possessed,' and the other larger portion of which was to 'be distributed throughout the country, so as not to leave even the smallest integral part or division without a resident guide, guardian, and instructor.' "[4]

In a condescending remark of trivial import, Ingham interprets the preservation of the passage as a sign of Hardy's "familiar devious-

---

[3] Ian Small discusses the process in *Conditions for Criticism: Authority, Knowledge, and Literature in the Late Nineteenth Century* (Oxford: Clarendon, 1991).

[4] Linda Dowling, *Language and Decadence in the Victorian Fin de Siècle* (Princeton, N.J.: Princeton University Press, 1986), xiv–xv, 28, 29.

ness" (37). In a reading that makes sense of the passage exclusively in terms already well known within the culture in which it was produced, she negates Hardy's charged approach to sexual politics by referring to what he, in the postscript to the preface of the first edition, called "the marriage theme."[5] Contextualized in this way, sexual politics is restricted in effect to questions about the reform of divorce law. In the postscript, however, Hardy disavows this thematization and attributes it not to himself but to "a learned writer" who had commented on the novel (vii). The marriage theme is, then, a product of the institution-alization of *Jude* carried forward in later editions that include the post-script. In pedagogy, the "theme" becomes a matter of strictly antiquar-ian interest.[6] Yet Sue's predicaments can be contextualized in relation to a variety of issues, such as the control of sexual touch, intimate rela-tionships, and reproduction, that are as troubled today as they were in 1895. Her difficulty in finding adequately compensated, emotionally and intellectually satisfying work is also pertinent, as are the difficulties she faces in developing supportive relationships with other women.

In sum, all three of Ingham's foci (textual, biographical, thematic) use the apparatus of scholarship to exclude the question of address. This question has been much more difficult to avoid in relation to Forster's posthumous publication. In the early 1970s, readers of Forster suddenly faced a body of work previously unpublished on the grounds that publication would expose the author to prosecution under the terms of the same amendment under which Wilde had been tried and found guilty.[7] Forster reserved *Maurice* and the short stories until after his death, three years after the Sexual Offences Act of 1967 had partially decriminalized male homosexual behavior. Beforehand,

---

[5] Hardy, *Jude the Obscure* (Toronto: Macmillan, 1969), vii; quoted in Ingham, 169.

[6] Technically, the postscript is a paratext, "the set of [texts] that surround the central text: things like prefaces, dedications, notebooks, advertisements, footnotes, and so forth" (Jerome J. McGann, *The Textual Condition* [Princeton, N.J.: Princeton University Press, 1991], 13). Following Gérard Genette, McGann argues that "they are consistently regarded as only quasi-textual, ancillary to the main textual event" (13). But the example that I have chosen indicates that a paratext can be used to affix a particular thematic interpretation to a text.

[7] Forster, "Terminal Note," in *A Room with a View; Howard's End; Maurice* (New York: Quality Paperback, n.d.), 250.

his career as a major novelist was believed to have ended with the publication of *A Passage to India* in 1924.

The appearance of new material posed serious questions internal and external to the Forster canon. Do the gay texts and the nongay ones constitute separate bodies of work? Should surveys continue to conclude with a discussion of *A Passage to India* as Forster's chef d'oeuvre, or should they now have a final chapter on the gay writing, which, by virtue of appearing last, becomes the telos toward which his development moves? Should the gay writing be relegated to the margin as expressing a minority interest that has in fact been outdated by legal reform? Or should readings of Forster interleave the gay writing, some of which was done before World War I, with his more conventional work? Should the claim be made that his writing is really about a desire between men that remains masked, for better or possibly for worse, in novels that follow an apparently heterosexual trajectory?

To whom are either or both bodies of work addressed? If the gay texts seem to imply a gay readership, are gay readers likely to accept Forster's ambivalent response to desire between men as in any way a representation of their own response? How can the cultural gap be bridged between a man whose lifelong response to homosexuality was affected by his terror, at age sixteen, of what happened to Wilde versus the young men and women who, in the immediate aftermath of 1967, were inventing gay liberation? If only Forster had been fortunate enough to die not in his ninety-second year but in his eighty-second, publication might have helped cut short the decade of delay between issuance of the report of the Wolfenden committee and the implementation of its recommendations. Then, at least, what by 1971 seemed too late an appearance would have done some good.

And what about Forster's familiar liberal readership? Do the gay texts address them? How are they now supposed to read the credos, in the novels and the journalism, for which Forster became renowned? Everyone knows that in 1938 he had declared that "I hate the idea of causes, and if I had to choose between betraying my country and betraying my friend I hope I should have the guts to betray my country." But not everyone knew that for Forster the word *friend* carried a particular inflection. And what was one to make of his insistence in "What I Believe" on "trust," "natural warmth," "love," and "creation" when, except for a passing reference to "Brünnhilde's last song," that love is never described as heterosexual?[8]

Similarly, there is the well-known statement that Margaret Schlegel voices in *Howard's End* in response to the "incomplete asceticism" of Henry Wilcox: "Only connect! That was the whole of her sermon. Only connect the prose and the passion, and both will be exalted, and human love will be seen at its height. Live in fragments no longer. Only connect, and the beast and the monk, robbed of the isolation that is life to either, will die."[9] But Henry isn't listening, and the reader of Philip Furbank's biography of Forster will know that for a number of years after the publication of this novel he continued to live the life of a "monk," all too aware both of his "isolation" and of the "beast" that a sexual desire without habitation can produce.

His frustration inhabits his paeans of romantic love. His anger at the violence done to him and his resistance to compulsory heterosexuality inflect his utterance within liberal discourse, which is often mobilized as a reverse discourse in the strict sense of that term as Foucault describes it:

> Discourses . . . can . . . circulate without changing their form from one strategy to another, opposing strategy. We must not expect the discourses on sex to tell us . . . what ideology—dominant or dominated— they represent; rather we must question them on the two levels of their tactical productivity (what reciprocal effects of power and knowledge they ensure) and their strategical integration (what conjunction and what force relationship make their utilization necessary in a given episode of the various configurations that occur).[10]

This double siting deeply offended some liberal reviewers of *Maurice*, because it challenges the idea that "civilization," to use a term that Forster favored, can be defined in terms of "a common measure of fact, a universal conceptual currency, so to speak, for the general characterization of things. . . . By [this phrase] . . . I mean that all facts are

---

[8] Forster, "What I Believe," in *Two Cheers for Democracy* (London: Edward Arnold, 1972), 66, 68.

[9] Forster, *Howard's End* (Harmondsworth: Penguin, 1968), 174–75.

[10] Foucault, *An Introduction*, vol. 1 of *The History of Sexuality*, trans. Robert Hurley (New York: Vintage, 1980), 102. Kaja Silverman quotes the passage in *Male Subjectivity at the Margins* (New York: Routledge, 1992), 343.

What I Believe, by Paul Cadmus (detail). "Forster, with an uncharacteristic upstick-ing tuft of hair, is at the back; Isherwood reading in foreground" (Francis King, *E. M. Forster* [London: Thames and Hudson, 1978], 115). Private collection, cour-tesy Midtown Payson Galleries, New York.

located within a single continuous logical space, that statements reporting them can be conjoined and generally related to each other, and so that in principle one single language describes the world and is internally unitary. . . . 'Only connect' is an intelligible and acceptable ideal."[11] Forster's posthumous publication scandalizes by dispelling the fiction that "all referential uses of language ultimately refer to one coherent world, and can be reduced to a unitary idiom" (Gellner, 21). That the fugitive enunciation within the texts published earlier is also, to use Marshall Brown's phrase, "feminine or feminized" likewise violates the silent but oppressive law of gender that operates within discursive univocity.[12]

Some reviews indicate why Forster's prestige declined during the 1970s. Walter Allen, a leading expert on moral realism in the English novel, tried to minimize the damage by describing *Maurice* as "the least in literary value" of Forster's novels.[13] In a review in England's leading liberal organ, the *Manchester Guardian*, Julian Mitchell referred to the book as "a fairy tale in the worst possible sense" (Gardner, 440). But if reviewers shied away from Forster, the responses of some gay polemicists were harsh. Forster's belated appearance as a gay writer scarcely earned him acceptance, much less acclaim, from the voices of gay liberation in the post-Act, post-Stonewall decade of the 1970s. Occurring when it did, the publication of *Maurice* and the short stories prompted people to ask why Forster had waited so long. Why had he failed to come out during his lifetime? In an important British pamphlet, *With Downcast Gays* (1974), Forster is the one gay man singled out for attack by name. According to the coauthors, Andrew Hodges and David Hutter, Forster kept silent because he was unwilling to put at risk

> his privileged status as the Grand Old (heterosexual) Man of English Letters. . . . Throughout his life Forster betrayed other gay people by posing as a heterosexual and thus identifying with our oppressors. The novel which could have helped us find courage and self-esteem he

---

[11] Ernest Gellner, *Nations and Nationalism* (Oxford: Basil Blackwell, 1983), 21; quoted in Michael Holquist, "Response," *Yale Journal of Criticism* 5 (spring 1992): 154.

[12] Brown, "Contemplating the Theory of Literary History," *PMLA* 107 (1992): 22.

[13] Quoted in Philip Gardner, ed., *E. M. Forster: The Critical Heritage* (London: Routledge and Kegan Paul, 1973), 438.

only allowed to be published after his death, thereby confirming belief in the secret and disgraceful nature of homosexuality. What other minority is so sunk in shame and self-oppression as to be proud of a traitor?[14]

Dennis Altman, a leading theorist of gay liberation, observes that "homosexual love is a constant spirit in Forster's writings, requiring only a sympathetic reading to materialise." But in 1977 even Altman concluded: "The real significance of Forster's homosexuality seems to me to be that it forced him to be false to himself. He was false in his writings, because he had always to describe heterosexual relationships."[15] Although Altman, Hodges, and Hutter are all critics of liberal discourse, their remarks share the assumption that there is "a universal conceptual currency" in which the flip of a coin can turn up a Forster who is either true or "false."

Responses like these forget that homosexual polemicists before Forster, such as Walter Pater and Oscar Wilde, critiqued the claims of identity, general consciousness, and universal truth that one finds enforced within English studies and other disciplines fashioned during the nineteenth century. Forster's critique of the heterosexual contract radically qualifies his investment in patrician liberal ideals of high culture, individual sensibility, and personal relationship.[16]

The attack on Forster has not been confined to the first phase of gay liberation. It continues in John Fletcher's recent criticism of the "pessimism and political resignation" of the "Terminal Note" to *Maurice*.[17] Fletcher adapts Eve Kosofsky Sedgwick's model of male homosocial relations in order to describe the relationship with Edward Carpenter and his working-class lover, George Merrill, which provided Forster with the impetus for his novel. Fletcher further draws on Jean

[14] Hodges and Hutter, *With Downcast Gays: Aspects of Homosexual Self-Oppression*, 2d ed. (Toronto: Pink Triangle, 1979), 24–25.

[15] Altman, "The Homosexual Vision of E. M. Forster," in *Studies in E. M. Forster, Cahiers d'études et de recherches victoriennes et édouardiennes*, nos. 4–5 (1977): 91, 92.

[16] Tom Nairn refers to "the traditions of patrician liberalism" in *The Break-up of Britain: Crisis and Neo-Nationalism*, 2d ed. (London: Verso, 1981), 65.

[17] Fletcher, "Forster's Self-Erasure: *Maurice* and the Scene of Masculine Love," in *Sexual Sameness: Textual Differences in Lesbian and Gay Writing*, ed. Joseph Bristow (London: Routledge, 1992), 64.

Laplanche and Jean-Bertrand Pontalis in order to describe the "primal scene" in which *Maurice* originates: "In conceiving and bearing the novel, Forster becomes the site, at once intellectual and unmasculine, of what must resist or discomfort the mythic resolutions of manly love" (72). Yet Fletcher forgets perhaps the most important point that Laplanche and Pontalis make: namely, that the subject is liable to mobile identifications with positions and predicates within fantasies of the primal scene.[18]

If Forster is to be identified with characters in the novel, as Fletcher believes, there is little reason to insist as Fletcher does that this identification occurs primarily with one character. Fletcher neglects to exploit the element of resistance that he notes in Forster's production of the text. Instead, he contends that Forster was a mommy's boy who could not overcome his identification with the forbidding figure of his deceased father. For this reason, the novel ends by investing its author in the figure of the self-suppressing intellectual, Clive. En route, Fletcher reproduces a photograph of Forster's mother and very young son, "all Little Lord Fauntleroy locks and possessive embraces" (86). This metonym "explains" a subjection to the paternal superego that accounts for Forster's cathexis with Clive. Castration likewise explains Forster's failure to come out by publishing *Maurice* earlier. As long ago as 1948, however, H. Montgomery Hyde dismissed the accusation, made at the time against Wilde, that he had been perverted by his mother's having "dressed him in girl's clothes during his childhood days, decking him out with jewels which made him look like 'a little Hindu idol.'" Hyde remarks: "Victorian mothers were accustomed to dress their children of either sex in petticoats and skirts until they were six or seven years old."[19]

Forster repeatedly inscribes *Maurice* within a structure of surveillance. In a letter that he wrote to Christopher Isherwood after Isherwood had read the novel in manuscript in 1938, Forster remarked that he feared that publishing it would result in the harassment of his married, working-class intimate, Bob Buckingham ("Everyone connects

---

[18] Laplanche and Pontalis, "Fantasy and the Origins of Sexuality," in *Formations of Fantasy*, ed. Victor Burgin, James Donald, and Cora Kaplan (London: Routledge, 1989), 22–23.

[19] Hyde, *The Trials of Oscar Wilde* (New York: Dover, 1973), 51.

him with me").[20] In the "Terminal Note" of 1960, Forster writes: "The Wolfenden recommendations will be indefinitely rejected, police prosecutions will continue and Clive on the bench will continue to sentence Alec in the dock. Maurice may get off" (255). Forster could have excised these sentences after passage of the Sexual Offences Act of 1967. Why didn't he? The answer, I think, is historical: Forster perceived that the class structure of sexual and emotional ties between men persisted and that relations between men continued to be subject to the law even after 1967. This view is not, as Fletcher believes, pessimistic. It is observant, warning against renewed outbreaks of police entrapment, which have in fact occurred. Forster's irony, directed toward the Clives, Alecs, and Maurices, is polemical. The recognition that one is judged is itself a judgment against the world that judges.

Fletcher also dislikes the "apolitical pastoralism" of the novel (65). But the genre of pastoral was highly politicized in late-Victorian sexual politics. Forster explains: "A happy ending was imperative. I shouldn't have bothered to write otherwise. I was determined that in fiction anyway two men should fall in love and remain in it for the ever and ever that fiction allows, and in this sense Maurice and Alec still roam the greenwood" ("Terminal Note," 250). The upbeat ending made the text particularly liable to prosecution: "The lovers get away unpunished and consequently recommend crime" ("Terminal Note," 250). The "imperative" that dictates this ending is obviously political. But just as Forster's implicit anger denegates the irony with which he presents desire between men as on trial in court, he negates the utopian vista of the "greenwood" into which Maurice and Alec escape.

Acknowledging that two world wars had "transformed" England, Forster disavows Maurice and Alec's ability to step outside the law:

> Our greenwood ended catastrophically and inevitably. Two great wars demanded and bequeathed regimentation which the public services adopted and extended, science lent her aid, and the wildness of our island, never extensive, was stamped upon and built over and patrolled in no time. There is no forest or fell to escape to today, no cave in which to curl up, no deserted valley for those who wish neither to reform nor corrupt society but to be left alone. People do still escape,

[20] Forster, *Selected Letters*, ed. Mary Lago and Philip Furbank, vol. 2 (Cambridge, Mass.: Belknap Press of Harvard University Press, 1985), 159.

one can see them any night at it in the films. But they are gangsters not outlaws, they can dodge civilization because they are part of it. ("Terminal Note," 254)

As with the image of men in court, Forster ends by emphasizing that escape does not negate the law. There is no place outside the law; nor is there a maternal womb to which to return. Instead, Forster insists on temporal difference—between 1960 and the time before World War I when he wrote the novel. This recognition requires that men with sexual and emotional ties to other men continually place themselves and their struggles in a set of historical reflections from which there is No Exit.

This insistence has been a continuing source of offense. In the early 1970s the goals of personal and social transformation that animated activists paradoxically required that they suppress awareness of the very oppressions and outrages in whose name they demanded change. To bring the existence of sexual minorities into visibility, it was necessary to negate the conditions that militated against doing so. In Nietzsche's words: "'Being' is merely a continual 'has been,' a thing that lives by denying and destroying and contradicting itself." He argues that those who wish to achieve modernity have to suspend memory; otherwise they will not be able to escape its limits. Amnesia, however, requires an act of will that is continually in danger of lapsing. This tendency renders the loss of memory always incomplete. The question is whether what comes back is useful or damaging.

Forster chose to emphasize the aspects of destruction, contradiction, and deferral in the process of becoming. His attention to memory is offensive to those who seek to transform gender and sexuality, since such a transformation can occur only if the subject forgets those relations as they have existed. But forgetting is costly, including the loss of memory of past individual homosexuals and queers; of their networks and subcultures; and of their political struggles, bafflement, and occasional success. This is the price that action can exact. "In the smallest and greatest happiness," Nietzsche observes, "there is always one thing that makes it happiness: the power of forgetting, . . . the capacity of feeling 'unhistorically' throughout its duration" (6).

Forster's posthumous publication insists, to the contrary, on the noncoincidence of intention, act, and effect in cultural and political

interventions. In refusing to let differences, gaps, and reversals be forgotten, he offends against the ethic and politic of gay liberation as that
term was defined two decades ago. Yet today, in the 1990s, his offense
begins to appear necessary. The impacts of AIDS have made feeling
"unhistorically" seem like a betrayal of those who have died. Nascent
queer theory, under the impress of AIDS, emphasizes resistance, intro-
jected loss, and deferral in the constitution of the subject. At such a
moment, the insistence on temporal difference in Forster's representation of queer existence as *he* experienced it can contribute to a
renewed sense of purpose. In Nietzsche's phrasing:

> To fix this degree and the limits to the memory of the past, if it is not to
> become the gravedigger of the present, we must see clearly how great is
> the "plastic power" of a man or a community or a culture; I mean the
> power of specifically growing out of one's self, of making the past and
> the strange one body with the near and the present, of healing wounds,
> replacing what is lost, repairing broken molds. (7) [21]

Forster alters the structure of literary history by inserting his texts
into it in a new mode of temporal allegory. Paul de Man has distinguished allegory from symbol by arguing that "whereas the symbol postulates the possibility of an identity or identification, allegory desig-
nates primarily a distance in relation to its own origin."[22] The desire
for an authentic text is for one in which authorial intention and "tem-
perament," to use Ingham's word, coincide with a stabilized text (169).
An allegorical text, in the sense in which I use the term, is one that,
because of the materials entrusted to posterity by the writer, always differs from itself. In Hardy's case, the non-coincidence of three versions
places the novel in an allegorical relationship with itself. Within the
terms of Forster's posthumous publication, individual texts function
as systems of signs dialectically related by means of temporal differ-

---

[21] For an important statement of queer theory see Judith Butler, "Imitation and
Gender Insubordination," in *Inside/Out: Lesbian Theories, Gay Theories*, ed. Diana Fuss
(New York: Routledge, 1991), 13–31. This and the preceding paragraph are
indebted to Paul de Man, "Literary History and Literary Modernity," in *Blindness and
Insight: Essays in the Rhetoric of Contemporary Criticism* (New York: Oxford University
Press, 1971), 142–65.

[22] De Man, "The Rhetoric of Temporality," in *Interpretation: Theory and Practice*,
ed. Charles S. Singleton (Baltimore, Md.: Johns Hopkins University Press, 1969), 191.

ence.[23] Neither the fiction published before 1925 nor the fiction published after 1970 can properly be identified with Forster. Henceforth the meaning of Forster and of each fiction needs to be assessed in relation to both sets of texts as well as to the contexts of production that account for their appearance a half century apart. Such an assessment will always be further marked by an implicit or explicit evaluation of the place of sexual politics in cultural politics now, which depends in turn on continually shifting realities in the mobilization of homophobia in a wide range of politics.

Neither cultural radicals nor literary historians who read Hardy and Forster can expect their texts to authenticate expressed or tacit moral or sexual truths. Instead, as Foucault urges, readers need to question what "reciprocal effects of power and knowledge" are "ensured" by the deployment of particular discourses at particular moments. The predicate that Foucault uses, *ils assurent*, is equivocal.[24] Like the English word *assure*, the verb can mean "to declare or promise confidently." It can also mean "to guarantee" or "to make certain of." Like the English word *insure*, the verb can mean "[to contract to] protect against damage or loss."[25] There is a significant difference between promising an outcome and making it certain. The distance between the two makes it possible to detour and derail discursive practices. I have argued that a framework that restricts interpretation to the terms deployed within historical discourses will provide an unsatisfactory account of such effects. Nor can one hope that the "truths" of contemporary discourses will enable adequate comprehension of texts. What is necessary is a double framing that exploits the possibilities of temporal difference in order to put in question both historical and contemporary truths. In this process, textual politics can never be freed

[23] Forster's posthumous publication presents a special case of what de Man refers to as "writing": "The ambivalence of writing is such that it can be considered both an act and an interpretative process that follows after an act with which it cannot coincide" ("Literary History," 152).

[24] The clause reads: "quels effets réciproques de pouvoir et de savoir ils assurent" (Foucault, *La Volonté de savoir*, vol. 1 of *Histoire de la sexualité* [Paris: Gallimard, 1976], 135). I would like to thank Linda Dowling for puzzling over this sentence with me.

[25] *Webster's New World Dictionary of the American Language*, s.vv. "assure," "insure" (modified).

from sexual politics. But the reverse is also true. The latest assertions about the truths of sex and gender are marked by the traces of struggles in the past, and nowhere more so than with regard to the texts that I have discussed here. For this reason, those texts should be neither forgotten nor impugned; they should be recalled.

THE PEDIGREE OF THE
WHITE STALLION:
POSTCOLONIALITY AND
LITERARY HISTORY

Rukmini Bhaya Nair

Has anyone noticed the absence of weather in *Kim*? The influence of climatic conditions on history as well as on individual character forms, as we know, a crucial element in the orientalist narrative from Pierre Sonnerat through James Mill to William Arnold;[1] we know, too, that *Kim* spreads itself across Upper India like one of those detailed surveyor's maps that its hero is trained to draw. And if we compared *Kim*, certainly the cult novel of high colonialism, to the great Indian anti-*Kim*, Rabindranath Tagore's *Gora*, so replete with descriptions of seasonal changes, we could hardly help remarking on the significance of Kipling's omission. Toward the end of this essay, I shall, indeed must, return to these signs of strange literary weather in *Kim* and *Gora*, but first, we may need some of the equipment basic to writing any kind of history at all: a rough specification of time and terrain.

A coincidence of dates, 1901, 1910, 1990—zeroes, nines, and pristine ones, encircling the century—initially caught my attention. I must admit I was taken with the symmetry of this roundel until it dawned on me that coincidences, like jokes, do not cross cultural boundaries; even the sassiest of them retreats at the fences of history. The audience of the present collection will pick out 1901 as the date when *Kim* appeared on the literary horizon, but few among even this academic community are likely to be aware of the complex patterns that con-

---

[1] Sonnerat, *A Voyage to the East Indies and China between 1774 and 1781* (Calcutta, 1788); James Mill, *The History of British India* (London, 1817); and Arnold (brother of Matthew), *Oakfield; or, Fellowship in the East* (London, 1854).

nect *Kim* to *Gora* (1910) or to *The Trotternama* (1990), rumbustious
post-*Kim*.[2] They remain texts of radical estrangement. Marked only by
their absence in the Western imagination, they cannot spark off the
instantaneous recognition that is the epistemic basis for an apprecia-
tion of coincidences, jokes, and, by extension, textual congeries.

What will an American readership make, for instance, of the forbidding silence that Tagore maintained about *Kim* or, indeed, of the
filial license that Allan Sealy, author of *The Trotternama*, has latterly
taken with *Kim*? These questions drag behind them the trawl of recent
subcontinental history. Without the facts and theories entangled in it,
they are weightless, insubstantial, undecipherable; with them, they
might just bring in a catch—a trout in the milk, perchance. [3]

The biographical facts are boring; they belong, rightly, to the
underworld of footnotes. That they surface here, in the middle of my
text, has less to do with their inherent interest than with my lack of
confidence that I share this litter heap of facts with my current readership. But for what they are worth, here goes. Tagore (1861–1941) and
Kipling (1865–1936) seem to have led lives that ran coldly parallel,
like railroad tracks designed not to touch even by accident. Kipling, of
course, has always been identified with the heyday of the Empire; of
Tagore's historical placement, Ketaki Dyson writes that "his lifespan
was roughly coeval with that of British imperial rule in India, his birth
coming within three years of its formal commencement and his death
just six years before its dissolution."[4] The timing makes it laughably
easy to discover a series of "resemblances" between the lives of the two
authors. Born to bourgeois families in Indian metropolises, Tagore in
Calcutta and Kipling in Bombay, each, inevitably—for how can one

[2] *The Trotternama* first appeared in America and Europe in 1988, which, it would
seem, rather ruins my "coincidence"; however, it was published in India by Penguin
only in 1990, so I continue to think of 1990 as the relevant date for its subcontinental incarnation.

[3] This phrase from Thoreau, which forms the title of Lawrence Lipking's essay,
is embedded in the sentence "Some circumstantial evidence is very strong, as when
you find a trout in the milk." The search for circumstantial evidence of the colonial
and postcolonial "hand" ☞ (or agency) in the case histories of literary texts is not
unimportant in my essay, although the sense Lipking emphasizes—"of surprise,
delight, and the unexpected"—is very much intended as well.

[4] Dyson, introduction to *I Won't Let You Go: Selected Poems*, by Rabindranath
Tagore, trans. and ed. Ketaki Kushari Dyson (New Delhi: UBSD Publishers, 1992), 17.

resist the power of legend?—had what Doris Lessing has called "the best apprenticeship for a writer . . . not necessarily an unhappy but a *stressed* childhood" as a lonely boy raised mainly by family servants. A recent Tagore biographer, Andrew Robinson, mentions the common fascination that the Grand Trunk Road held for Kipling and Tagore as children, adding that Tagore was particularly enamored of the idea of traveling the length of the road by bullock cart—a possibly endless journey.[5] In time, these two most acclaimed men of letters from the Indian subcontinent carried off Nobel Prizes in literature within a few years of each other, Kipling in 1907 and Tagore in 1913; Kipling refused a knighthood twice, and Tagore promptly returned his after the Jalianwala Bagh massacre. Widely traveled, especially in the New World, both authors had predictably illustrious but, it appears, mutually exclusive circles of friends. Among Kipling's literary admirers were the Anglo-American contingent—Thomas Hardy, Edmund Gosse, Rider Haggard, Robert Louis Stevenson, Cecil Rhodes, and Mark Twain—and among Tagore's the internationalists—William Butler Yeats, Wilfred Owen, Pablo Neruda, Gabriela Mistral, Victoria Ocampo, Juan Ramón Jiménez, Leonard Elmhurst, William Rothenstein, and Edward Thompson, not to mention Mahatma Gandhi, Jawaharlal Nehru, and pretty much all of Bengal. The deaths of two of Kipling's three children (Elsie in 1899 and John in 1917) and of three of Tagore's five (Renuka in 1903, Shomi in 1907, and Madhurilata in 1918) provide another point of poignant comparison. One could go on like this for pages, but what could be less revealing than this tedious catalog? Like Marx's definition of history replayed, it reduces even tragedy to farce.

Infinitely more remarkable is one stark observation: neither Kipling nor Tagore seems to have so much as *mentioned* the other, ever, in the course of their long and concurrent lifetimes, which was also, as we have remarked, roughly the lifetime of the Empire, *although, although* . . . Much hinges in my argument upon the analysis of this echoing *although*. For while nothing in their public lives indicates that the one knew the other existed, the novelistic masterpieces of both

[5] Rabindranath Tagore, *My Reminiscences* (1917; rpt. Delhi: Rupa, 1992), 212n; see also Krishna Dutta and Andrew Robinson, *Rabindranath Tagore: The Myriad-Minded Man* (London: Bloomsbury, 1995).

authors choose precisely the same curious motif. Each is about Irish foundlings brought as "Indians."[6]

Gora, Kim, and, nearly a century later, *The Trotternama* turn out to be texts that insist on talking to each other, with or without the cooperation of their authors. The rest of this essay concerns itself with the ways in which history shackles its authorial agents while allowing, apparently, for the most permissive unions between the texts that they father. How are such literary genealogies created? Who holds copyright over a contested history, such as that of colonization? How can recently developed methods of historical interpretation help us understand the subject(s) of literature? I take these questions to be as important as any to the discipline of literary history.

Astride the gun Zam-Zammah.[7]—Historiography in a postcolonial state is an energetic art. It gathers up all the recondite theories of reading and extravagant agendas for political subversion that, in societies more confident of their own cultural pasts, are left to literary criticism or philosophy. Historians, not critics, are the missionaries of interpretation in postcolonial India. For this simple contextual reason I propose to explore the relationship between literary history, which in India at any rate summons up only the most staid images of old-maidish scholarship, and its dashing, unconventional sister, subalternist historiography. Literary history has always conversed in subdued tones of the ways in which literature exposes the interiors of history and brings point of

---

[6] The "Irish Question" was a matter of concern among the Bengali intelligentsia as early as the 1820s. Raja Ram Mohun Roy, founder of the Brahmo Samaj, of which Tagore's father, Debendranath Tagore, was a stalwart member, strongly opposed the British occupation of Ireland. Roy actually sent money to the famine-stricken Irish and wrote against their oppression in his *Mirat-ul-Akbar*. The activities of the Brahmo Samaj form an important narrative element in *Gora*. Tagore therefore inherits a tradition of intellectual sympathy for the Irish, which facilitates his against-the-grain reading of the *Kim* theme in *Gora*. Incidentally, at the age of eighteen, the impressionable Tagore had also heard Gladstone and Bright speak on Irish home rule in the British Parliament.

[7] This quotation and the one heading the next section are from Rudyard Kipling, *Kim* (Calcutta: Rupa Paperback, 1989), 7, 97; the next two sections are headed by quotations from Rabindranath Tagore, *Gora* (Madras: Macmillan, 1989), 338, 19; and the final two sections by quotations from Allan Sealy, *The Trotternama* (Delhi: Penguin, 1990), 173, 255, where the hand, I should emphasize, is a quite integral part of the text.

view, subjectivity, to bear on brute fact, but current subalternism has little patience with this gentle twittering. It uncompromisingly politicizes the subject. By privileging the class-based notion of subject position over the individualistic point-of-view perspective traditionally favored in literary criticism, subalternism insists on the futility of *any* discussion of subjectivity, even the most esoteric, without reference to collective consciousness or power relations.

In short, there exists a school of historiographers in India today who themselves form a collective of considerable intellectual power. Writing, therefore, from the place that I imagine I occupy on a rather badly drawn cultural map of the world, I would have to be an ostrich of truly magnificent proportions to ignore compelling subalternist modes of analysis, which have decisively shaped our understanding of what it "means" to be a postcolonial. Any ideas on literary history that I might want to suggest must first negotiate the historiographical channels that have already been charted and have already begun a trade in rich intellectual properties—rumors, bodies, boundaries, calamities, crises, insurgencies, strategies, collectivities, patriarchies, female territorialities, moments and discontinuities, agencies, instrumentalities, alterities, consanguinities, lineages . . .

Kim stakes out, with sardonic accuracy, the site of conflict in its famous opening scene.

> "Off! Off! Let me up!" cried Abdullah, climbing up Zam-Zammah's wheel.
> "Thy father was a pastry-cook, Thy mother stole the ghi" sang Kim. "All Mussalmans fell off Zam-Zammah years ago!"
> "Let me up!" shrilled little Chota Lal in his gilt-embroidered cap. His father was worth perhaps half a million sterling, but India is the only democratic land in the world.
> "The Hindus fell off Zam-Zammah too. The Mussalmans pushed them off. Thy father was a pastry-cook —" (Kipling, 10)

Eavesdropping on the exchanges of street children seems to lead the omniscient narrator in *Kim* to draw the startling categorical conclusion that "India is the only democratic land in the world." Because there is a politics of belief to be read into this initiatory, as well as initial, exchange of ritual insults, I hope to discuss next how the historiographical studies that have burgeoned in postcolonial India help us explain the sincerity conditions that attach to the enigmatic assertion about Indian democracy in an avowedly imperialist text.

Edward Said, analyzing the connections between "culture and imperialism," presents the unusual argument that the vision of India in *Kim* is benign because "its author is writing . . . from the perspective of a massive colonial system whose economy, functioning and history has acquired the status of a virtual fact of nature. Kipling assumes a basically uncontested empire." "For Kipling *there was no conflict*" between an attachment to India and the conviction that it was best for India to be governed by the British.[8] But Said's shrewd observation is undercut by an anxiety about the unreliability of historical forces. History, like the weather, is a chaotic system. Kipling's uncertainty about the permanence of political control is evident even in that scene where children squabble simultaneously over pedigree and power. In the series of "racial" displacements of control over Zam-Zammah—of the Hindus by the Muslims and the Muslims by the British—there seems to be no guarantee that the last occupation is the final one. *Everyone* is liable to insult and the vagaries of fortune. Indeed the text itself ruptures nervously, with Kim breaking off literally in midsentence: "He stopped; for there shuffled round the corner, from the roaring Motee Bazar, such a man as Kim, who thought he knew all castes, had never seen" (Kipling, 10). The dramatic entry of Kim's *guru*, the lama, at a moment of unresolved "truth" may have implications contra Said for our reading of authorial attitude and intentionality—sincerity—in *Kim*.

Eye-rishti—that was the Regiment—my father's. There is a piece of paper that flutters around *Kim*. Where that paper flies, flies History, swooping over the crowded rooftops of Lahore, via the trading *kafilas* of the north country, up to the spacious bungalow of Creighton Sahib and down the Grand Trunk Road, straight into the shadowy territories of the Five Kings. Now, it is true that, during these picaresque proceedings, history very closely mimics local color—garish, painted scenery wheeled in and out all through the action—but the effect, like so much else in *Kim*, turns out to be double bluff, illusion. History fools you; when war is planned, a takeover foiled, or a deal struck, the air

---

[8] Said, *Culture and Imperialism* (London: Vintage, 1994), 162, 176.

thickens with confusion. That thickness is history, or at least the literary version of it, a miasma of subjectivities. Geertz today might term it "thick description"; the lama in *Kim*, as much a "wallower in the ontic,"[9] calls it, simply, "the Wheel of Things," a mill of desire to which everyone in history is strapped. The main props that establish the layered ambiguities of history in a colonial state do not, as we might expect, consist of names, places, actions. If history takes place not onstage but behind the scenes, as *Kim* repeatedly insists, then its secret workings are to be discovered in the most unlikely place of all: on paper, the classic metaphor of the human mind, of mental spaces.[10]

Documents are the surest signs of power in *Kim*; agency, not to mention sexuality, is heavily invested in the novel's peddlers of paper. Every one of the principal players in the text, including the lama, Creighton, the spy E.23, Hurree Babu, Mahbub Ali, and Kim himself, controls the movement not of troops or women but of letters, coded messages, certificates, wondrous ethnographic maps, scriptures, and bureaucratic notes. The flags of history marking regimental advances (red bulls on green fields) constitute only vulgar signals of a far more subtle exercise of the will to power.

> Kim stole out and away, as unremarkable a figure as ever carried his own and a few score thousand other folk's fate slung round his neck. . . .
> Presently forth came an Englishman, dressed in black and white, humming a tune. It was too dark to see his face, so Kim, beggar-wise, tried an old experiment.
> "Protector of the Poor!"
> The man backed towards the voice.
> "Mahbub Ali says—"
> "Hah! What says Mahbub Ali?" He made no attempt to look for the speaker, and that showed Kim that he knew.
> "The pedigree of the white stallion is fully established."
> "What proof is there? . . ."
> "Mahbub Ali has given me this proof." Kim flipped the wad of folded paper into the air, and it fell on the path beside the man, who put his foot on it as the gardener came round the corner. When the ser-

---

[9] I owe this phrase to Richard Rorty, who used it in a conversation with me at Dartmouth in 1992.

[10] See Gilles Fauconnier, *Mental Spaces: Aspects of Meaning Construction in Natural Language* (Cambridge, Mass.: MIT Press, 1985).

vant passed he picked it up, dropped a rupee,—Kim could hear the clink,—and strode into the house, never turning around. Swiftly Kim took up the money; but, for all his training, he was Irish enough by birth to reckon silver the least part of any game. What he desired was the visible effect of action. . . .

"And all that trouble," said he to himself, thinking as usual in Hindustanee, "for a horse's pedigree! Mahbub Ali should have come to me to learn a little lying. Every time before that I have borne a message it concerned a woman. Now it is men. Better. The tall man said they will loose a great army. . . . There are also guns. It is big news!" (Kipling, 44–45)

Confronted with this sample of classic imperialist Kipling, how would a subaltern historiographer reach for the subjectivity displayed—or is the more appropriate word *concealed?*—in the text? Would he or she even admit literary representation as historical testimony? Because historiographers are professional metatheorists concerned with critiquing the foundations of historical knowledge, including all those grandstanding judgments about causality, determinism, contingency, and so forth that legitimize historical "truth," it might be supposed that they have a natural affinity for epistemological radicalism. So far, I have tacitly promoted this view by considering only one kind of historiographer, the subalternist, but there are others who, by enlarging the part that nonhuman agents (weather, climate, floods, earthquakes, microbes) might play in historical processes, conservatively delimit the absolute revolutionary powers that could otherwise be conferred on human agents in the "creation" of history.[11] But whatever their political convictions, all historiographers, given the range of documents they have themselves made use of, as well as the nature of their craft, would probably agree that any text can be mined for its historical content—but this is to make a very weak argument.

Raise the stakes, then: are *literary* texts, in particular certain genres, somehow more valuable as historical documentation? My perhaps not frightfully original but keenly felt contention in this essay, based on the texts of *Kim* and *Gora*, is that the capacious genre of novel, with its warren of crisscrossing subjectivities, is the obvious hideout for writers

[11] See Emmanuel Le Roy Ladurie, *The Mind and Method of the Historian*, trans. Sian Reynolds and Ben Reynolds (Brighton, 1981).

who wish to "betray their class," in both senses of this duck-rabbit phrase.[12] How else but through the passageways of the novel can members of the ruling classes—the tag applies fittingly to both Rudyard Kipling and Rabindranath Tagore—ever catch up with the vanquished ghosts that they are apparently bound by honor to suppress? Hamlet-like, the author of the colonial text must deliberate over a hapless choice of fathers—the dead—or the guilty, which may indicate why the description *children's fiction* has always applied a little uneasily to *Kim*, a novel about the tethered attachments of a *son* and not really about the innocent amusements of a boy. Because in life we are, on the whole, stuck with our parents, local histories, and the cocooning protocols of the quotidian, we remain unprepared for the difficult counterfactual question that *Kim, Gora,* and *The Trotternama* all pose: *How, if we could, would we negotiate a choice of fathers?* The schizophrenia of the two Kiplings, imperial apologist and fixated lover of India, has, of course, been discussed to distraction; I restrict myself now to a consideration of the ways in which consanguinity might intersect with the issue of subject position, that special preoccupation of the subalternist, in *Kim* and, next, in *Gora*.

I emphasized earlier that the subaltern historian construes the notion of the subject as a collectivity. Now I am going to suggest that in the scene we have just read in *Kim*, the boy from the "hot and crowded bazaars . . . [where mix] the press of all the races of Upper India" is the metonymic extension of this crowd. A subalternist perspective might home in on this single feature in the portrait of Kim. In the colonial transaction between "class" and "mass," that bourgeois *politesse* captured in the phrase *loss of face* is replaced by the awful alternative of faceless*ness* if a member of the ruling race, as it were, enters subhistory. Recall the scene:

For the most part, Kim literally lies underfoot, in imminent danger of being trampled on like a worm in the grass ("Flat on his belly lay Kim"), his gaze directed upward at the remote Englishman. Subject positioning? But there is more. In this passage we have an early demonstration of Kim's aptitude for surveillance, which later facilitates

---

[12] See Ludwig Wittgenstein's famous drawing of perceptual ambiguity in *Philosophical Investigations*, trans. G. E. M. Anscombe (Oxford: Basil Blackwell, 1958), 194.

his entry into the Ethnographic Survey, where he will become a proxy player in the "Great Game" of history by spying for the cause of empire.[13] In the present, though, Kim and Creighton, the unidentified Englishman who will turn out to be head of the survey and Kim's mentor, meet not face-to-face ("It was too dark to see his face") but in a typically faceless encounter, conducted through the clink of silver, ventriloquist voices ("He made no attempt to look for the speaker, and that showed Kim that he knew") and, most crucially, a "wad of folded paper." Homi Bhabha, analyzing Fanon's *Black Skins, White Masks*, writes:

> The primal moment [occurs] when the child encounters racial and cultural stereotypes in children's fiction. . . . Such dramas are enacted *every day* in colonial societies, says Fanon, employing a theatrical metaphor— the scene—which emphasizes the visible—the seen. I want to play on both these senses which refer at once to the site of fantasy and desire and to the sight of subjectification and power. In the act of disavowal and fixation the colonial subject is returned to the narcissism of the imaginary and its identification of an ideal ego that is white and whole. For what these primal scenes illustrate is that looking/hearing/reading as sites of subjectification in colonial discourse are evidence of the importance of the visual and auditory imaginary for the *histories* of societies. I suggest that in order to conceive of the colonial subject as the effect of power that is productive—disciplinary and "pleasurable"— one has to see the *surveillance* of colonial power as functioning in relation to the *scopic drive*.[14]

Oscar Wilde, Kipling's senior contemporary, might have appreciated the Lacanian-Foucauldian-Barthesian point that Bhabha makes, for Wilde himself, old roué, certainly recognized sexual voyeurism when he saw it. Of Kipling's work he said pithily, "One feels as if one were seated under a palm tree reading life by superb flashes of vulgarity. . . . [Kipling] has seen marvellous things through key-holes, and his backgrounds are real works of art."[15]

With Wilde and Bhabha in tow, the claim that the very first transaction between Kim and Creighton marks a "site of subjectification in

---

   [13] Kipling's interest in codes, ciphers, and secret societies is well documented. For a useful guide to this aspect of Kipling see Norman Page, *A Kipling Companion* (London: Macmillan, 1984).

   [14] Bhabha, *The Location of Culture* (London: Routledge, 1994), 76.

   [15] Wilde, *Intentions* (London, 1891).

colonial discourse" seems too obvious to defend. The scene not only coalesces all the elements of a primal meeting between a "native" son and his stereotypical object of desire—a father "white and whole"— but exposes the tacit "consent" so necessary to an eroticism of conceal- ment. While the ubiquitous "servant" of the colonial text pads around, demarcating the area of danger, Creighton and Kim begin to acknowl- edge each other's presence in secrecy; in this silent recognition consists the thrill of reciprocal surveillance, of two nations eyeing each other, Bhabha's titillatory "scopic drive." Furthermore, the iconography of gesture and voice seems wonderfully to magnify the seen (Creighton, the Englishman), while the agent who sees (Kim, the ambiguous Irish- Indian boy-man) turns into the very background to which Wilde refers so perspicaciously. For example, a neat perceptual payoff results when Kim, situated reflexively among the undifferentiated poor, uses a con- ventional pseudo-patronymic to first draw Creighton's attention to him- self. Against Kim's plural anonymity, the figure of Creighton, "Protector of the Poor," stands out boldly, singular and capitalized.

In this scene, as in others in the novel, Kim obviously symbolizes India's unidentifiable masses ("as unremarkable a figure as ever car- ried his own and a few score thousand other folk's fate slung round his neck"). Not only does he think in Hindustani, but even his English words and phrases tend to break through an invisible line of linguistic control (*Irish* becomes *Eye-rishti* and *Nicholson*, *Nikal Seyn*)[16] into phone- mic and semantic equivalents of the much-discussed variations of dress, or changes of skin, so to speak, that he puts on so adeptly. Kim is "Indian" because he constitutes what Partha Chatterji might call a "fragment" of the Indian crowd and merges into that collectivity, becoming background and witness, skin and all, in a way no "true" Englishman ever could. The delicious irony, we all know, is that Kim is Irish. In this respect the metonymic device of Kim as a crowd offers

---

[16] The Nikalsenis (Kipling spells it *Nikal Seyn*: "Ahi! Nikal Seyn is dead—he died before Delhi! Lances of the North, take vengeance for Nikal Seyn" [67], quavers the old soldier in *Kim* who, unusually, fought on the British side during the 1857 insur- rection) were a "religious sect" of the Punjab who formed a kin group (no, *not* a Kim group) based on their "relationship" with Captain John Nicholson—another fascinating instance of how the mythic pedigree of the white stallion transfers in colonial history. Fortuitously, the word *seni* or *sena*, deriving from the *-son* in *Nichol- son*, happens to mean "soldier" in Hindi.

"evidence of the imortance of the visual and auditory imaginary for the *histories* of societies"—colonized societies, different, like all crowds, yet all the same.

India alone by reason of her restraint has been able to survive. The postcolonial historiography that we have taken as a guide so far maintains that it endeavors to recover unwritten histories, the mostly unrecorded subjectivity of the masses. One way to do so, obviously, is to study the representational strategies in contemporary novels like *Kim* and *Gora* that consciously take on the burden of capturing an alien subject positioning. Indeed, the whole enterprise of literature itself could be viewed, from a postcolonial perspective, as a subhistory. Literature deals with categories of experience not directly accessible to historians or, for that matter, to any third party, yet important for some kinds of historical record. To use one of Kipling's favorite metaphors, literature could be described as history "in code," in that it invites, even demands, repeated displays of interpretative skill, of reading between the lines, precisely because of the underground nature of its categories. That, of course, is where the literary historians come in. They are experts at paperwork.

So far I've argued that in *Kim*, the "press of India," the unruly ruled, make contact with their rulers not directly but through a wad of paper. Control over paper crudely equals power over history or, to put it differently, power over the vast collectivities whose presence is mandatory in the Western narrative of colonial hegemony. For a respectable bunch of rulers needs not only territory but subjects, who in turn need external authority to organize them. Need, we must not forget, is a predicate of desire, of the subjectivity of dependence. But why is paper so important in the representation of subjective states? Familiarly, because it is the ambivalent tool of power in the hands of the makers of history (facts, proofs, "the visible effect of action") as well as of the makers of literature (feelings, suggestions, illusions).

Three important observations are to be made about "the pedigree of the white stallion" in *Kim*: it is *fake*; the "proof" is given, or fakery perpetrated, on paper; and the coded document that Kim brings to his "English father" Creighton explicitly uses the key words *white* and *pedigree*. Deciphering the code requires its interpreters—us—to make certain nonobvious connections between the "false" claims of literature and the actual violence of history. My own conjecture is that *Kim*'s claim to be a novel about India depends more on its absolute faith in paper to create an illusion of governance than on its lashings of local color—although color is not unimportant. I also hope, as I have indicated, to understand something of the disciplinary relations between literary history and postcolonial historiography through the management of documents in three literary texts.

The title of the second text, *Gora*, literally means "white, fair." It hardly needs emphasizing that Tagore intends to foreground the debate on "the pedigree of the white stallion." More than eighty years after it was written, *Gora*, the unlikely tale of an Irish baby orphaned during the 1857 uprising and brought up as an orthodox Bengali brahmin, in complete ignorance of his own pedigree, remains unquestionably *the* Indian novel of high bourgeois nationalist aspiration. Translated, unlike *Kim*, into most major Indian languages, *Gora* is like *Kim* in its contrariness. Nirad Chaudhuri once famously categorized *Kim* as "the finest story about India—in English"; today, U. R. Ananthamurthy describes *Gora* as "the best nationalist novel—by an ardent anti-nationalist."[17] These textual dissonances can be usefully interpreted by the literary historian.

Tagore consistently wrote and lectured against "the cult of nationalism," which he associated with fascism in Europe and with political exclusions in India. Like Kipling, Tagore is fascinated by the idea of the Indian collectivity, in his case "the nation"; understandably, however, he conceptualizes his subject differently. From the middle of the nineteenth century, the bilingual (Bengali, English) elite in Bengal made it "a cultural project to provide its mother tongue with the necessary linguistic equipment to become an adequate language for 'modern' culture . . . belonging to that inner domain of cultural identity,

[17] Ananthamurthy is president of the Sahitya Akademi (Indian Academy of Letters) and one of the country's best-known writers. He expressed this opinion in one of our conversations about *Gora*. Comparing *Kim* with *Gora* is almost a cottage industry among literary academics in India, although the activity is not often recorded in print. One of the few pieces that has been published appears in Ashis Nandy, "The Novels," chap. 2 of *The Illegitimacy of Nationalism* (Delhi: Oxford University Press, 1994), 34–50 ("Loss and Recovery of Self"). It is among the best essays I've read on the social psychology of these two texts.

from which the colonial intruder had to be kept out; language therefore became a zone over which the nation had first to declare its sover-
eignty and then had to transform in order to make it adequate for the
modern world."[18] There is little doubt that, in the Indian imaginary,
Gora still stands as the most substantial contribution to the language-
based print capital so crucial to the enterprise of modern nationalism.

In *Kim* money does *not* equal power, and democracy negatively
consists in the pushing of the little Hindu, Chota Lal, off Zam-
Zammah despite his father's being worth "perhaps half a million sterling." Instead, intellectual capital in *Kim* is invested, on my reading, in
paper. Likewise in *Gora*. Thus, Tagore argues with Kipling not face-to-
face but novel-to-novel. He responds systematically to each trope in
Kim—paper, pedigree, whiteness, and the Indian masses—so that they
serve the nationalist cause in *Gora*. And he fills in the two most obvious
blanks in *Kim*: the missing women and the absent weather.

In effect, Tagore replaces Kipling's query about individual identity, "Who is Kim? What is Kim?" with another gigantic refrain, "What is
India? Where is India?"[19] The entire four-hundred-odd pages of *Gora*
make up an answer, but the essence of Tagore's response occurs as
early as page 17:

> "And where is this India of yours?" pursued Binoy. "Where the point of
> this compass of mine turns by day and by night," exclaimed Gora, plac-
> ing his hand on his heart.
>
> "There,—not in your Marshman's *History of India*."
>
> "And is there any particular port to which your compass points?"
> continued Binoy.
>
> "Isn't there!" replied Gora with intense conviction. ". . . that Port of
> a great Destiny is always there. That is my India in its fullness—full of
> wealth, full of knowledge, full of righteousness. Do you mean to say
> such an India is nowhere? Is there nothing but this falsehood on every
> side! This Calcutta of yours, with its offices, its High Court, and its few
> bubbles of brick and mortar! Poof!"

[18] Partha Chatterji, *The Nation and Its Fragments: Colonial and Postcolonial Histories*
(Princeton, N.J.: Princeton University Press, 1993), 7.

[19] Did Kipling know that the Sanskrit homonym of *Kim* means "what"? The text
is an absolute net of interlinguistic puns, but, tantalizingly, one cannot always distinguish the coincidental from the intentional.

Clearly, Tagore is bidding for rights over history. Marshman's textbook is suspect, and so is the entire apparatus of the Empire—justice, education, administration. The British picture of India is not just ill conceived; it is false, illusory, worthless "bubbles of brick and mortar." In its stead Tagore projects another phantasm: an ideal India. But if adversarial positioning were all, the move would not be particularly rewarding for literary historians to follow through. What makes *Gora* an intriguing novel is the sophisticated textual strategy it uses both to reduce the potency of and to draw on the *Kim* stereotype.

Rather than reject the central anxieties in *Kim*, Tagore moves, pythonlike, to *ingest* that novel. He absorbs the motifs of *Kim* into a larger counternarrative that Kipling himself could never have conceived of and would not have countenanced. This is Rabindranath's po-faced joke—hah, got you, Rudyard! If Said tells us, in pursuit of his thesis of a conflictless *Kim*, that "Kipling was untroubled by the notion of an independent India" (176), then *Gora* is equally holistic in its vision of an India whose independent status comes from a mature *containment* of its antagonisms. In *Gora* the argument that self-control has been India's primary means of surviving repeated waves of conquest seems to be advanced in deadly earnest. The task before "Young India," then, is to "modernize," the age-old policy of restraint through the agency of educated bilinguals at ease with the belief systems of both the Gita and Thomas à Kempis, that is, to alter readerly perceptions of the power relations between colonizer and colonized by a subtle substitution of the oral street culture on display in *Kim*.[20] Historians of "modern India" would by and large agree, I think, that the distinctively nonorientalist coloring of *Gora* derives, despite its incongruous "white" hero, from its author's very conscious inclusivism and pluralism. Tagore's anti- (or supra-) nationalism consists precisely in a vehement denial of political boundaries, alterities. The greatly extended literary world of *Gora* is not just self-indulgent; it is meant to facilitate a reverse expansion of intellectual territory.

In contrast to Kipling, who in line with Macaulay dismisses Indian

---

[20] Kipling uses the phrase *Young India* in his review of Prafulla Chandra Roy's translation of the *Mahabharata*; it signifies the "modern," "Westernized" India of the cities (*Civil and Military Gazette*, August 1886, rpt. in *Kipling's India: Uncollected Sketches, 1884–88,* ed. Thomas Pinney [London: Macmillan, 1986], 175–78).

classical learning as "unprofitable, and to the Western mind at least, foolish" (review), Tagore is careful not to show hostility for the Western canon. *Gora*, in fact, bonds intertextually with a number of occidental master texts, ranging from *The Imitation of Christ* to Dryden's "Alexander's Feast." The hijacking (an anachronism, I know, but we are in postcolonial airspace, where anachronisms are never really out of turn) of *Kim* is in line with these other gestures. Tagore does a Professor Higgins on Kim, who emerges as an articulate defender of "nationalist" values, capable not only of a self-critique of India's "ancient" past but also of laying confident claim to "the best of the West."

Paper was never used for more subversive purposes. Not just any rival text would do, only "the finest story about India—in English." Quite simply, Tagore's portrayal of "India in its fullness" requires him to dine off the great Kipling. By invoking *Kim* as the literary ancestor of *Gora*, Tagore accepts the challenge, swallowing the guilt of the Empire along with its pride. His act has now imprinted itself on the community memory of the subcontinent as part of its textual/sexual politics—a backhanded compliment, an ironic reversal as well as a ritual caste insult: "Thy father was a pastry-cook, Thy mother stole the ghi."

He has a face like a bulldog and calls us babus "baboons." "There exist obsessive ideas, they are never personal; books talk among themselves, and any true detection should prove we are the guilty party."[21] Guilt, fathers and mothers, obsession, detection—Eco sets us back on the investigative track. I have suggested that texts authored under colonialist conditions were forced by the violent circumstances of their production to make an unnatural choice. Dead fathers or guilty ones, the victims or the murderers—whose side were their authors on? I have answered that novelists like Kipling and Tagore occasionally take advantage of their professional license to slip across "to the other side" of the race/class/gender/nation barrier. The frisson in *Kim* and *Gora* comes from literature's having done what history will not allow. In history, to choose one's father is an impossibility; individuals are always victims of contingencies. In literature, *au contraire*, fate can be man-

---

[21] Umberto Eco, *Reflections on "The Name of the Rose,"* trans. William Weaver (London: Minerva Paperback, 1994), 81.

aged. Tagore and Kipling offer their heroes generous latitude. At least three fathers are made available to each hero: the lama, Creighton, and the curator (a figure based on Kipling's own father) to Kim; Krishnadayal the foster parent, Paresh Babu, and his own biological father to Gora. These ersatz sons bond with their chosen fathers through the sacred *guru-chela* (master-student) relationship, a traditional intellectual attachment among males that is made much of in both books. The Tagore-Kipling war of tropes ("There are also guns. It is big news!") has to be understood in terms of choice of paternity. Tagore need not have picked Kipling's story to revamp; he might well have summoned up other ancestors. That he chose Kipling places him, piquantly, as *chela* to Kipling's great white *guru*.

Still, a fin de siècle downer prompts me to ask whether any of this matters. Why has the struggle between the two old troopers not been consigned to history by now? But the retort is plain. Postcolonies inherit institutional memory through entrenched bureaucratic structures; within our universities and our offices, a massive inertial equilibrium preserves almost intact the thought processes devised during the Raj. *Kim* and *Gora* remain stalwart texts in university syllabi; worse, English, a language of transnational power, persists as the writ of elite dominance in India, which in turn continues to be a poor, brown, "third-world" country. Thus, many issues *Gora* discusses—population, agricultural poverty, community divisions, casteism, Babu-dom, educational responsibility, national pride and the role of Western thought in a modern democracy—remain contentious in our political discourse. Even when Gayatri Spivak today debates whether a subaltern can speak, she seems to follow the trajectory Tagore traced for bilingual intellectuals: Address the white man by not addressing him; take *in* all Western learning if you want to take the West *on*.

But the main reason *Gora* possesses such iconic value for a post-independence generation is that it is a hopelessly optimistic work. It recognizes that there is a logical, as well as an emotional, problem with the notion of "India," as there is with any human collective. Whether it is sixteen thousand American professors of English, or "the middle classes," or four million street children, the delicate subjectivity of each member of any "type" must be made to yield to a totalizing group identity. Rewards have to be shared as well as competed over. Only some individuals are fully represented. A collective thus encourages emotional distancing, even *within* itself, and, when it has "problems," immense cynicism. A collective like India, huge, diverse, impoverished, is simply too hard to comprehend as a whole, so why would anyone be foolish enough to believe that its problems can be understood and resolved as a whole? Tagore's literary answer still works. There is no cause for pessimism, he insists in *Gora*, because the idea of India (carried in the heart, not described by Marshman's externalized *History*) has managed to survive even the intellectual repression of colonialism. Now, when the idea of a collective is so indestructible, the forces that would fissure it must be less potent than the integrative powers that keep it together.[22] In other words, India's multifarious problems can only be resolved in toto, although paradoxically her "unity" can only be described in fragments, through the ideational structures of fiction. And at this point literary history integrates with that other historiographical concern: the politics of the local.

Gora forces us to notice that it, unlike the mythic and ambulatory *Kim*, is modern realist. Except for its hero's ideologically motivated forays into the countryside to share "the joys and sorrows" of "potters, oil vendors, and other low-caste men," the novel is anchored in Calcutta. However, that hinterland of villages is critical for Tagore's co-optation of Kipling, for through it he remodels the Indian masses. In tactical terms, Tagore achieves an elegant victory in *Gora* by robbing *Kim*'s India ("It was . . . beautiful to watch the people, little clumps of red and blue and pink and white and saffron, turning aside to go to their villages") of the one thing vital to all orientalist accounts: color. The masses that Gora encounters in the villages are dull, worn out by poverty, crushed by the tyranny of caste. For *his* collectivity Tagore retains Kipling's essentialist division of Hindus, Muslims, and Englishmen (remember Zam-Zammah) but reduces them all to the status of *victims*, specifically those of successive colonizations, Aryan, Mogul, British.

---

[22] *Gora*, written in Bengali, assumes, unlike *Kim*, a cultural milieu where the dominant Sanskritic literary tradition has always had to contend with a plurality of histories and literatures in the regional languages. Hence it has long been accepted in India that richness, a multiplicity of texts, entails some loss of "authenticity" but never a total depletion of resources, because reproduction via orality and translation is more or less guaranteed.

If Kim is a metonym of the Indian crowd, Gora is its antonym. He has, for all his burning desire to merge with the crowd, nothing in common with it. Whereas Kim looks up at Creighton, Gora is often portrayed looking down from a "height," his own six-foot frame or the top deck of a Ganges steamer. The collective becomes a context for elite soul-searching and self-criticism:

> The more he saw of their lives the more . . . [he] saw that among these village people the social bondage was far greater than among the edu-cated community. . . . When in his educated community, Gora had writ-ten, argued and lectured, it was natural for him to paint in rosy colours . . . a fascinating picture of what was in reality a mere useless ruin. . . . Gora tried night and day, because of his intense love for his mother-land, to cover everything behind the screen of his own brilliant feel-ings . . . but when he got out among the villages . . . he found it no longer possible to look at the truth through any kind of veil. (367)

Kim escapes into his Indian crowd; it is a symbol of freedom. Gora must redeem his Indian crowd; it is a symbol of bondage and oppres-sion. Thus, the "white man's burden" is implicitly reclaimed in *Gora* through a critique of the fake nationalism that is satisfied with a pre-fabricated, romantic India "paint[ed] in rosy colours."

White, as much a color as any other, is in *Gora* stripped of the fetish value it has acquired via the *Kim* stereotype. It is Gora's superior Bengali upbringing and the education imparted to him by his step-mother, Anandamoyee, and his eventual guru, Paresh Babu, that truly mark his pedigree. Although the deus ex machina of "whiteness" frees Gora from the tyranny of brahminical caste observances toward the end of the novel, when he discovers his origins, the question of color is trivial, and trivialized. The Victorian pattern of orphanhood and adop-tion is much more significant, because it encodes Tagore's attitude toward the myth of origins or, to put it another way, toward the "loss and recovery of self under colonialism."[23] Both Sucharita, the heroine, and Gora are adopted orphans; Gora's best friend, Binoy, is an orphan. Since the adoptees are clearly the genuine article, we may conjecture that Tagore is directing readers to view them not as the free spirits of *Kim* but as test cases in the nature-nurture debate. Color does not mat-

[23] Ashis Nandy, *The Intimate Enemy: Loss and Recovery of Self under Colonialism* (Delhi: Oxford University Press, 1983).

ter, but culture and character do—in that order. The proof of pedigree follows not in the shape of paper fetishes strung around the neck
but from inscriptions upon—where else?—the heart.

There is never any question of Gora's return to the English fold.
All the Englishmen in *Gora* are pompous idiots. Only the least
admirable characters, such as Gora's rival in love and ideology, Haran,
are taken up with British ways. The true hero is, irony of ironies, the
Bengali Babu. Although the Babu in *Kim* belongs to the select group
who spy for Creighton, he is ridiculed as a "whale," a product of "the
monstrous hybridism of East and West." Said says that the Babu is
treated so badly in *Kim* because Kipling cannot make himself take Indians, even erudite ones, seriously. I suspect the titter is much more nervous, because the bilingual Babu, whose desire to be elected a fellow of
the Royal Society matches Creighton's but whose scholarly qualifications are probably better, constitutes the real threat to British power.
By comparison, the melodramatic plotting of the Five Kings is, literally,
child's play.

In the Babu, a creature forged on the anvil of empire, the tribal
aggression of empire is hammered into scribal energy. It is not for nothing that one of the most important buildings in Calcutta is called the
Writer's Building to this day. The business of governing the masses of
Bengal is still conducted from this citadel of Babu-dom, of paperwork,
or of what I think of as a savagely scribal culture, the hallmark of postcoloniality.[24] So it does not surprise me that *Kim*'s stock of animal insults
carries over directly into *Gora*, where, as in the quotation at the beginning of this section, the British officer calls the Babus "baboons" and is
promptly compared to a bulldog by them. The slight decentering of the
anthropomorphism of both novels through the figure of the Babu—
the type includes Gora, who sports "fists like the paws of a tiger" and
whose brahminical caste marks are described as "warpaint"—has exactly
the democratizing effect Kipling had said was typical of India. The

---

[24] One of the many ironies of postcolonialism is that it is a left-wing, Marxist
government, probably the most long-standing and least corrupt of all the state governments in India, that now operates out of the Writer's Building. Marx's own views
on the ills of "oriental" states, deriving directly from Mill, make these circumstances
of occupation even uncannier. The subalternist historiography I've relied on in this
essay also originated in Calcutta.

Babu, when properly reddened in tooth and claw, as in *Gora*, does get back on Zam-Zammah, after all.[25] *Gora* pieces together shards from *Kim* into a dream of independence in which the Babus assume responsibility for the masses, so that India realizes her true "Destiny."

History will not record it, Mik. That is an illusion. Finally: enter Kim as a postmodern. I called *Gora* an optimistic work; not so *The Trotternama*. Allan Sealy, himself one of "them," uses every trick in the book of the nineties—bricolage, parody, pastiche, oodles of serious historical research—on his quest for the lost tribe of "Anglo-Indians." *The Trotternama*, as its name implies, travels everywhere in its almost six hundred pages and is a must-read for anyone interested in contemporary Indian writing, but here I confine myself to the audacious claim it makes on *Kim*. *The Trotternama* places *Kim* within another subaltern collective, that of the truly marginalized Anglo-Indians.

In their contemptuous dismissal of this hybrid community, Tagore and Kipling are, for once, united ("Their eyes blued and their nails blackened with low-caste blood," snorts Kim, while the omniscient narrator breaks in hurriedly, "We need not follow the rest of the pedigree"). But Sealy is determined to rescue the Anglo-Indians, as Tagore rescued the "monstrous" Babus, from historical oblivion and textual abuse by following through on their pedigree. And what better guarantee of class than descent from Kipling's magnum opus?

Sealy fires his first shot with anastrophe. Kim becomes Mik, short for Michael: General Mik Trotter, independent mercenary. It's cruel enough to turn Kim into a soldier (recall the original text: "'*Gorah-log* [white folk]. No-ah! No-ah!' Kim shook his head violently. There was nothing in his nature to which drill and routine appealed. 'I will *not* be a soldier!'" [Kipling, 105]), and then to make his rival in war an *Irishman*. But worse outrages follow. Sealy dyes his Mik indigo, reminiscent of Krishna, the cowherd god, as well as of the infamous colonial plantations. Then, when the sun bleaches Mik during his travels, Sealy has him expose "the one part" that the sun does not reach to prove his

[25] Further support for my thesis concerning the fabling of the Babu through zoomorphic traits can be found in Bankimchandra Chattopadhyay's (1838–94) mordantly self-debunking prose. See, for example, the long passage translated from the *Bankim Rachanabali* by Partha Chatterji (69–70; see n. 18).

succession to his patrimony. Still later, Kipling's chaste hero, in the form of his Mik doppelgänger, fathers a son among the very low-caste sellers of ghee whom he despised so much, while the all-white Rose Llewellyn Begam, Mik's official wife, takes over the upbringing of the child as if it were her own ("She scooped up the bundle, muttering the old refrain with a new assurance: '*Proof! Proof! Proof!*'").

Accretion is the style of *The Trotternama*; detail by detail, indignities begin to press upon the nerves. No-ah! No-ah! you suddenly find yourself squealing; you can't do this to *Kim*, unspoiled text of my childhood. But by the time Sealy is done with Kipling, your faith in the simple proof of pedigree that *Kim* offers has been blown to bits. *The Trotternama* simply will not allow *Kim* its blissful innocence; it rips up the colonizer's history as if it were the paper it is written on, interleaving Mik's story with "other" historical records that reveal the Raj's shabby treatment of the Anglo-Indians. Like Kim, Sealy is skilled at surveillance; he, too, gazes up at an imagined father—Kipling—but his sight is the sight of a postcolonial. Hence, the eroticism of Sealy's text derives not from the maintenance of a secret pact but from the *publication* of the scandals inherent in it. On one of his many escapades from school, Mik and his *guru*, the lama, coolly indulge in a couple of unexplained arsons. Buildings burn down, but what does it matter? "History will not record it, Mik. That is an illusion." If a community is simply erased from history, can it matter whether its acts have been criminal or blameless?

Conversely, if another collective sings its own praises after emerging as colonial victors, what proof exists of its sincerity? Pushed off the official maps and ethnographies, the Anglo-Indians can turn for redress neither to the proud bourgeois nationalist tradition that *Gora* endorses nor to their ungrateful patrons, the British. In limbo, the despised collective can discover a sense of self only through a perverse fiction. Here *The Trotternama* ceases to be a huge intertextual spoof and becomes a record of the collective anguish that must interest subalternist historiographers. From *The Trotternama* a traveling conversation aboard a plane:

> "A strange monadic people," Peter Jonquil went on.
> "Nomadic?"
> "Monadic. They live in a kind of bubble—or many bubbles. They

speak a kind of English. . . . They fantasize about the past. They impro-
vise grand pedigrees. It's like a Raj novel gone wrong." (Sealy, 560)

We know which novel, and how badly it has gone wrong. There is a
curious combination of despairing love and immoderate textual
assault and battery in *The Trotternama*; it is almost a rape of *Kim*. I hesitate to find in this medley of emotions a facile psychology of the child
abused by his parents, the ambiguous loyalties of the illegitimate off-
spring of empire. Yet the conclusion is intuitively plausible, given the
savagery of Sealy's "humor." Because its textual structure so bitterly
mimics the invasiveness of the official mythmakers, who leave out so
much, especially of pain, *The Trotternama* succeeds better than many
fictions in rendering the blind spots, the lacunae in the colonial
annals, that subalternism has theorized for us.

☞ *The locket is missed.* When Mark Twain wrote that everyone talked
about the weather but no one did anything about it, he could not have
had Kipling in mind, for the author of *Kim* did do something about
it—simply by not talking about it. Consider the evidence. *Kim* is an
outdoor novel that prances all over Upper India for several years during the hero's adolescence, but is he ever drenched by the monsoons,
oppressed by the heat, frozen in the snowy Himalayan passes? No. Just
two fleeting references to rain occur in *Kim*; the "spokes" of the sun
turn steadily "broad and golden" throughout. Three hypotheses present themselves. First, the weather is absent in *Kim* for the same reason
that as Borges once conjectured, no reference is made to a camel in
the Koran: it is simply there, too much a part of the landscape to pick
out.[26] However, this explanation is unconvincing, given the minute
attention Kipling pays to the human and the natural environment. Second, the weather works as a species of pathetic fallacy, embodying the
purely benevolent view of a remembered India that Said credits
Kipling with. Again, I cannot agree, having already argued against
Said's sanctioning of an unconflicted equilibrium in *Kim*.

[26] Cf. also Wole Soyinka's comment on "negritude" in Afro-Caribbean literature;
while acknowledging that it might have been a necessary development, Soyinka
points out that tigers do not seem to feel a similar compulsion to advertise their
"tigritude" (cited in "African and Caribbean Literature," in *Guide to Modern World
Literature*, 3d ed., ed. Martin Seymour-Smith [London: Macmillan, 1985], 2).

And third? My inclination is to pull two rabbits, one big, one small, out of the colonial hat. The small rabbit first: brolly-talk, conversations around the weather, is a quintessentially English pastime. By eliminating the weather from *Kim*, Kipling makes it in one stroke a *non-English book*, a discourse about elsewhere. By invoking a specific nomenclature of Indian seasons, Tagore reclaims that initiative. In fact, reading *Gora*, with its repeated reminders of the rich literary culture around seasonality in Bengal, alerted me to the absence of weather in *Kim*. Had I been born to a different linguistic history, would I have been led to believe the lack existed?

Now the big rabbit. Everyone in *Kim* is frightfully energetic: Kim, the lama, the bazaar boys, E.23 the spy, the widow and her retinue. Even the fat, unfit Hurree Babu never rests for one moment; the interlinguistic pun on his name should alert us to the rush he's in. India itself is in a constant frenzy of activity; indeed, the narrative's picaresque structure largely depends on it. For example, when Kim speculates about his identity, he reflexively sees himself as "one insignificant person in all this roaring *whirl* of India" (italics mine). And if, as I have suggested, he is not just part of the manic energy but its metonymic embodiment, then what price the thesis that the Indian climate enervates its masses so that they loll about all day long, unable to bestir themselves at any cost?

It will not do to answer that the weather and climate are different entities, for the weather is only a day-to-day manifestation of a climatic range; it would not snow in the tropics, for example, nor would the mean tropical temperature drop below twenty degrees Celsius in the current geological age. That the characters in Kim, "lazy" Orientals for the most part, show no signs of lassitude whatsoever contradicts, in effect, a long ethnographic tradition in which climate offers a causal explanation for every oriental ill, from "despotism" to technological "backwardness" to sheer lack of willpower.

I suggest that *Kim* and *Gora*, in their different ways, mark a hiatus in the literature of colonization when the weather begins to lose its preeminence as the villain. The Indian masses—the "population problem," as we refer to it today—are taking their place as the preferred narrative complication, since the problematic of the crowd is intrinsically linked to the "new" politics of democracy and nationalism. History now attaches itself to this equally volatile agency. Although neither *Kim* nor *Gora* ever dwells on the possibility that the Indian crowd will turn into a mob or an insurgent threat, the dark of 1857 clouds the horizon of both novels. Kipling and Tagore deal with the metamorphosis of (destructive) weather into (dangerous) crowd a little differently, though, the former by erasing the potential embarrassment of the weather almost completely from his imperialist novel, the latter by exuberantly including the weather in almost every chapter as part of the emotional context of Indianness ("In the whole world our country is the only one which has six seasons").

When we surmise that population is supplanting weather in the imaginative history of the subcontinent, the balance is tipped in favor of the hypothesis by one crucial factor: the impact of India's early censuses. Our friends the bureaucratic Babus and the Indian masses meet over the census, which displays for the first time "the roaring whirl of India" tabulated and arranged. The conjunction signals the emergence of forms of institutional power we still live with. Climate may be passé as an explanation of "who we are," but the office of the Babu and his control over our huge population remain subjects of grave concern in historiography.

The first partial census of India was undertaken in 1881, but the widespread dissatisfaction with it led to a new, much fuller census twenty years later (and decennial censuses ever since). The date? 1901. Can it be mere coincidence that *Kim* was published in the same year? According to *The Trotternama:*

> It is not everyday that the poet-and-chronicler . . . is called upon to answer for coincidence. Weighty matters, yes: tragedy, moral uplift, character—these are our daily cup. . . . But *coincidence*—what is it to the great mind? . . . History books! We shall know what to do with them. Now a *chronicle*—there's something. . . . And if a soupcon of coincidence (so called) enliven the brew, what of it? Is it not plain FATE that these asses are now exercised over? Why not call it by its proper name? (Sealy, 261)

Coincidence, then, is the misnomer with which historians humble a once-grand literary device, fate. Kim carries the "fate" of "a few score thousand" about, albatross-fashion; Gora talks of India's "Destiny," no less. But their texts are robbed of rhetorical *gravitas* by mealymouthed histories. The poet-chroniclers (literary historians?), whose trade requires them to call things by their "proper names," must come to the rescue by pointing out historical absences, which, by erasing connections, contrive to make fate look like mere coincidence.

In the 1901 census of India there are separate columns for men and women. "It appears to me," Binoy explains to Gora, "that in our love for our country there is one great imperfection. We only think of half of India. . . . We look on India as a country of men. . . . for you the idea of our country is womanless, and such an idea can never be a true one" (Tagore, *Gora*, 83). Binoy hopes to persuade his conservative friend (Kim in Indian nationalist garb) to enroll women in his struggle to free the "Motherland," and by the end of the novel Binoy has made his case. So has Tagore, who unabashedly helps advance Binoy's cause by making three of the novel's most revolutionary thinkers women: Anandamoyee (Gora's stepmother), Sucharita (the heroine), and Lolita (Sucharita's friend and Binoy's eventual wife). The "half of India" that *Kim* left out is repopulated in *Gora* by a phalanx of articulate women.

In this literary context, the census can be seen as a prelude to universal suffrage in India. By making women numerically visible, it foreshadows their role in the processes of democracy. Yet the potential power conferred on women has to be converted from the faceless statistics of the census to the "print capital" of personal subjectivity. Tagore, sensitized to the historical absence of women, sets himself the "nationalist" task of filling it, for as his narrator remarks, "a deed or document is not finished with when it has merely been written." Precisely.

A stereotype like the one Kipling brought into being in *Kim* has a certain horrible vitality. Unlike jokes and coincidences, the stereotype is an inveterate boundary crosser; it returns, succubuslike, at times of crisis or shifts of perspective, in literary history. In this respect, it functions as one of the few means by which we bind together the fragile, necessarily fragmented consciousness of nations and other large collectives. Within the parameters of this century, we have witnessed *Kim*'s reappearance not only in the two novels I've discussed but also in M. M. Kaye's widely televised bestseller, *The Far Pavilions*—a noticeable absence in my own essay that students of popular culture might indict. Curiouser and curiouser, Timeri Murari, another popular novelist, has recently managed to publish not one but two sequels to *Kim*.[27] Historiographers of postcoloniality, therefore, could find literary stereotypes in general, and the *Kim* stereotype in particular, useful as seismographic devices to detect tremors in subterranean patterns of subjectivity. Where will *Kim* appear next? Fanciful though it may seem, I would like to suggest in the dying minutes of this article that the stereotype actually underlies the terms under which I have written it.

Stock markets the world over would tell us at once that the "wad of folded paper" through which Indian academics communicate with their American counterparts still carries a subtext of white pedigree. Nor is there any doubt of the systems of "tacit consent" underlying these transactions. Think of the scenario closest at hand. Ceteris paribus, for an American to publish in an Indian journal is a momentary curiosity; for an Indian to publish in an American journal is a minor triumph. Quality is not the issue; the politics of exposure is where we're at: visibility, the clink of silver, and the thrill of being at the "scene of the seen"— Creighton's lawn, America, Europe, certainly not India.

Taking my cue from subalternist historiography, I have suggested that the trope of the crowd has superseded that of the weather in key subcontinental texts, and that the process offers us an insight into how postcoloniality is often represented today through a construct called "the population." There is also some inductive evidence that India configures as a mass, or even a mess, in the minds of most Americans. When I write in India, for Indians, my response to this observation is simply a shoulder-shrugging "So what?" The situation changes when I "speak as" a postcolonial internationally. Then I become a metonym, like Kim, the extension of a populace, not just a representa*tive* but a representa*tion*, a stereotype.

Entering the metanarrative of postcoloniality in this fashion is disconcerting.[28] Having problems is one thing, being a problem quite

[27] I am grateful to Sujit Mukherjee for having alerted me to Murari's double sequel to *Kim*.

[28] Because the *Kim* of this essay has been located entirely in relation to *Gora* and *The Trotternama*, it seems to have lost much else in the metanarrative of postcoloniality: nostalgia and immigrant consciousness in Britain, the exoticization of the Orient in America, its commodification and neo-fascist repression in Europe. This fracturing, we know, is inevitable; it belongs *within* the story. Cf. Said's "two his-

another. The first is an epistemic state, the second an ontological category. Representationally, I am now the population problem for my readers; *that* is what metonymic status as a postcolonial implies. It means stepping out of one's head and into someone else's already defined mental space. It means leaving the collective in order to be perceived as part of the collective—a disjunction.[29]

Thus stripped of context, of subjectivity, what can a stereotype convey? My essay has developed cracks, grown misshapen, become overly long, quote-studded, a Frankenstein's monster, under the strain of answering this question. It has meant bodily dragging *Gora* and *The Trotternama* into an arena where I was convinced they had no place yet ought to belong. That I could not assume a context of easy knowledge, of deictic reference ("☞ The locket is missed"), even of moral agreement, throughout this essay alarmed me. It was a sharp reminder that postcoloniality is the self-effacing state of mind that makes Kims of us all. In India, the justification for writing literary history, if any is needed, is that it works as an antidote, produced in kind, to that selectively amnesiac culture of postcolonial bureaucracy. Scribal note taking, after all, is not to be confused with taking note. Our multilingual literary histories offer us some of the most durable safeguards against the terrors of self-doubt and communicative breakdown that accompany the acceptance of stereotyped self-images. They do so by reminding us of some incredible continuities. Kim begat Gora begat Mik begat . . .

---

toriographies, one linear and subsuming, the other contrapuntal and often nomadic" (xxix). In the second format, the postcolonial, the locket, is, as always, missed.

[29] I've used the word *collective* interchangeably for large groups, populations, and crowds in this essay; it has seemed a particularly appropriate word to me in the colonial and postcolonial contexts because, of all the officials of the Raj, the Collector (the term nicely elides the fact that what he was collecting was rent, or tax) was possibly the most important link between the bureaucracy and the masses of India. "To the people of India the Collector is the Imperial Government," says a contemporary "sketch" by G. R. Alberigh-Mackay (Sir Alibaba K.C.B.) entitled "Twenty-one Days in India, 1897," rpt. in *British Life in India*, ed. R. V. Vernede (Delhi: Oxford University Press, 1994).

THE VICTIMS OF
NEW HISTORICISM

Walter Benn Michaels

The title of this essay is prompted by a series of recent attacks on the New Historicism, most of which take the form either of suggesting, as does Carolyn Porter, that New Historicists "ask themselves whether and when [their] kind of analysis becomes complicit in the cultural operations of power it ostensibly wants to analyze" or of more bluntly asserting, as does Donald Pease, that New Historicism is a sort of "linguistic colonialism" that fails to recognize its "affiliation with actual colonialist practices."[1] In these (and in many other) accounts, whatever methodological problems the New Historicism may have are subsumed by its politics. It is described not simply as a mistaken account of the past but as a political practice that contributes to various forms of injustice. Hence the assumption of my title—that, as a political practice, the New Historicism may have victims, and hence also the question I want to begin by raising—who are the victims of the New Historicism?

Both Porter and Pease are primarily concerned with Stephen Greenblatt's essay "Invisible Bullets," and it might be argued in the context of the present essay that his victims, at least, are the Algonkian Indians whose "potential cultural agency" and ability to "speak for themselves" are, according to Porter, "eradicated" by Greenblatt's discussion of them (773). And if there is something a little odd about

---

[1] Porter, "Are We Being Historical Yet?" *South Atlantic Quarterly* 87 (1988): 781; and Pease, "Toward a Sociology of Literary Knowledge," in *Consequences of Theory*, ed. Jonathan Arac and Barbara Johnson (Baltimore, Md.: Johns Hopkins University Press, 1991), 119, 145.

thinking of the Algonkians as Greenblatt's victims—Isn't he too late? How, with the best will in the world, can he silence people who have been dead for over four hundred years?—this oddness cannot be described as entirely inappropriate to Greenblatt's own conception of his historical practice. "I began," he says in the first sentence of *Shakespearean Negotiations,* "with the desire to speak to the dead."[2] Once you think of yourself as trying to hear the dead speak, surely you license others to think of you as trying to shut the dead up. So even if it seems implausible to think that the New Historicism's victims could be people whose victimization had more or less definitively taken place long before the New Historicism was invented, it may not be so implausible to think that at least some versions of the New Historicism (and of historicism more generally) are nevertheless committed to a concept of the historian's relation to the past that, in its assertion of the essential continuity of past and present, makes such accusations imaginable.

Porter's main point, however, is not to protect the Algonkians from Greenblatt; the real victim of New Historicism, as she sees it, is history itself. Her answer to the question asked by her title, "Are We Being Historical Yet?" is no; the New Historicism's "effacement" not only of "marginal groups and subordinated cultures" but of "the 'social' itself" constitutes a kind of "colonialist formalism" in which the "social discourses" supposedly used to "historicize" literary texts are instead transformed into more literature (780, 779, 752). From this standpoint, the New Historicism is not only insufficiently committed to making literature historical but also inappropriately committed to making history "literary." In response "to the question of how you relate text to reality," she argues, you can't just say that "reality *is* a text, and then proceed to read it, like a New Critic, for its paradoxes, tensions, and ambiguities" (780). Porter understands the New Historicism to be textualizing history in just the way that a certain vulgar deconstruction textualizes the real.

But if you can't just say that reality is a text, you *can* just say that texts are real—what else could they be? And if you can't make history literary, you can't help but make literature historical. What's wrong

---

[2] Greenblatt, *Shakespearean Negotiations: The Circulation of Social Energy in Renaissance England* (Berkeley: University of California Press, 1988), 1.

with New Historicism, in other words, is also what's wrong with Porter's critique of it: the project of historicizing literature requires us to imagine a literature in need of historicizing. We can be urged to connect literature with history only if we can be convinced that literature has been disconnected from history, as if the publication of poems, say, were somehow less historical than the promulgation of statutes. But, of course, the act of writing a poem and the act of writing a statute both take place in history, and any attempt to understand either act is an attempt to understand a historical event. Thus the familiar imperative "Always historicize" is one that we can't help obeying. Every reading of a literary text is an interpretation of a historical act or acts, and every reading is an account of the effects of that act or those acts, even if the effects in question consist of nothing more than the critic's response to the text. The idea that by talking about a text's participation in other social phenomena—say, imperialism or the critique of imperialism— we make the text more historical depends on the idea that other things a text might do—say, foreground the materiality of the signifier or call into question the possibility of determinate readings—are somehow less historical. But foregrounding the materiality of the signifier is as historical as critiquing imperialism. When we disagree about which of these two things any given text does, we are disagreeing not about whether to historicize it but about how to historicize it. Indeed, it could easily be shown that every critical or theoretical argument about whether a reading is historical is in fact an argument about whether its history is the right one. There are no more or less historical readings; there are only differently historical readings.

If this is true, then certain familiar problems about the relation of literature to history (above all, the very idea that there can be a problem about the relation of literature to history) disappear. We need not worry, for example, about whether historical approaches inevitably fail to appreciate what is distinctively literary about literary texts. Since the distinctive literariness of literary texts must itself be understood as a historical fact, any attempt to characterize it will inevitably take the form of historical explanation.[3] Poems, in other words, may be differ-

---

[3] This is not to say that it is impossible for a historical reading to fail to appreciate the distinctively literary character of a text, but only that such a failure could not be understood as a consequence of the historical character of the reading.

ent from statutes, but they are not less historical than statutes, so questions about the distinctive nature of literature, like questions about the distinctive nature of statutes, will be historical questions producing historical answers. By the same token, we need not worry about whether our accounts of the nonliterary turn historical reality into just another literary text. Nothing is more historically real than literary texts. So the problem of how to bridge the gap between the text and reality, between literature and history, disappears. The problem of how to bridge the gap between literature and history can exist only if there *is* a gap between literature and history. Since there isn't, there is no problem.

But my point is not really to defend historicism by making certain problems disappear. For one thing, it is perfectly obvious that if there are real problems in talking about the relations between poems and statutes (or poems and other poems, statutes and other statutes), those problems are not solved by the reminder that both poems and statutes are historical. For another thing, historicism, if I am right, doesn't need defending. My point instead is to raise the question of why it nevertheless is not only defended but promoted. What are we being told when we are told to historicize? Why are we being urged to do something that we can't help doing?

We can get at least one answer to this question by remembering the debate that may be said to have dominated self-proclaimedly historicist criticism in the 1980s, the debate over literature's relation to what can most generally be called the "culture" in which it is produced. Does American literature, say, resist or oppose American culture? Is literature complicitous with it? Does it both resist and comply? It is tempting to think that what's wrong with these formulations is the generality of "literature"—surely different literary texts may do different things. But the real problem is with the generality of "culture." If we think of a culture as the totality of beliefs and practices among a given group of people at a given time, then it is obvious that neither resistance to it nor complicity with it is imaginable. The demand of turn-of-the-century American feminists, for example, that women be allowed to sell their labor resisted patriarchy in the name of possessive individualism. But since both patriarchy and possessive individualism were elements of late nineteenth-century American culture (if they hadn't been, there would have been no possibility of or point to resistance), what sense does it make to think of this demand as resisting American culture? The point is not that resistance or complicity as such are impossible but that what one resists (or is complicitous with) is never one's culture.

Seen in this light, the debate over resistance and complicity is just a rerun of the old debate over the possibility of truly radical political change, a rerun made possible by the historicist appropriation of an essentially deconstructive model of political difference. Difference in deconstruction is crucially subversive, which is to say— translated to the level of culture—that differences within a culture must be understood as the difference of the culture from itself. This claim generates the two forms of pathos circulating in historical arguments about resistance. From the standpoint of those who sympathize with the resistance, the pathos is that it can never quite succeed: since resistance to the culture is resistance of the culture to itself, the resistance will always be the thing it resists. From the standpoint of those (if any) who sympathize with the oppressors, the pathos is that resistance can never quite fail: the culture can never eliminate the resistance to it, because the resistance to it is part of it.

On this model, political problems are understood as problems in locating a ground from which to produce a critique of one's own society.[4] Thus, for Brook Thomas, the value of literary history is that, in a world where "it has become increasingly difficult to imagine alternatives to our present situation," "historical hindsight" can show us that "different actions and ways of constructing the world could have set it on a different path," "thus provoking us to grope for alternative ways of world-making."[5] The idea is that knowing that things

[4] Hence the characteristic commitment to self-consciousness; Porter, for example, calls for "a politically self-aware critical practice" (744), as opposed to one that is simply politically aware. The pathos now is personal: the historian's *own* resistance and complicity become the privileged objects of attention.

[5] Thomas, *The New Historicism and Other Old-Fashioned Topics* (Princeton, N.J.: Princeton University Press, 1991), 172, 211. Thomas too is committed to the primacy of self-consciousness; he thinks that reading "texts from the past" can "give us a sense of the otherness of our own point of view" (211). But while it's easy to see how reading texts from the past might change our point of view or confirm it or make us more or less confident of it, it's hard to see how reading texts from the past

might have turned out differently in the past can give us reason to hope that they might turn out differently in the future. And this apparently innocuous observation, when linked to the debate over resistance and complicity, is given a certain political bite. For the complicity historian's claim that there couldn't be resistance is now translated into the politically conservative claim that there can't be resistance, and the resistance historian's claim that there could be resistance is translated into the progressive political claim that there can be resistance. In other words, the exhortation to historicize, translated into the exhortation to recognize that things could have been different in the past, emerges as the conviction that things can be different in the future and thus as the proclamation of a progressive politics.

This scenario makes sense of what has otherwise seemed a rather baffling aspect of contemporary intellectual life, the tendency to conflate people's views of what happened in the past with their desires about what will happen in the future. But it does so only by transforming the pathos of history into the bathos of politics. For the problem with the debate over complicity and resistance is, as we have already seen, that it idealizes resistance, requiring it to be resistance not to some particular aspect of the culture but to the culture itself. And only this idealization can justify the claim that our current political predicament consists in our inability to imagine "alternatives." For only if the alternatives must be understood not as alternatives available within our culture (even if only as reports of what other cultures do) but as alternatives to our culture (practices we can't even conceive) does imagining them become a problem. And when it does become a problem, it becomes an insoluble one. For, in fact, it's *easy* (not difficult) to imag-

---

(or anything else) can make our own point of view come to seem to us other while allowing it to remain "our own." What Thomas wants is a change not in what we know but in the ground of our knowing. In other words, his frequently proclaimed "antifoundationalism" consists not in an indifference to foundations but in a commitment to having the right attitude toward them. The antifoundationalist reminder that our point of view is, after all, only our point of view must be supplemented with the exhortation to think of it as other. And literature, Thomas thinks, is particularly useful in this regard, since it is, "by accepted convention," antifoundational (172). What it might mean for anything to be "by accepted convention" antifoundational is beyond the scope of this essay, but it seems worth noting that the stipulation that literature is commits literary history to the absolutely foundationalist values of self-consciousness right from the start.

ine "alternatives to our present situation," and it's *impossible* (not difficult) to imagine truly "alternative ways of world-making."

The political point of the debate over complicity and resistance is
thus to make wishful thinking a progressive—indeed, the only truly
progressive—political position. Since no possible commitment on any
available issue—abortion, defense, affirmative action, whatever—can
count as resisting one's culture, the mark of a truly progressive politics
becomes the insistence that things might have been (and so might still
become) otherwise.[6] But if, from this standpoint, the exhortation to
historicize is a way of asserting that things could be different, it is,
more frequently and more powerfully, a way of asserting that some
things have stayed the same, which is most obvious in the current
vogue for thinking of historical inquiry as a form of memory. When
William J. Bennett claims that "memory is the glue that holds our
political community together" and describes "history" as "organized
memory," or when Annette Kolodny urges the contributors to the
Columbia and Cambridge histories of American literature to "compose a literary history that recovers the integrity of memory," what's
being asserted is the primacy of identity, not difference.[7] For insofar as
historians are understood to "remember" the past they study, that past
is transformed into *their* past. History becomes a way of asserting the
radical continuity between past and present, radical not because past
events are thought to have caused present events but because the per-

---

[6] And what appear to be more moderate forms of this argument—the reduction of the irresistible culture to the at least comparatively resistible dominant culture, for example—empty it of its point altogether. For the effect of making the
resisted culture merely dominant is to make it possible to resist, and the reason that
the resister can resist it is that he or she is no longer understood as belonging to it.
If, in other words, you think of your culture as the totality of the beliefs and practices
of your society, then what you resist cannot be your culture. And if, instead, you
think of your culture only as your *own* beliefs and practices, then you still can't resist
it, since what you will be resisting is someone else's culture. No one, so far as I know,
has ever denied that people can resist (whether successfully or not is another question) *other* cultures.

[7] Bennett, *Our Children and Our Country: Improving America's Schools and Affirming
the Common Culture* (New York: Simon and Schuster, 1988), 165; and Kolodny, "The
Integrity of Memory: Creating a New Literary History of the United States," *American
Literature* 57 (1985): 300.

son who participated in those past events is thought to be in some way the same as the person who records them.

This is what it means for the past to be remembered instead of learned, and, when it isn't learned, for it to be forgotten. "History is a source of personal identity," Bennett says, and this sense that we study history in order to learn who we are is as powerful among those, like Kolodny, who explicitly oppose Bennett's version of that history as it is among those who support it. Indeed it is only because people on both sides think that this is a debate about their own identities that there is a debate. It is, for example, because we think people should learn about themselves that we think the racial makeup of the students in our schools should be reflected in the racial makeup of the authors whose books we assign to them. And even if we vary the argument and insist that our students should learn also (or instead) about the history of others, we remain committed to a model of historical inquiry that identifies some parts of the past as elements of our own identity and other parts as elements of someone else's identity. But since almost none of the things done in the past were in fact done by us, why do any parts of it have either more or less to do with *our* identity? When we learn things that we never knew, why should we think of ourselves as remembering them? Who is the historical subject who, when he learns about some things that didn't happen to him, thinks he is studying his own past and, when he learns about other things that also didn't happen to him, thinks he is studying someone else's past?

The most common answer to this question today is the racial subject, and there can be little doubt that contemporary historicism plays a real if limited role in the ongoing racialization of American life. This is obvious in those cases where race as a biological entity is asserted as a link between the living (present) and the dead (past). But it is even more powerfully true when history itself is called upon to supply the racial link, when people are imagined to belong to the same race not because of their genes but because they are part of a common history. That history cannot, in fact, perform this function, Kwame Anthony Appiah pointed out several years ago: the common history that is supposed to produce a nonbiological race cannot count as common unless the biological racial entity is already in place.[8] And the increasingly frequent repudiation of racial history in favor of cultural history doesn't change things. Insofar as people's culture consists in whatever they learn to believe and do, there can be no way to specify in advance which culture they should be understood to belong to, so there can be no way of deciding whether the culture whose history they study is properly theirs. When Bennett asks why we should study Western civilization and answers, "First . . . because it is ours" (194), he is begging the question, not answering it.[9] If we are studying something we don't know, it cannot yet be ours, and, whosoever it once was, once we *have* studied it, it will become ours. If all Americans read only Chinese literature, an intimate knowledge of Chinese literature would instantly be a fundamental aspect of American culture. Culture can no more be used to take the place of race than history could be used to support the idea of race.[10]

If, then, the question with which I began—who are the victims of New Historicism—was asked in a somewhat skeptical spirit (skeptical because the objects of historical study have generally, insofar as they are victims, been victimized long before the historians get to them), the identitarianism of much current historicist thinking—the conviction that in studying the past we are studying ourselves—turns out to make my initial skepticism somewhat inappropriate. This is not because we *can* somehow revictimize long-dead Algonkians but because the idea that we can—the idea, in other words, that the past we study is ours—requires technologies of identity that do play a role in contemporary politics and that may indeed produce real victims. From this standpoint, the current debate over which past is ours serves above all to legitimate the idea that *some* past is ours, and, since the primary technologies deployed to connect us with our pasts are racial or (what amounts to the same thing) cultural, the current commitment to

---

[8] Appiah, "The Uncompleted Argument: Du Bois and the Illusion of Race," *Critical Inquiry* 12 (1985): 21–37.

[9] Bennett's second answer, however, "Because it is good," is theoretically (although perhaps not factually) impeccable.

[10] For extended discussion of this point, see Walter Benn Michaels, "Race into Culture: A Critical Genealogy of Cultural Identity," *Critical Inquiry* 18 (1992): 655–85.

historicism should, as I suggested above, be understood as a modest contribution to keeping racial identity a central fact about American life. Whether the maintenance of racial identity is a good or a bad thing is beyond the scope of this essay; my point here is only that if it is a bad thing, its victims will in some degree be the victims of historicism.

Literature as History

PREFACE TO A
LYRIC HISTORY

Susan Stewart

To imagine the relation between poetry and history is to bring
forth immediately the problem of genre as fixed form and the
problem of history as a discourse of reference. *Genre* is a problematic
term because it implies fixed categories of the literary that, if they do
not transcend, at least endure temporal change. It is quite easy to call
into question all of the essentialism, or nominalism, or idealism that
such a stance implies about cultural forms.[1] And *history*, as we commonly use the term to refer to a narrative of event or events, raises
questions of rhetorical convention and, ultimately, ideology as condi-

---

[1] See, for example, *Encyclopedia of Poetry and Poetics,* ed. Alex Preminger (Princeton, N.J.: Princeton University Press, 1965), s.v. "lyric," 460–70. The authors begin
by saying that lyric is not narrative or dramatic; then they speak of the "musical"
quality of lyric, qualifying it as a criterion and adding brevity, expression, and other
defining features. "Most of the confusion in the modern (i.e., 1550 to the present)
critical use of the term 'l[yric],' is due to an overextension of the phrase to cover a
body of poetic writing that has drastically altered its nature in the centuries of its
development" (460). One argument for the usefulness of generic categories and
against the frequent materialist assumption that the only alternative to local modes
of explanation is a transcendent model can be found in Norman Bryson, *Looking at
the Overlooked: Four Essays on Still Life Painting* (Cambridge, Mass.: Harvard University
Press, 1990), 12: "I strongly sympathise with this materialist objection [to a higher
Platonic realm]. . . . But the objection brings with it an exceedingly drastic consequence, if the only way forward would seem to be to abandon and disown the concept of generic series even though such series exist objectively and historically.
Whenever a series is *dis*continuous, and jumps from one specific cultural milieu to
another, it would seem that materialist analysis must close its eyes, or issue an auto-
matic accusation of idealism to anyone who thinks it is still a series. But it may be that
the analysis is not being materialist *enough*."

tioning the possibility of historical perceptions from the outset.[2] My
goal here is to think dialectically regarding the relations between lyric
and history by paying attention to lyric as a structure of thought medi-
ating the particular and the general; that is, terms of generality and
specificity that appear in the tensions between genre and history are
the very ones that the art form takes as its task to determine. It may be
that the mediation of the particular and the general characterizes the
production and apprehension of any art form and, indeed, that the
aesthetic and the historical have shared the task of determination
since the emergence of "the aesthetic" in the eighteenth century. To
this extent, as Rodolphe Gasché has suggested, aesthetic experience
poses the maximal conditions enabling concrete individuality to
escape reification by moving between the poles of totality and particularity. Yet lyric specifically both produces and reflects upon conditions
of subjectivity.[3] Lyric process itself (as a tradition of both accumulated

[2] We are reminded here of Althusser's distinction between ideology in general,
which has no history, and particular ideologies, which are subject to history, and of
his claim that the concept of history is itself not historical ("Ideology and Ideological
State Apparatuses," in *Lenin and Philosophy*, trans. Ben Brewster [New York: Monthly
Review Press, 1971]). Althusser's attempt to find a metahistorical term under which
historical critique might proceed constantly appears as a gesture of transcendence
under which all limits to transcendence are articulated.

[3] Gasché, "Of Aesthetic and Historical Determination," in *Post-Structuralism and
the Question of History*, ed. Derek Attridge, Geoff Bennington, and Robert Young
(London: Cambridge University Press, 1987), 139–61. In his study of the implications of Baumgarten's *Reflections on Poetry* for the philosophy of determination,
Gasché shows the mutuality of history and art and points out that "poetry, as the discourse in which concrete individuality is brought about by total determination, [is]
the very goal of the historiographic ideal" and that "the converse is [also] true, and
history as the discourse of all inclusive determinateness becomes the telos of poetry."
He concludes that determination (*Bestimmung*) links the poetic and historical as
both different and complicitous "modes of totalisation through limitation." The
"transcendental" structure governing determination as destination and limitation is
posed by Gasché as the precondition of any poststructural "discovery" of history
(159–60). A suggestive analogue to Baumgarten can be found in W. K. Wimsatt's
statement "The Concrete Universal," in *The Verbal Icon* (Lexington: University Press
of Kentucky, 1954), 69–100, especially in Wimsatt's discussion of metaphor and
character as realizations of such a "concrete universal." Steven Knapp, *Literary Interest: The Limits of Anti-Formulism* (Cambridge, Mass.: Harvard University Press, 1993),
49–87, discusses the concrete universal. His argument that "affective experience, if
it is communicable at all in the way presupposed by the cognitivist account, must

and lost practices) has been and can continue to be distinguished from the spatial arts of sculpture and architecture, from painting, from music, from narrative and dramatic literature by means of its particular relations to subjectivity, language, and temporality.

Even privileging the aesthetic as the encompassing term here, we can say that this topic "has" a history. That is, it is possible to find accounts of these problems regarding poetry and history, the universal and the particular, as stemming from quite opposed philosophical traditions. In what might be placed as the first of these traditions, Aristotle in a famous passage in chapter 9 of the *Poetics* contends that "the poet's function is to describe, not the thing that has happened, but a kind of thing that might happen. . . . [The distinction] consists really in this, that the one describes the thing that has been, and the other a kind of thing that might be. Hence poetry [narrative and lyric verse] is something more philosophic and of graver import than history, since its statements are of the nature rather of universals, whereas those of history are singulars."[4] In this emphasis upon events that, once reflected upon, turn out to be generalizable, we find the continuing bias of a Platonic idealism wherein poetry acquires status over history because it is universal, but ultimately loses status to philosophy because it is hypothetical and fictional.

Throughout this tradition of thought—extending, somewhat ironically, from Aristotle to Augustine's division between perception and conception to seventeenth-century empiricism and its consequences— a split between subject and object, between "inner" and "external" phenomena, is maintained regardless of the varying values placed upon either term. Perhaps its most delicate balance is effected in the mixture of Neoplatonism and Aristotelianism of Sidney's *Defence*,

---

have a built-in generality that already complicates any stark opposition between private emotion and public knowledge" (83–84) provides a helpful supplement to the positions of Baumgarten and Wimsatt.

[4] Aristotle, *De poetica*, trans. Ingram Bywater, in *The Basic Works of Aristotle*, ed. Richard McKeon (New York: Random House, 1941), 1464. Aristotle then says that narrative poetry requires its maker to be "more of the poet" than "verses" do, for narrative works necessitate the imitation of actions: "And if he should come to take a subject from actual history, he is none the less a poet for that; since some historical occurrences may very well be in the probable and possible order of things" (1464).

where poetry is poised as the middle term between the overparticular-
ity of history and the overgenerality of philosophy.[5] Even in Hegel's
dialectic, aspects of Platonism appear in the rendering of art as the
ideal in sensual particulars. For Hegel, art is, therefore, a more primitive form on the path to *Geist* than the forms of religious and philosophical thought, respectively. Because of poetry's stronger tie to the
sensuous materiality of language, it is still an adequation, rather than
an expression, of the ideal.[6]

But there is another, nonmimetic tradition of thought, also promoted by Hegel, that imagines the subject-object dichotomy as a false
problem, claiming that expression is prior to subjectivity, that ideology
is a consequence of form, and that thought is productive of culture,
including its concepts of nature, rather than a mere reflection upon it.
This tradition is perhaps most vividly articulated by Giambattista Vico,
but it can be linked to a more general view of historiography if we see
it as a facet of the break with medieval thought enabling the establish-
ment of modernity. In broad terms, as classical aesthetics emphasizes
imitation, morality, and the analysis of rhetorical effects, modern aesthetics emphasizes expression, the imagination, and autonomy of production. Within the modern aesthetic tradition, lyric's role appears in
the expression of pain and the corporeal senses; in the imaginative

---

[5] Sidney, *A Defence of Poetry*, ed. Jan Van Dorsten (Oxford: Oxford University
Press, 1966), 31–42. For an important discussion of the psychology of the "defense"
as a genre see Margaret W. Ferguson, *Trials of Desire: Renaissance Defenses of Poetry*
(New Haven, Conn.: Yale University Press, 1983).

[6] See the discussion of romantic art in G. W. F. Hegel, *The Philosophy of Fine Art*,
trans. F. P. B. Osmaston, 4 vols. (New York: Hacker Art Books, 1975), 1:118–20.
"Mind, in short, here determines this content for its own sake and apart from all else
into the content of idea; to express such idea it no doubt avails itself of sound, but
employs it merely as a sign without independent worth or substance. Thus viewed,
the sound here may be just as well reproduced by the mere letter, for the audible,
like the visible, is here reduced to a mere indication of mind. For this reason, the
true medium of poetical representation is the poetical imagination and the intellectual presentation itself; and inasmuch as this element is common to all types of art it
follows that poetry is a common thread through them all, and is developed independently in each. Poetry is, in short, the universal art of the mind, which has
become essentially free, and which is not fettered in its realization to an externally
sensuous material, but which is creatively active in the space and time belonging to
the inner world of ideas and emotion" (120). In note to this passage Osmaston says
that Hegel underestimates the sonorous quality of poetry. A similar criticism is made

reconfiguration of nature through such devices as onomatopoeia, personification, and other modes of projection; and as the coordination of various modes of temporal experience necessarily *preceding* any narrative forms.

Following Vico, one could claim that lyric cannot be the subject of history, for lyric is necessarily prior to history. Lyric is not denotation; it is rather a process of enunciation, expressing the passage from not knowing to knowing through which we represent the world to ourselves. Vico conjectures that early peoples "created things according to their own ideas. But this creation was infinitely different from that of God. For God, in his purest intelligence, knows things, and, by knowing them, creates them; but they, in their robust ignorance, did it by virtue of a wholly corporeal imagination. And because it was quite corporeal, they did it with marvelous sublimity; a sublimity such and so great that it excessively perturbed the very persons who by imagining did the creating, for which they were called 'poet,' which is Greek for 'creators.'"[7] Under the influence of two central tenets—history is made by humankind, and thought is under constant modification— Vico explains that the imagination stems from the senses and is moved to represent itself by anthropomorphizing nature and by giving being to inanimate things. Fashioned from nature as Jove is fashioned by the first humans from their experience of lightning, these "inventions" eventually become narratives (74). And as narratives harden into ideologies, authorization and legitimation give such ideologies ethical force.

Vico merges his account of the ontology of poetry and culture with an agenda of ideology critique: "All that has been so far said here upsets all the theories of the origin of poetry from Plato and Aristotle down to Patrizzi, Scaliger, and Castelvetro. For it has been shown that it was a deficiency of human reasoning power that gave rise to poetry so sublime that the philosophies which came afterward, the arts of poetry

---

by Charles Taylor, *Hegel* (Cambridge: Cambridge University Press, 1975), 478–79. Yet Hegel would find it impossible to allow any sonorous aspect of the lyric to remain unworked, that is, not subjected to the cognitive transformation whereby every material element transcends itself.

    [7] Vico, *The New Science*, trans. Thomas Goddard and Max Harold Fisch (Ithaca, N.Y.: Cornell University Press, 1970), 75.

criticism, have produced none equal or better, and have even
ed its production. . . . This discovery of the origins of poetry
uoes away with the opinion of the matchless wisdom of the ancients so
ardently sought after from Plato to Bacon's *De sapientia veterum*. For the
wisdom of the ancients was the vulgar wisdom of the lawgivers who
founded the human race, not the esoteric wisdom of great and rare
philosophers" (79). Vico continues with the claim that the origins of
poetry precede the origins of languages and letters, including histories. He contends that humankind developed from muteness to the
articulation of vowel sounds by singing, then to stammering out the
first consonants. And, like Rousseau, he says that passion was the impetus behind the first utterances, which, shouted, led to diphthongs,
songs, and, eventually, heroic verse—that form most closely allied with
"extremely perturbed passions."[8]

Vico arrives at the stunning conclusion that memory "is the same
as imagination. Imagination is likewise taken for ingenuity or invention. . . . Memory thus has three different aspects: memory when it
remembers things, imagination when it alters or imitates them, and
invention when it gives them a new turn or puts them into proper
arrangement and relationship" (260). In this account of the place of
memory we find the dual relation of memory to historical and poetic
thought. Memory is the method of history, but it is intelligible only
through the imagination's determination and organization of its elements. And determination and organization pose the thematization,
the particularization of parts in accordance with a totality or end, of
both forms: poetry's own history is internalized and displayed in its

[8] Ludovico Castelvetro's neo-Aristotelian claim that history must have come first
and then poetry, for history addresses the true and poetry is an imitation, is refuted
by Vico: "Inasmuch as the poets came certainly before the vulgar historians, the first
history must have been poetic" (257). Sidney makes a similar argument in the
Defence, but in mythological terms rather than textual ones. He claims that the legends of poets precede any histories: "And even historiographers (although their lips
sound of things done, and verity be written in their foreheads) have been glad to
borrow both fashion and perchance weight of poets. . . . So that truly, neither
philosopher nor historiographer could at the first have entered into the gates of
popular judgments if they had not taken a great passport of poetry" (Sidney, *An
Apology for Poetry*, ed. Forrest G. Robinson, Library of Liberal Arts, 74 [Indianapolis,
Ind.: Bobbs-Merrill, 1970], 9).

perfected form; history, shaped by processes of memory informed by imagination, is a consequence of poetic activity.

Vico's thoughts on poetry therefore foreground the nexus of aesthetics and a critical historiography we have come to associate with later thinkers. We find here an idea of the redemptive, future-oriented account of the past hoped for in Benjamin's "Theses on History" and a position furthered in Habermas's recent utopian project of a history mobilized toward intersubjective action.[9] Yet an earlier and more direct connection can be drawn to Vico's most prominent modern follower, Benedetto Croce, who relates this way of thinking more particularly to historiography. Contending that there are no "non-historical facts," but only "unthought facts,"[10] Croce draws, within a discussion of chronicle and period in history, an analogy to metrical form:

> It has sometimes been said that every periodization has a "relative" value. But we must say "both relative and absolute," like all thought, it being understood that periodization is intrinsic to thought and determined by the determination of thought. However, the practical needs of chroniclism and of learning make themselves felt here also. Just as in metrical treatises the internal rhythm of a poem is resolved into external rhythm and divided into syllables and feet, into long and short vowels, tonic and rhythmic accents, into strophes and series of strophes, and so on, so the internal time of historical thought (that time which is thought itself) is derived from chroniclism converted into external time

[9] This emphasis is particularly found in Benjamin's thesis 18 (A): "Historicism contents itself with establishing a causal connection between various moments in history. But no fact that is a cause is for that very reason historical. It became historical posthumously, as it were, through events that may be separated from it by thousands of years. A historian who takes this as his point of departure stops telling the sequence of events like the beads of a rosary. Instead, he grasps the constellation which his own era has formed with a definite earlier one. Thus he establishes a conception of the present as the 'time of the now' which is shot through with chips of Messianic time" (Benjamin, *Illuminations*, ed. Hannah Arendt, trans. Harry Zohn [New York: Schocken, 1968], 263). Habermas discusses the "Theses" in *The Philosophical Discourse of Modernity: Twelve Lectures*, trans. Frederick G. Lawrence (Cambridge, Mass.: MIT Press, 1990), 10–16.

[10] Croce, *Theory and History of Historiography*, trans. Douglas Ainslie (London: George Harrap, 1921), 108–10: "There is no fear of going astray in history, because, as we have seen, the problem is in every case prepared by life, and in every case the problem is solved by thought, which passes from the confusion of life to the distinctness of consciousness" (110).

or temporal series, of which the elements are spatially separated from one another." (113)

If we take Croce's statement apart, we find a number of key insights into lyric's relation to history. First, Croce's emphasis upon the *relative* value of periodization brings forward the intersubjective ground upon which historical judgments are made, their orientation toward an intelligible version of both the present and the future. But the *absolute* value of periodization stems from the problem articulated in Augustine's theory of time. In returning to Augustine's concept of the coincidence of divine knowing and making, we properly remember, in fact, an important antecedent to Vico's thinking on this subject.

For Augustine, the being of time is established in a threefold, dynamic present: the present of past things, or the memory; the present of present things, or direct perception; and the present of future things, or expectation. Through the extension of the subjective mind in the present, measurement extends outward. But the basis of the quantification of time is not the movement of things in the world. Rather, both movement and rest, or interval, are determined by the projection or extension of time from the subject. In a well-known example Augustine links a sound that starts, continues, and stops resonating to the past; the "not yet" under which we speak of the stopping of resonance exemplifies the future spoken of as the past and the present under which we are able to say that the sound "is resonating." This present is already disjunctive, however, to the presence of resonance. Thus we speak of the very passing of the present already in the past tense. Augustine asks, "Is there a way to measure time passing both when it has ceased and while it continues?" He considers how, in memorizing a hymn by Saint Ambrose, his mind forms impressions of the relative terms of duration. Long and short syllables are quantified in relation to the whole. In recitation, this expectation regarding the whole poem turns then toward what remains of the poem, enacting the process by which the present relegates the future to the past. The past increases as the future diminishes until the future is wholly absorbed in the past. Augustine's example of the song that bears an internal system of duration and yet is actively engaged in both continuing and ceasing does not, therefore, merely illustrate the experience and knowledge of duration. It is also an example of the simultaneously active and passive situation of the subject, who is passive in relation to sense experience, memory, and expectation and active in relation to a present alteration of those terms. I will return to the situation of the subject soon, but my point now is that Croce's discussion of interval in history has a profound connection to the much older argument that the experience of duration is contingent on an internal time consciousness that itself is contiguous to the experience of language.

Croce, following Augustine and Vico, must define history as that which is *thought* and therefore *made*, so that the measurement of time is not dependent upon some external nature. From a dialectical analysis of the relations between "general" history and "special" histories (between history as a narrative of the past and the particular histories of phenomena and discrete "moments") he concludes that "nothing exists but general history." Not surprisingly, the formulation is both an homage to and a critique of Hegelian teleology: "All doctrines that represent the history of nations as proceeding according to the stages of development of the individual, of his psychological development, of the categories of the Spirit, or of anything else, are due to the same error, which is that of rendering periodization external and natural" (Croce, 115).

In Croce's critique of periodization and his claim that a general history must be constructed from a constant dialectic between particulars and abstractions, including "general history," we find a parallel to the critique of Hegel's "restricted economy" of thought in Georges Bataille's call for a "general" economy capable of addressing the limits of any functional, or teleological, version of dialectic.[11] Just as Vico objects strenuously to Leibniz's neat summation of the function of history, so Bataille claims that the dialectic's relentless absorption of all contradiction is based upon a repression of both the grounds of its system and any element resisting incorporation. Here it is useful to note that any theory of lyric history that celebrates the so-called marginal

[11] Bataille, *Visions of Excess: Selected Writings, 1927–1939*, trans. Allan Stoekel, with C. R. Lovitt and D. M. Leslie (Minneapolis: University of Minnesota Press, 1985), 116–29. See also Jacques Derrida, "From Restricted to General Economy: A Hegelianism without Reserve," in *Writing and Difference*, trans. Alan Bass (Chicago: University of Chicago Press, 1978), 251–77.

status of lyric, that posits lyric as deviation, or that imagines lyric consciousness only within the hackneyed terms of free expression and spontaneity is necessarily a functional theory incapable of addressing the complexity of lyric's relation to subjectivity and narrative. Both cognitive anthropology and comparative poetics frequently claim that lyric exists in tension with speech, on the one hand, and song, on the other, but the fixed terms of such a model of genre cannot accommodate the temporal nature of lyric experience. Nor can a static model acknowledge the complexity of the subject's passage from reception to expression in the work of lyric as it moves between aspects of received tradition, such as metrical convention; aspects of sense impression, such as rhythm and interval; and individuation of utterance.

Hence the impasse at which any current lyric history finds itself: first, the contradiction of a constantly varying and multiple "form" that emerges from the classical aesthetic view; second, the hardly disinterested formulations of historical context posed as "surrounds" of various lyric practices that emerge from the modern aesthetic view. In any formalist account of lyric history, lyric will be the subject of a larger "framework" that resists any encroachments that would threaten an intelligibility of form. We have only to think of how the very binding of *The Norton Anthology of Poetry* makes its contents seem equally alike and equally different. Yet we must avoid confusing lyric with narrative and dramatic verse. And we must avoid as well any dissolution of lyric into either its material element (the "mere" verse Aristotle derides) or its abstract element (philosophy, politics, etc., "posing" as poetry).

If we look at the formal qualities most often attributed to lyric, musicality and timelessness, we see that form is defined by the absence of certain features as much as by the presence of others. Further, musicality and timelessness are suggestively self-canceling, for music, as the intended unfolding of sound in time and the grounds under which duration might be conceptualized, is precisely the quality lyric must have and yet the abstract form it must resist becoming. In its resistance to fixed identity, lyric is defined as that which maintains music as one quality in tension with others. Here is the key to lyric as enunciation, for lyric's defining formal feature, paradoxically a presentation of temporal alteration, is the condition under which the semantic is brought forward from the somatic.

In theories of lyric we constantly return to the site of enunciation. How is this site to be imagined? It is the situation of the person spoken by sound who becomes the person speaking—the cry of the senses coming forward beyond will is transformed into the person of volition and consequence, thus necessarily a person articulated by speaking and being spoken to. To put it another way, it is the situation of the emergence of subjectivity both ontologically, that is, in general, and historically, that is, in particular. But the reconciliation of this model as a structural problem and a historical practice is not a simple one. How can lyric be both the repetition of an ontological moment and the ongoing process or work of enunciation by which that moment is recursively known?

In the formalist studies of Julia Kristeva and others, lyric practice becomes the repetition of a "deviation" from fixed linguistic forms:

> In the case, for example, of a signifying practice such as "poetic language," the *semiotic disposition* will be the various deviations from the grammatical rules of the language: articulatory effects which shift the phonemative system back towards its articulatory, phonetic base and consequently towards the drive-governed bases of sound-production; the overdetermination of a lexeme by multiple meanings which it does not carry in ordinary usage but which accrue to it as a result of its occurrence in other texts; syntactic irregularities such as ellipses, non-recoverable deletions, indefinite embeddings, etc.; the replacement of the relationship between the protagonists of any enunciation as they function in a locutionary act . . . by a system of relations based on fantasy; and so forth."[12]

But following Vico's critique of imitation theories, we readily can see that Kristeva's "transgressive" concept of poetic language reifies linguistic usage into fixed forms and cannot account for linguistic, let alone poetic, transformation. Such transformation could be construed not simply as a matter of historical "fact" but as demanded by our drive toward expression under changing circumstances. The imitation of a lost primal relation to the somatic posed by Kristeva is not a "natural" enunciation but the pale reflection of its own sentimental ideology of nature. We could say of the theory, as well as of the forms of predictable transgression it espouses, what Theodor Adorno says of lyric

[12] Kristeva, "The System and the Speaking Subject," in *The Kristeva Reader*, ed. Toril Moi (New York: Columbia University Press, 1986), 28–29.

in general: "Even lyrical creations which are untouched by conventional, material existence, by the crude world of material objects, owe
their high worth to the power the subjective being within them has, in
overcoming its alienation, to evoke an image of the natural world.
Their pure subjectivity, apparently flawless, without breaks and full of
harmony, actually witnesses to the opposite, to a suffering caused by
existence foreign to the subject, as much as it shows the subject's love
toward that existence."[13] Adorno's argument refutes a formalist one by
concluding that the temporal enunciation of the subject counters both
a reification of the subject and any finite determination of subjective
lack. Whereas Kristeva's model is ultimately compensatory, Adorno
places lyric practice within a more general history of a temporally
determined subjectivity emergent in practices of enunciation that are
not secondary to some fixed linguistic "dominant."

Lyric challenges any possible dichotomy between the subjective
and objective on several fronts. First, in theories of lyric from Vico forward, the enunciation of pain at the origin of lyric must appear before
the emergence of the subjective. To equate pain with subjectivity is to
equate the body with subjectivity and so to confuse the most collective
with the most personal. Pain has no memory, but necessitates the intersubjective invention of association and metaphor.[14] The situation of
the person resides in the genesis of the memory of action and experience in intersubjective terms, that is, in the articulation and mastery of
the originating pain. The organization of memory, the determination
of feeling, the articulation of point of view in space and time—these
qualities of lyric are not the eruption of the somatic in an already
determined framework of perception; rather, they characterize the

---

[13] Adorno, "Lyric Poetry and Society," trans. Bruce Mayo, *Telos* 20 (1974): 59.

[14] I follow Vico and Nietzsche in arguing that pain necessitates the invention of
metaphor. This argument rests upon the assumption that lack motivates the desire
for the production of form and that a trajectory from pain to pleasure is created
through such production. It is important to distinguish such an ontological argument from the thematic of pleasure or pain in works of art. That producing a thematic of pain might be a cure for pain and a consequent form of pleasure is
addressed early in Aristotle's *Poetics*, with its discussion of the pleasure taken in viewing an exact representation of a corpse. Another key text would be Wordsworth's
preface to *Lyrical Ballads* for its complex presentation of the interrelations of pain
and pleasure in poetic composition.

transition toward subjectivity, just as reflection upon them transforms the terms of subjectivity and consequently the terms of objectivity so that neither can provide the "context" for the other.

> The specific paradox belonging to the lyric poem—this subjective, personal element transforming itself into an objective one—is bound to that specific importance which poetry gives to linguistic *form*, an importance from which the primacy of language in all literature (prose forms as well) derives. . . . The most sublime lyric works, therefore, are those in which the subject, without a trace of his material being, intones in language until the voice of language itself is heard. . . . Lyric poetry shows itself most thoroughly integrated into society at those points where it does not repeat what society says . . . but rather where the speaking subject . . . comes to full accord with the language itself. . . . It is not a moment of compulsion or force, not even of force against the speaking subject. . . . Language itself first speaks when it speaks not as something foreign to the subject but as his own voice. . . . language . . . would otherwise submit to the process of reification and disintegrate as it does in everyday speech. (Adorno, 62)

Adorno's argument is that subjectivity articulates itself as a singular voice when it is most objective, when it takes itself to the limit of what linguistic experience might be able to produce and there articulates itself in fullest particularity. We might be reminded here of Coleridge's position on metric as an act of will: "which strives to hold in check the workings of passion. It might be easily explained . . . in what manner this salutary antagonism is assisted by the very state which it counteracts; and how this balance of antagonists became organized into meter . . . consciously and for the foreseen purpose of pleasure." Coleridge explains that in the "frequency of forms and figures of speech" we find "offsprings of passion" that are also "adopted children of power."[15] Yet the mastery of pain through measurement is not merely repressive; it is as well a matter of coming to knowledge and expression, as in the transforming interpolations of Gerard Manley Hopkins ("fancy come faster," in "The Wreck of the Deutschland") and Elizabeth Bishop ("write it!" in "One Art"). Coleridge's explanation echoes the Augustinian formulation of a subject coming into activity out of a passive

[15] Coleridge, *Biographia Literaria*, ed. J. Shawcross, 2 vols. (Oxford: Clarendon, 1907), 2:49–50.

relation to sense experience, memory, and expectation. The figures and forms created are those of a subjectivity enunciating itself.

Divergence in lyric is thus not between language and music but between a subject and his or her transformations from the somatic both toward and against the social. The history of lyric is thereby the history of a relation between pronouns, the genesis of *ego-tu* and *ego-vos* in the reciprocity of an imagination posing and composing itself and its audience via the work of time. It is almost unbearable to imagine lyric outside of these terms of subjectivity. As W. R. Johnson writes in *The Idea of Lyric*: "No experience in reading, perhaps, is more depressing and more frustrating than to open a volume to Sappho's fragments and to recognize, yet again—for one always hopes that somehow this time will be different—that this poetry is all but lost to us. . . . Even though we know that Greek lyric is mere fragments, indeed, *because* we know that Greek lyric is mere fragments, we act, speak, and write as if the unthinkable had not happened, as if pious bishops, careless monks, and hungry mice had not consigned Sappho and her lyrical colleagues to irremediable oblivion." In the famous lyric *phainetai moi*, beginning (in Symonds's Victorian translation), "Peer of gods he seemeth to me, the blissful / Man who sits and gazes at thee before him," the speaker describes her reaction to her own merely voyeuristic position as one of hushed voice, broken tongue, fire beneath the flesh, tremors, pains, sweat, and blanched limbs. The fragment contains an additional line, usually omitted by translators: "All must be dared since one who is poor . . ." Yet in the progress of this lyric, if one includes the missing line, is a resolve to a position of action and a movement away from the depiction of fragmented internal states. At least since Longinus, who preserved in his treatise on the sublime the only existing record of the lyric, this fragment, *without the final line*, ironically has exemplified the sublime unity of classical lyric. "Do you not marvel," Longinus writes, "how she seeks to make her mind, body, ears, tongue, eyes, and complexion, as if they were scattered elements strange to her, join together in the same moment of experience? In contradictory phrases she describes herself as hot and cold at once, rational and irrational, at the same time terrified and almost dead." He praises "her selection of the most vital details and her working them into one whole which produce the outstanding quality of the poem." [16] The third-person viewpoint, the imposition of an external position, effects the unity here, linking the work of writer and critic and crossing the threshold between the somatic and the social.[17] But as Johnson emphasizes, "the sublime unity" of Sappho's lyrics is as compensatory to their material loss as Longinus's judgment is to the somatic shattering described.

From such fragments as *phainetai moi,* which explain the most intense contexts of feeling and perception within the abstraction of an addressee who is both herself and the third-person viewpoint, to the voyeurism implicit in Donne's overheard forms and Herbert's pedagogy in the guise of abstracted prayer, the triangulation of desire in lyric structure characterizes a reversal and recognition between subject and object. Yet the process is historical, not natural; the ideology of the "natural" subject, who speaks from feeling, from the heart, from disinterestedness, is a consequence rather than a source of lyric history.[18] How noncoincidental, then, that innovations in discursive lyric (Pindar's reinvention of the vatic and Jonson's reinvention of the Pindaric; eighteenth-century minor poetry's striving after oral effects; aspects of such a syncretism between the oral, the written, the archaic,

[16] Johnson, *The Idea of Lyric: Lyric Modes in Ancient and Modern Poetry* (Berkeley: University of California Press, 1982), 25; Longinus, *On Great Writing (On the Sublime),* trans. G. M. A. Grube (Indianapolis, Ind.: Bobbs-Merrill, 1957), 18.

[17] For the place of pronouns and pronominal terms in the construction of subjectivity, see Emile Benveniste, *Problèmes de linguistique générale* (Paris: Gallimard, 1966); Charles Altieri, "From Expressivist Aesthetics to Expressivist Ethics," in *Canons and Consequences: Reflections on the Ethical Force of Imaginative Ideals* (Evanston, Ill.: Northwestern University Press, 1990), 225–53; and the discussion of "the third party" in M. M. Bakhtin, "The Problem of the Text in Linguistics, Philology, and the Human Sciences: An Experiment in Philosophical Analysis," in *Speech Genres and Other Late Essays,* ed. Caryl Emerson and Michael Holquist, trans. Vern W. McGee (Austin: University of Texas Press, 1986), 103–31.

[18] Contrast, for example, Bruno Snell's arguments for lyric subjectivity as an invention of Greek culture in *The Discovery of the Mind: The Greek Origins of European Thought* (Oxford: Basil Blackwell, 1953), 42–70, and *Poetry and Society* (Bloomington: Indiana University Press, 1961), with the position of the authors of *A History of Private Life,* who write: "Ronsard, and with him the group of poets known as La Pléiade, can be credited with originating lyric poetry as the Romantics would later define it: poetry that expresses private feelings and experience" (vol. 3, *Passions of the Renaissance,* ed. Roger Chartier, trans. Arthur Goldhammer [Cambridge, Mass.: Belknap Press of Harvard University Press, 1989], 368).

and the "modern" in Keats, Yeats, Brooks, and others) have typically been accompanied by accusations of a certain failure in audience. These breaks in practices signify the recomposition of audience and are not merely instances of authorial innovation.

It is something of a commonplace in aesthetic theory to argue that single-point perspective determined, in its initial appearance in the classical period and in its rediscovery in fifteenth-century Florence, the individual subject as rational observer and nature as "scene" or pictorial space.[19] This commonplace has enabled formalism in all the plastic arts and has made such terms as *property, landscape, viewpoint, work,* and *field* the "natural" vocabulary of the critic. But despite the superficial coherence between single-point perspective and the solo singer, only a weak analogy can be made to lyric. As lyric has come forward in language, it has necessarily come forward in processes of cultural catachresis and transformation. Virgil, Horace, and the Latin elegists faced enormous technical problems in reviving Greek meters and themes in Latin. In relying on *hyperbata,* they emphasized the violent mastery of time implicit in any metrical revival. They remind us that in consequence of its transformation of syntax, poetry necessarily affects our very concepts of causality and temporality (see Johnson, 123–26). English meter, in its break with pure accentual forms, turned to accentual syllabics only through invasion and contamination and through the loss and rediscovery of Chaucer's iambics. And the choice of "quantitative meter" (always a fiction of approximation) or iambics or any other system becomes ideologically laden—a matter of an attitude toward the past, toward nation, toward authorship. Further, the revival of forms has meant by definition the imposition of inappropriate context either generally, in the sense that revival is always accompanied by an accretion of nostalgia, or specifically, as when the ancient system of decorum (classical iambics for conversation; heroic hexameter for epic and pastoral eclogue; the couplet for inscription, epigram, satire, and epistle) is dirempted by the application of old meters to new situ-

[19] See, for example, Charles Taylor, *Sources of the Self: The Making of the Modern Identity* (Cambridge, Mass.: Harvard University Press, 1989), 199–207; and Michael Baxandall, *Painting and Experience in Fifteenth Century Italy* (Oxford: Oxford University Press, 1972).

ations (stressed decasyllabics for the stage, iambic pentameter adapted for high and low forms, couplets for heroic verse in Renaissance practices).[20] The great break with song and narrative effected in Baroque lyric is not simply a consequence of new forms of conversion, spiritual discipline, and meditative practices; it is as well a matter of attention to the duration of perception, a formal change coincident to transformed and transforming concepts of subjectivity.[21] I am thinking particularly of Traherne's remarkable inscription of the genesis of subjectivity in sense perception and of the instability of narrative and point of view in Crashaw's attempts to represent states of ecstasy.

If musicality is not only an abstract quality of lyric but also a specific historical practice, whereby even the concept of musicality appears as ideologically laden, this is just one aspect of the temporally bound nature of lyric "timelessness." Lyric by definition appears in the unfolding web of memory, perception, and expectation so continually described in lyric theory from Augustine to Benjamin. The vaunted spatiality of lyric after the advent of print is only in fact an exaggeration of this position of ephemeral, yet significant, enunciation. And the poignant anxiety regarding the material status of lyric utterance that we find in the sonnets of Shakespeare and Spenser, for example, both foregrounds and undermines this newly found spatial stability, this uncertain fixity. Temporality unfolds in all lyric on many levels at once. We should consider not only the ways in which the future becomes past but also such aspects of lyric as the following: the tension—or, as

---

[20] John Hollander, *Vision and Resonance: Two Senses of Poetic Form* (New Haven, Conn.: Yale University Press, 1985), 172–73. See also in this volume the discussions of quantitative meter (59–70) and of Campion's attempts to adapt English meters to musical systems (71–90). Hollander's work is an important guide to issues of formal transformation. See his position on aurality, emphasizing the tension between repetition and time, in Hollander, *The Figure of Echo: A Mode of Allusion in Milton and After* (Berkeley: University of California Press, 1981); and Hollander, "Breaking into Song: Some Notes on Refrain," in *Lyric Poetry: Beyond the New Criticism*, ed. Chaviva Hošek and Patricia Parker (Ithaca, N.Y.: Cornell University Press, 1985), 73–89. For an authoritative contemporary meditation on the relations between subjectivity and lyric practice see Allen Grossman, "Summa lyrica," in *The Sighted Singer: Two Works on Poetry for Readers and Writers*, with Mark Halliday (Baltimore, Md.: Johns Hopkins University Press, 1992), 205–383.

[21] See, for example, the discussion of "time as a means of structure" in Lowry Nelson, *Baroque Lyric Poetry* (New Haven, Conn.: Yale University Press, 1964), 19–84.

Hopkins practiced it, the counterpoint—between metrical structure and the shifting progress of the individual line; the lexical transformation implicit in rhyme with its simultaneous link across time and denial of repetition; the tension between pronounced speech and fixed inscription; the reversal and reorganization of syntax and the disjunctions between syntax and rhythm; the fluctuating stability of stanzaic structure and the spatial and temporal breaks effected by such forms as the caesura and the volta; and the historical accretions, borrowings, and metaphorical approximations of "metrical structure" itself in practices such as contrafacta, parody, and other modes of metrical allusion.

The temporal impossibility of any pure repetition is emphasized in lyric by the creation of redundancy on the level of the somatic, where sensual information offered to sight and sound appears to be the same. Lyric synesthesia emphasizes that figuration is accomplished by sound and that spatial interval makes sound intelligible and subject to measure. And because that measure does not fade as the semantic burden increases, any semantic transformation remains inseparable from the somatic. We could think, for example, of the emotional and literal burden of Dickinson's recurring slant rhymes, such as *port* and *chart* (in "Wild Nights") or *spar* and *despair* (in "It Was Not Death, for I Stood Up") or *grace* and *price* (in "Publication Is the Auction"); the deadening and deadly insistent exact rhymes in Plath's "Daddy," and the refusal of rhyme and breaking of pattern in the final lines of many stanzas in Wilfred Owen's work. In the objectification of what is most individual, what is brought forward is the subjective view of the social; what is felt is brought to the light of what can be known via the intersubjective work of speaking and listening in time. Lyric here departs from the narrative tradition in its break with teleology and closure. It departs from dramatic tradition in its resistance to the typification of subjectivity. And lyric is anticathartic in its resistance to the abstraction of audience and in its promotion of the temporal reformulation of judgment. Even in such simple features of ballad as incremental repetition and the testament, we find this movement forward through the transformation of expectations and the anticipation of response.

Every formal feature of lyric is thereby a social-historical feature. Truisms such as the natural lightness of trochaic meters and the comic resonance of triple rhymes depend on the stability of conventions produced by recurrent historical practices of speech and writing in general and not just lyric in particular. Lyric timelessness may be promised by sight and hearing as those senses most capable of being mobilized in a project of overcoming distance. But as the media of poetry, sight and hearing also *define* distance. Unheard melodies, things not yet imagined, selves unsullied by the world, appear only by means of their negation, only in a relation both historical and material. However, they also draw us back from any paradoxical idealism regarding the status of the historical and the material. When accounts of lyric have forgotten the practice's cognitive and spiritual dimensions and its capacity for cultural transformation, the result has been a distorting artifactualism of the kind we find in attempts to unify classical lyric fragments or to read such poets as Edward Taylor and Christopher Smart as products merely of belated reception.

As we survey the current methods for imagining lyric history, at least among English-speaking critics, positions ranging from formalism to contextually based historicism yet fall within the range of what Croce would call "special histories" and are not dialectically sufficient to bring forward as practices of general history. Contextual historicism has made the error of assuming the coincidence of subjectivity and the body and hence has confounded its own basis in sensation with a universal interest. If the body is the lowest common denominator of human history, the task of lyric has been to move the subjective forward toward more complex structures of agency and engagement. And functional models are fixed upon the attribution of simple cause and so have little cognitive utility. The merit of general history is its capacity to critique ideology and to refuse reification regarding language and subjectivity. My reader will no doubt seize upon this goal as an example of a hidden agenda of emancipation. But I suggest that emancipation is precisely what is promised falsely by the formalist method in its claim of literary transcendence and by any historicist method claiming contextual explanation. The special history of literary transcendence is ultimately unintelligible and idiosyncratic; its meticulous particularity, a refusal of judgment. And the dioramas of context offered by a narrow historicism are the projection of a model of history neces-

sarily aestheticized in the first place by its drive toward closure of explanation.[22] Lyric history holds out no promise of emancipation, only an
incremental progress of subjectivity, only a continual haunting by
music, only a future altered by memory and the imagination that is
memory forgetting itself.

[22] For a critique of "historical contextualism" see David Perkins, *Is Literary History Possible?* (Baltimore, Md.: Johns Hopkins University Press, 1992), 121–52.

CAN WE BE HISTORICAL EVER? SOME HOPES FOR A DIALECTICAL MODEL OF HISTORICAL SELF-CONSCIOUSNESS

Charles Altieri

In writing my *Painterly Abstraction in Modernist American Poetry* I encountered problems that make me glad to have this opportunity, especially since it comes with the space restrictions here requiring me to engage them so abstractly. How does one write a history of a movement intensely critical of narrative modes of historical representation? If we historicize modernist strategies for dealing with history, do we evade the force of their critical resistance to narrative, and even to the primacy of historical over structural analytic stances? Or is this resistance itself to be treated as a screen or symptom best grasped by understanding their historical moment from a contemporary perspective? Is this modernist work further grist for our historicist mills? Or can modernist resistance guide us in developing different options for treating historical phenomena, for example, by showing us how to take seriously writers' claims to be able to bear witness for their culture, or even to exemplify acts of mind that take on transhistorical force?

I doubt that we can resolve such questions from within the disciplines devoted to historical understanding. At stake are fundamental ethical and political choices (themselves in constant conflict) involving the degree to which we honor what seem agents' intentions and the degree to which our projects justify placing intentions in larger contexts that might even make the agents reinterpret their own behavior, especially in terms of how the intentions mask actual political interests and forces. Here, however, I cannot take up the ethical questions as such. Instead I will reverse the valences by treating the ethical issues as instruments indicating the complex tensions that historians must con-

tinually address, at least insofar as they study the arts. For I am convinced that the more complex our sense of historical agency—both in
the actions we study and in the persons we become in the studying—
the more likely we are to recognize the need for dialectical models
of the historical enterprise. In fact, dialectics can be defined as an
interpretive stance devoted to showing how such tensions between
honoring and recasting intentions remain both inescapable and irreducible for the historian. Dialectics concentrates on the constant reciprocal modification between historians' analyses of intentions from the
past and their understanding of their own position in the present, so it
can provide a clear model for the ethical and political implications of
historical research.

I will begin with one dialectical moment where these tensions seem to
me especially salient, then try to sketch some theoretical concerns that
emerge from the example. This moment is a struggle within modernism: it wished to free itself from the narrative historicism dominating its public culture, yet it also wanted to resist the increasingly powerful positivist principles that treated such teleology as mere myth,
from which positivism alone could save us. By the late nineteenth century Hegel and Darwin appeared allies, since both thinkers offered
narrative histories shaped by and sustaining prevailing ideological
dreams of progress, even though the empiricists found little trouble
exposing the contradictions and slippages in the version of dialectical
thinking shaping those narrative modes. There was and still is no easy
way to correlate how history narrates with what it claims to be the
object of its narration. On the simplest level, as Hayden White has
stressed, the rhetorical stances historians take have substantial effects
on their actual historical claims. But the issue is even more interesting
on the phenomenological level, where we face another apparent no-
win situation. One desires to locate a historical reality, a level of experience that does not depend on the rhetorical shape given by representational structures. Or, if we can show how rhetoric itself becomes
an aspect of cultural experience, with specific tasks to perform and
with specific traps it imposes on both agents and historical analysts,
then we can explain the gaps between rhetoric and experience. But
how then can we describe what might resist a given rhetoric (without

appearing to be just another rhetoric)? And how do we establish principles allowing us to make judgments among available rhetorics?[1]

To appreciate modernist art fully, we must track its efforts to open an alternative perspective on history. All the ladders must begin with a foregrounding of the fundamental gulf between what is represented and what goes into the representing, so that the more powerful any single picture appears, the more suspicious we must be of what underlies it. We can find relevant speculations in thinkers as diverse as Freud, Dilthey, and Heidegger, each in his own way pursuing what forces might determine representations. But because such work is confined to proposing discursive alternatives, we must shift to examples from art in order to appreciate modernism's richest models for dialectical thinking about history. In modernist art the very conditions of acting and meaning get transformed. Rather than focus on the truth of specific claims, even about the forces that go into representations, modernist art asked how forces are embodied in actions and hence offer society models for value that depend on how experiences are constructed more than on what we can then say about them. This shift in focus might even yield artistic versions of the impersonal principles that positivism made the necessary condition for appealing to public agreements.

Although theoretical analogues exist in Freud the therapist, in William James, and preeminently in Wittgenstein's *Investigations*, Cézanne provides the richest example for our purposes. His obsession with how we see, and with how the intense desires we bring to seeing can be correlated with the objects of sight, led him to transform the very idea of landscape and hence figuratively any idea of subject-object relations. Cézanne focuses less on the object of vision than on the life of the eye, which gives dynamic value to the activity of seeing. So he can envision an exemplary artistic will manifest in the ways that the brush seems to characterize the activity of seeing at its most intense. Similarly, Picasso's 1906 *Self-Portrait* treats the painter at his easel as relying not on a brush but on his arm itself as the artist's instrument, since what painting makes visible is the very activity of composing sight's powers within the world.

---

[1] Jonathan Rée gives a good account of historicism and shows how its faith in explanation runs counter to an adequate sense of "historicity" ("The Vanity of Historicism," *New Literary History* 22 [1991]: 961–84).

Wilhelm Worringer used what Cézanne made visible in order to turn dialectically against Renaissance representational ideals. In his *Abstraction and Empathy* Worringer argued that after four hundred years of carrying out the positive aspects of Renaissance artistic ideals, the time had come to understand also how these ideals functioned negatively. And on that basis it might become possible to locate displaced spiritual forces necessary to combat empiricist appropriations of those Renaissance ambitions. For this project Worringer turned to the antinomy between representations and representing: by idealizing the mimetic features basic to representational art, the Renaissance tradition suppressed both the demonic and the daemonic aspects of the energies that go into the representing. Bound to the display of skill in controlling the world, these artists lost both the mysterious energies of the creative psyche and the incursion of a transcendental otherness not containable by our images. So once we reorient that skill, as Cézanne did, art might be seen as providing culture very different resources.

If we recast Worringer for the theory of history, we find a basis for showing how the poles of our antinomy between representation and representing constitute one another's contrary and limit. The historian's ideal of representation requires attempting to recuperate from some moment of the past the texture of felt life, and thus of immediacies for subjects, approachable only by ideals of experience and intuition developed by Dilthey and the phenomenological tradition. But no self-consciousness within the historical moment can capture the forces at work upon and within the processes of representation. For this analytic work historians need abstract hypothetical frameworks, either like those proposed by Marx, Weber, Spengler, and Freud or like those facilitated by the empirical tools of the demographer and economist. Hence just as modernist art requires recasting what we can mean by intentional agency, modern historical thinking must begin to explore modes like genealogy that can at least register the complex forces that oscillate between these poles.

Now the basic challenge emerges. Can the prevailing theoretical perspectives on historical analysis respond adequately to this sense of necessary contraries, and can they use the contraries to open some third realm where we understand what is at stake in focusing on their interplay? There can be no doubt that sophisticated contemporary work understands the conflicts involved and provides sharp ironic methods both for teasing out the forces at play in historical self-representations and for recasting claims about experience so that we see the experiences themselves as material effects of rhetorical practices. But as a result of that sophistication, contemporary historians often seem cyborg versions of Antaeus who gain strength the more they can unsettle any ground on which historical agents might hope to stand. We are superb at exposing the gaps and fissures that open because of contradictory regimes of representation. Yet our acuity leads us to make oppositions into absolutes (however mobile) rather than seek within contradiction a generative power bearing dialectical force.

Perhaps it then should not be surprising that this contemporary history ends up producing a disturbingly symmetrical reversal of the modernism that it aims to overcome. For the emphasis on gaps and fissures and delusions seems to embrace modernism's ironic sense of the tensions between what represents and what is represented, but then to build positive theories simply by overturning the old emphasis on the object represented. "Sophisticated" historical work recasts representations of the past in order to emphasize hitherto unrepresented interests, and it tries to disclose through elaborate homologies the extent of cultural power maintained by the dominant order. And then the more ironic aspects of New Historicism delight in showing how these representations misrepresent interests and needs and structures that we now realize governed their behavior. So whether we deal with the left or the right, we find neither having to worry about granting sufficient depth or dignity to the historical agents whom it studies, because neither tries to reconstruct a historical density sufficient to challenge its own allegories, positive or negative. One might also say that these views prove compatible because, mercifully, the theoretical framework often dissipates before the allure of difference and particularity that draws most of us to historical work.

Unfortunately, the allure of particularity is not a sufficient theoretical position from which to seek alternatives to these contemporary stances. An adequate alternative must have a language for building on the limitations inherent in making a positive goal out of the undoing of representation, so that we need not be content with working through the needs and lacks that the undoing of representation reveals. For this additional task we need dialectical principles that articulate the productive force generated by specific antinomies. No longer content with the options of teleological historicism and positivism, or with the deconstructive or genealogical-constructivist inversion of those positions that locate singularity or political force only in terms of what generalizations cannot grasp, a dialectical history must build generalizations precisely on the internal dynamics set in motion by the play of mutual limitations. This history need not seek an increasingly grand synthesis revealing an underlying teleology. It suffices to develop a third arena of questioning and speculating, based on how the opposites live one another's lives and die one another's deaths. Agents characterize their experiences within history in one set of terms; those who understand the events as occurring under historical conditions that the agent could not as fully grasp impose a second set. The task of dialectics is to put the two sets in productive tension, leading us to appreciate both the power in those moments when the historical agents find terms they need and the problems that attend to their working within inadequate categories. And this dialectics ultimately requires our attempting to understand how our own categories are shaped by the past that we attempt to understand. Thus we begin to develop new versions of Marx, Weber, and Freud based less on their positive claims than on the struggles we see them engaging to postulate concepts that we now must try to supplement because we are coming to appreciate what their struggles involved.[2]

Promulgating the need for dialectics is obviously the easy part of my enterprise. Now, given confidence by the space limitations of this forum, I must show how we can mold the conceptual building blocks that historians need to assume dialectical stances. The first prerequisite for dialectical historical analysis is to develop some version of Kenneth Burke's act-scene distinction: we must correlate the agent's terms

---

[2] I am indebted to a talk by Satcha Mohanty for my sense of the tension between experience claims and criteria for representations. I must also cite Tony Bennett's powerful analysis of how contemporary readings of history engage an established historical record (*Outside Literature* [London: Routledge, 1990]).

for experience with an analysis of the forces set in motion by the conditions framing that experience, and we must base our correlation on what can be claimed as internal to the tensions actually characterizing that historical situation. This entails occupying two positions at once, then showing that the third position empowers us to appreciate how each of the two perspectives necessarily modifies the other. While the experience term requires identifying with the agent's self-projections, the situation term establishes a distance enabling us to characterize the conditions that frame those projections and, if necessary, to redescribe the actions. We cannot adequately characterize a historical moment unless we have the means of asking how the agent's descriptions of the situation are influenced by the agent's relations to other persons, to the other, in the form of the demands coming from "elsewhere" that shape superegos and define practices, and to pressures locatable within large movements like industrialization or Braudelian shifts in cultural atmospheres. But we must also hold open the possibility that as agents become partially aware of those constraining conditions, they can act in ways that require us to modify those general concepts.

Cézanne clearly could not give an adequate account of how his bourgeois Catholicism and his rivalry with other painters, as well as with photography, led to his turning the entire impressionist enterprise into a profoundly psychological and even ethical project. To understand him we need to see what those like Braque and Picasso saw in his work. But then we can go back and see how he struggled to develop the principles that they would build from, so that how we shift the situation modifies how we then come to appreciate Cézanne's distinctive agency. And, correlatively, as we more deeply respond to that agency, the better positioned we are to understand how Cézanne changed the enterprise of painting in ways that he could not have comprehended. Once we can develop an alternative to Renaissance perspectival ideals, we become more clear on the price those ideals exacted because they cultivated myths of mastery over nature, and we see how the very idea of what it means to be a painter becomes open for reinterpretation and, more important, for reidealization, this time calling for struggles against the society that the Renaissance ideal called on the artist to serve.

The most important feature of this example is that it demonstrates the possibility that changing our models for historical analysis can also change our notions of what counts as historical knowledge (taking "knowledge" to mean agreement reached in accord with reasoned evidence). I think it fair to say that most historians, even those using genealogical techniques, still have epistemological models shaped by representational ideals. Thus they are still tempted by notions that we can only count as historical knowledge whatever can be given definite positive representations, whether these be facts or relations or discourses defining power structures. But if we pursue dialectical understanding, we must also grant that the inchoate becomes an important aspect of what we know about historical moments. We make claims not only about the facts of the matter but also about the possibilities surrounding those facts, in terms both of conditions that make them significant as facts and of events that create openings affecting other agents and other moments. When we know Cézanne's work, we also know how it opens possibilities affecting future directions for him and establishing complex networks of challenge and experiment for others. And we come to appreciate how this sense of possibility works on several levels, ranging from new aspects of the painter's art to new understandings of how that art can itself claim relations to a broader history, indeed to efforts like Worringer's to understand what can be said theoretically about that broader history. History too has its edges, and hence the history of art teaches something about the demands on history as an art.

The theory grounding such knowledge claims must show how the concrete interplay between act terms and reconstructions of the scene takes place on three basic levels, again in constant dialectical exchange. The first level is the dramatic one, where the fundamental dialectic is between situational factors that agents face and the capacities we attribute to them for grasping those factors, acting upon them, and revising self-understandings because of what they come to know about themselves. These situational factors comprise the relevant material conditions needed to set the scene, the specific pressures that seem to demand action and the underlying forces both shaping these conditions and establishing the frameworks within which agents in the past and present struggle to articulate their relation to those conditions. These encompassing frameworks will include both the general forces of production, conceived in Braudelian as well as Marxist terms, and cultural forces that influence the imaginative investments shaping what we take as necessary and significant actions. For we must be able to show how the same conditions of production can nonetheless call forth quite different actions, for example, if we compare those working under Christian dispensations with those shaped by therapeutic secular culture. More generally, we must be able to show that part of what constitutes cultural conditions is the range of different interpretations agents can propose for them, given the various needs, desires, capacities, and filiations shaping the individual responses. Finally, we must remember that each of these attributions will also involve correlating the agent's projected interpretation with how a distanced observer might characterize the action performed and the audience for whom it is performed.

For the principles we claim to underlie these historical dramas we must turn to a second, relational level of inquiry, where the central concern is less what happens than the status of what was, and is, available for characterizing what happens. In every historical analysis we must integrate what seems given, what gave intelligibility to the given, and what might have remained inchoate as tension and as potential within the agent's efforts to establish intelligibility. We cannot understand actions without a grasp of the practices that give them significance, but we also cannot be sure what the practice might have involved for the agent without careful attention to the bonds within and among groups that sustain and problematize the public quality of the practices. The very process of identifying with roles like that of professor or worker defines bonds to communities that leave the agent open to judgment, both by the self and by others. At the same time, these bonds open into supplementary roles and values that easily come into conflict with the initial group identification, so that agents can become anxious or rebellious about meanings. Then pressure builds to try alternatives, themselves defined in large part by the struggle involved in altering the complex initial filiations.

For example, modernist artists could not have rejected narrative history so thoroughly if they did not identify also with ideals of primi-

tive life and, more generally, with notions of mythic method. Those
identifications in turn created a climate of metaphors and values by
which modernism could also project an avant-garde responsible for
maintaining the distance from its society that primitivism reinforced.
Then modernist experiments took on a variety of social roles, from
strengthening group identifications and creating a distinctive cultural
capital to attempting to give psychological significance to the very distance it established from the dominant social order. But all these possible new directions remained haunted by some of the unintended or
unseen complications of the filiation with primitivism and the
metaphors emerging from it. Few modernists started out with fascist
tendencies, but primitivist ideals and experimental methods created
new, problematic relations to their own bourgeois origins, along with
fantasies of authenticity that led them to identify with culture-shaping
authoritarian claims, without realizing the full consequences of their
identifications.

Finally, we need a third level of analysis to handle how these relational factors get adapted, complicated, and recuperated when they
must be reconstructed by historical inquiry. On this level, all the tensions we have been observing get doubled because we must negotiate
between the modes of representation basic to the historical moment
and our own desires to bring to bear contemporary techniques, desires
intensified by a more general sense that we can know the past better
than it knew itself because we know the future it made and mediated.
The first task on this level is to explain what allows us to look back and
select particulars as somehow representative of significant historical
properties. For that work we need two additional sets of concepts. Historical analysis must establish criteria not only for understanding
actions in contexts but for developing ex post facto hypotheses about
which contexts most pronouncedly defined the situation, shaping even
the agent's understandings and desires. More important still, these
accounts must locate the ways in which both the actual deeds and the
institutional life fostering them and fostered by them opened or
blocked or modified certain paths through history.

Second, these interpretations must take on what we can call the
dimension of the "could have been," responsive both to the options
that were part of the historical situation and to how the roads taken

might be defined in terms of roads not taken. What agents failed or refused to do becomes a basic diacritical difference setting off the significance and the limitations of what did occur. By correlating the positive and the negative, we can make constant dialectical adjustments because our interpretations lead us back to richer versions of why agents in fact acted as they did. Modernist art had to be abstract to avoid the mutation of its antihistoricism and antiromanticism into empiricism, and the need not to succumb to the cultural practices involved in those options put the artists in a position where they could not be content with the formal qualities of their art, even as they could not rely on traditional representational content. So in order not to become what they had projected as alien, modernists had to invent new ways of understanding how the formal properties of art might also define and even testify to new psychic economies. These new models allowed them both to claim a lucidity like that fostered by empiricism and to recuperate the psychological bases for the religious beliefs that empiricism absolutely rejected.[3]

On this third level, our general claims are necessarily conditioned by our relation in the present to the very history we are trying to interpret. That is why circularity plagues any foundational version of objectivity. Dialectical theory, on the other hand, need not founder on that circularity, because its deep dream is to turn circles into spheres, as if we could learn to appreciate the circularity from the inside. The crucial measure of historical analysis becomes how well it can account for the historical process out of which one finds oneself locating the terms for one's own historical work.

I can envision three basic ways that historians can carry out the appropriate tests. First, historical interpretation can cast itself as responding to a call from the past—not some mystical appeal but a concrete sense of what is incomplete within it that has claims on the present. Then this particularity can be valued in two different ways: as significant singularity that we honor in its own right, and as materials that help us understand why we now feel the appeal or notice similarities.[4]

[3] I support my various comments on modernism in *Painterly Abstraction in Modernist American Poetry: The Contemporaneity of Modernism* (New York: Cambridge University Press, 1989).

I take the first of these options from a lecture by John Toews on the responsi-

A second arena for testing our responsiveness to historical phenomena derives from the generic filiations we make. Such filiations
narrow the past to specific fields, like military or literary history. But
what we lose in scope we gain in the concreteness of the demands for
explanation that we must encounter and in the clarity with which we
can draw direct relationships between the past and what it enables or
calls forth in the present. Here the most suggestive analogues are those
models of literary history, like Eliot's and Frye's, that try to treat the
past as partaking in a common conversation with the present. But we
must also recognize that these historical genres artificially cut up more
comprehensive fields, where affiliations with the present are more difficult to establish and where the pressure of historical contingency is
correspondingly much greater. As we work within genres, therefore, it
seems advisable to keep ourselves open to two basic dialectical concerns:
with how there can be clear internal relations among works from different temporal locales, and with the intricate relations between what can
be claimed as internal and what as external once we open our inquiry to
more general sociohistorical contexts. Ideally, we can project a synthetic
literary history based on showing that what seems internal depends on
external factors, while we also honor works of literature for attempting
to take that very externality within themselves. Once we make that projection, we understand why it is so difficult without dialectics to agree on
any single set of verbs by which to argue that what we say about texts displays significant relationships to the world beyond the text. Terms like
correlate with seem far too weak, while terms like *express the inner core* seem
to ignore the difficulties involved in making high art representative of
concrete social characteristics.[5]

This play of internal and external relationships also requires a
third level for testing dialectical claims. Heideggerian phenomenology
emphasizes a constant interplay between revealing and concealing

---

bilities we can be said to have to the dead. The second can be characterized as the
spirit of classical historians like Thucydides, for whom the past matters because
through it we can grasp our tendencies in the present and hence judge our options.

[5] Even a dialectic as subtle as Fredric Jameson's ends up using both families of
terms on the same page. See the shorter version of his "Postmodernism and Consumer
Society" reprinted in *The Anti-Aesthetic: Essays on Postmodern Culture*, ed. Hal Foster (Port
Townsend, Wash.: Bay, 1983), 113.

fundamental aspects of being. One could make the same claims about historical analysis. But since power is so central in that domain, the notions of revealing and concealing seem too innocent. We need instead to talk about the constant interplay between what is included and what is excluded from any given account. Indeed, that is the obsession of contemporary literary historians. But how do we go on to assess the leaving out and the including? Are those decisions simply matters of politics and ideology, or is there some abstract model of historical inquiry that can at least offer general criteria by which to organize concrete arguments on this topic? We can take steps toward proposing such a model by recognizing that the question of inclusion and exclusion also admits of several levels, most obviously one where such decisions are made in relation to specific stories, and one where the decisions are made in relation to genre considerations. For example, literary historians are likely to face many decisions about how their accounts enter into relations with the history of philosophy. They need that history, but they must also resist including details and arguments that would seem necessary for a historian emphasizing philosophical matters.

Thus making a history of literature that stresses philosophical matters is likely not only to produce a somewhat different sense of how literary works are embedded in their culture but also to raise questions about the literariness of certain philosophical works and concerns. Clearly, no criteria from within historical genres can adjudicate these pushes and pulls. In many respects there can be no criteria beyond the rhetorical power of the specific analysis. But we can imagine a dialectical model for at least shifting the evaluative discussion to a third level where we must justify our decisions about generic matters in terms of how our work can prove useful in addressing questions that lead beyond the discipline of history into the conflict of values played out as contemporary intellectual life. This does not mean that our histories ought to be written to take specific sides in contemporary arguments that may differ in form from the ones we analyze from the past. It does mean that we have a sense of how differences in the past might affect our understanding of conflicts in the present, if only to show why our own views are in many respects no better or worse.

Dialectics can somewhat clarify and extend this necessarily vague set of concerns by adapting J. L. Mackie's concept of bootstrapping.[6] Mackie uses the concept only to suggest that there are disciplines, like literary criticism and ethics, whose objects must be constructed from within the very discipline that goes on to analyze them. Dialectical historians could use the concept to project the ideal of showing how the social claims we propose for our work emerge from and partially fulfill the version of history we are trying to tell. This makes historical analysis the work of self-consciously taking on the burden of completing or resisting what we show we inherit. We test ourselves as historians by considering how what we learn seems to position us to engage the present itself as a historical product. Taking responsibility by bootstrapping not only defines our commitments but clarifies our own limitations, because we too become bound to a specific history. Our contingencies are indivisible from our capacities to ally with any history worth telling.

Modernism thought it could escape those limitations by opening itself to forces that transcended such localization (even if, as in Williams, localization was the means of transcendence). Dialectics finds in that failure at least the possibility of our realizing why how well we remember is inseparable from how well we live.

---

[6] Mackie, *Persons and Values*, ed. Joan Mackie and Penelope Mackie, vol. 2 (Oxford: Clarendon, 1985), 145–51. A "bootstrapping" discipline needs to decide not only what is part of the story but also what it means for something to be part of the story.

ON LITERATURE
CONSIDERED AS A
DEAD LANGUAGE

Denis Hollier

A literature always arrives at its destination.

As a working hypothesis, I'll oppose two generic models of literary history. According to the romantic one, literatures evolve from oral roots. According to the classical one, speech is not the origin, but instead there is a sort of arche-writing, the writing of a language no one speaks, a dead language. I will try to show why what is called postmodernism conforms to the second model. Which is to say, show that the regime of the uncanny within which postmodernism operates is the very definition of classicism.

In his book on nationalism, *Imagined Communities*, Benedict Anderson refers to "Marx's own failure to explicate the crucial pronoun in his memorable formulation of 1848 [in the *Manifesto*]: 'The proletariat of each country must, of course, first of all settle matters with *its own* bourgeoisie.'"[1] The following remarks are inspired by an analogous discomfort that some of us in literary studies feel as we observe the resurgence of possessive pronouns with their proprietary claims: *its own literature*, my literature, or, even worse, our literature. This is something we had thought to have done with, that we had hoped to have done with, about which we had decided to behave as if we had had done with. We were not prepared for the return of national rubrics.

A bit of history here, since it's history that returns and since structuralism itself has ended up by being a historical reference. Not that lit-

---

[1] Anderson, *Imagined Communities: Reflections on the Origin and the Spread of Nationalism* (London: Verso, 1983), 13.

erary history is necessarily nationalist, but its canonical form, shaped
by nineteenth-century national systems of education, is nonetheless
the history of *a* literature, which is to say, of a national literature. And
if someone like Lanson abjures Taine's geographical determinism,
refusing to open his *History of French Literature* onto a panoramic view
of the landscape of France, it's only to replace it with a portrait of the
Frenchman that adds the gratuitousness of bureaucratic psychology to
the profundity of the Guide Michelin.

The future we were preparing, twenty-five years ago or so, was
meant to protect us against or to cut us off from these ideological practices, these leftovers of the ideology of Frenchness. Should we, perhaps, look back to the 1960s, to the time when we were students? Following the New Criticism, the science or theory of literature was made
the order of the day precisely because it was seen as opening onto a
discussion of literature that could ignore the impositions of national
ideology. It was supposed to offer us access to a planet without borders
in which we could talk about literature without specifying in which
language we spoke, a literature where no visa was necessary. In the
structuralist shift from the history of literatures to the theory of literature, it was no less important to strip literature of its plural determi-
nations than to cross what was then called the epistemological frontier,
abandoning the empirical, contingent data of history for the laws of
science.

I borrow the model of this theory of literature from Gérard
Genette since, undoubtedly because of his background, he is the one
who sets it most forcefully in opposition to literary history. Genette sets
the right tone in giving an ironically Kantian twist to the text that lays
out his program: "Raisons de la critique pure" (Reasons of pure criticism), he calls it.[2] For, if one restores its Kantian meaning to the concept of purity (pure reason, pure practical reason, etc.), Genette's literary theory is above all a history of pure literature. Paul Valéry was
outraged by first lines of novels that go, "The Marquise left at five
o'clock." But the novel is not alone in suffering from this notational
arbitrariness. A pure history of literature is one that would escape
equally contingent formulations, such as "Montaigne wrote the *Essais*."

---

[2] Genette, "Raisons de la critique pure," in *Figures 2* (Paris: Seuil, 1969).

At this level, the anecdotal contingencies of Lanson's life-and-work case studies no longer enter into the account. Significantly, in Genette, the quotation that sounds most often is probably the sentence where Valéry imagines—in the opening lecture of his course on *poétique*— the possibility of a history of literature without proper names. In second place there would be the Borgesian utopia of a literature conceived "as a homogeneous and reversible space where neither the stylistic marks nor the inventive priorities of the individual author would have a place."[3] But, among the reversible features, we would probably place the linguistic ones. Borges's fantasy in "Pierre Ménard author of the *Quixote*" implies that *Don Quixote* could exist in French as well as in Spanish, that *Don Quixote* does not belong to a specific national language.

Two books marked a threshold, at least in the French context. Their titles had the status of a manifesto: *Theory of Literature*, the anthology of Russian formalist texts published in 1966 by Todorov in the Tel Quel collection, and *Literary Theory*, the translation of René Wellek and Austin Warren's famous *Theory of Literature*, which in 1970 inaugurated the Poétique series edited by Genette and Todorov. What literature were they talking about? It was neither French, nor American, nor South American. It was just literature. That was thirty years ago.

But at the time Wellek and Warren's book was already twenty years old, and the context in which it first appeared was not that of France in the 1960s but America in the 1940s. The stakes of its campaign for literary theory owed as much to World War II as it did to the New Criticism; which is to say, theory was promoted as the antidote to the nationalist fragmentation into which literary history was dragging literature. "Imparfait en cela que plusieurs" (Imperfect due to its very plurality), Mallarmé wrote, thinking of languages; it is even more true for nations; literary theory, however, must stand guard against its being true for literature. "Like humanity," wrote Wellek and Warren, "literature is one."[4] An essential part of literary theory's program is the separation of the teaching of languages from that of literature; one must not intermix

---

[3] Genette, *Figures* (Paris: Seuil, 1966), 125.

[4] Wellek and Warren, *Theory of Literature* (London: Harcourt Brace Jovanovich, 1975), 50.

the pedagogy of the multiple with that of the universal. The importance unduly given to linguistic barriers in literature is responsible, they said, for "the very close association between Romantic (mostly linguistic) nationalism and the rise of modern organized literary history" (51), to which the institutional association of "literature and teaching of a language" (51) attests. Literary history, responsible for joining the study of literature to that of language, leads literature into nationalist fragmentation. Literary theory aims at the reverse. "It is important to think of literature as a totality and to trace the growth and development of literature without regard to linguistic distinctions," they said (49). There is a Kantian spirit in these pages, too: you must, therefore you can; it is important, therefore it is possible.

The nationalism from which Wellek and Warren sought to extricate literature was European. In 1968, at the time of their French translation, the context was totally different: it had become an anti-European, postcolonialist third world's nationalism.

It's not absurd to imagine that when he registered his dissertation proposal in 1957 Derrida was intending to attack the dream of a pure criticism, of a history of pure literature. I cannot help regretting that he never wrote it. It's a dissertation I would have liked to read. He intended, he later wrote, to "bend more or less violently, the techniques of transcendental phenomenology to the needs of elaborating a new theory of literature."[5] Its very title, "The Ideality of the Literary Object," is not fundamentally different from the objective Genette set for a structuralist criticism, namely, determining "the modes of existence and the operating conditions of the literary object" (*Figures*). Wellek and Warren had also devoted a whole chapter to "the mode of existence of a literary work of art." But in their case, as in Genette's, the ideality of the literary object is what allows for pure criticism, what allows criticism to be pure, while Derrida opposes the very concept of pure criticism. For if the literary object is ideal, it is not free; its ideality is "chained" to a natural language, an actual language, defined by its historicogeographical inscription. In other words, contrary to Wellek and Warren's claim, it is not possible to protect literature from lan-

---

[5] Derrida, "The Time of a Thesis," in *Philosophy in France Today*, ed. Alan Montefiore (New York: Columbia University Press, 1983), 37.

guage: there is no literature without history, and the history of literature is not pure history because there is no pure literature.

The earliest texts by Derrida bear many marks of this very project.
For instance, in his introduction to *The Origin of Geometry*, after laying
out Husserl's theory of the ideality of the word—that is, the word as an
ideality that cannot be confused "with any of its empirical, phonetic or
graphic materializations"—Derrida cites the example Husserl uses for
his demonstration: the word *Löwe* (lion), as ideal as it may be, "in
being a German word rests essentially tied to a spatio-temporal reality;
in its very ideal objectivity, it continues its solidarity with the factual
existence of a given language, and thus the factitious subjectivity of a
speaking community."[6] There is no language without spacing. The literary object, as ideal as it might be, cannot shed the geopolitical
dimension of spacing. On the model of Freud's famous line, "The psyche is extended," we could say that literature is chained—if only by
the intermediary of the language in which it is written—to a geopoli-
tics that theory of pure literature knows nothing about and that it wants
to know nothing about.

I will not go into the problem here of whether Derrida, even if he
didn't write his dissertation, has ever stopped working over this question. But he has done it cautiously, never stepping over the line that
leads from natural language to national language: the speaking community is not determined by him as a national community. Quite the
opposite, as he said in a text on Jabès at the time: "Place is not the
empirical and national Here of a territory."[7]

The chaining of literature to the facticity of natural languages is not
enough to wear down one's resistance to what Sartre called the nationalization of literature. And, given this resistance, nothing produced as
strongly the feeling of a change of time in me as a page by Jameson
that, in concluding, I would like to comment on. It's the opening of
the essay where, on the occasion of rereading Claude Simon's *Les
Corps conducteurs*, Jameson looks back at the nouveau roman (the

[6] Derrida, introduction to *L'Origine de la géométrie*, by Edmund Husserl (Paris:
Presses Universitaires de France, 1962), 58, 62.

[7] Derrida, *L'Écriture et la différence* (Paris: Seuil, 1967), 101.

experimental prose that was contemporary with structuralism and the cult of *literarnost*, literature as such). Twenty years later, Jameson has reread the novel. He is shocked. It's not so much that the book has aged. Something stranger has happened to it. It has been national-ized. This book, on rereading, seems strangely French to him, more French than ever, French as never before, French as he would never have suspected it would be possible for it to become. And so he asks himself:

> Do we now feel the Frenchness of this work more strongly and oppres-sively than in previous decades (when writers like Simon simply repre-sented a non-national vanguard production of Literature as such)? Has the fission we associate with the "new social movements," micropolitics and microgroups, now fastened onto national traditions, such that "French literature" is fully as much a badge of local in-group member-ship as contemporary poetry, gay literature, or science fiction? Does not, meanwhile, the competition of the media and so-called cultural studies signal a transformation in the role and space of mass culture today which is greater than a mere enlargement and which may increas-ingly leave no space whatsoever for literary "classics" of this kind?[8]

I would like to pause over these questions. They eloquently show the distance we have traveled from a structuralist epistemology: we've passed from a space defined by the conjunction of literature and (nationlessness) nonnationality to a space that disjoins them. It's because we've stopped believing in literariness that we are retroactively seeing the marks of nationality burgeon on the pages of the *nouveau roman*. Yet somehow, this appearance of the national parameter does not require that we revise our hostility to literature's being involved in national programs. Better no literature at all than a nationalized liter-ature: and our wishes are granted. The nationalization of works of lit-erature is a function of our entry into the space of postliteracy (the postreaderly, the postliterary).

However, this national motive has a strange status. It comes back— but, precisely, not with a vengeance—it resurfaces desensitized, anes-thetized, disaffected, defused. This frozen quality reappears each time Jameson refers to a national theme. In the preface to *Postmodernism*, for

[8] Jameson, *Postmodernism; or, The Cultural Logic of Late Capitalism* (Durham, N.C.: Duke University Press, 1990), 131.

example, he writes, "The postliteracy of the late capitalist world reflects not only the absence of any great collective project but also the unavailability of the older national language itself." The postliterate unavailability of national languages condemns the literary work of art to the ontological status of the pastiche, which he defines as "the wearing of a linguistic mask, speech in a dead language" (17).

According to Valéry, every page of literature contains one message: I am a page of literature. Today it says: I am a page of the discourse "formerly called literature." I am an extinct species, speaking an extinct language. In relation to Pynchon, Jameson thus evokes the "non-great-power languages or extinct provincial traditions" (361). One has the strange feeling of a photographic negative, with all the so-called living languages uncannily frozen into dead languages. Just as, in Heidegger, utensils are noticed when they've stopped being functional, so national languages make their appearance in the postmodern space only because they are out of work. Literature has been mapped back onto the national, but only after the national itself has been disaffected, defamiliarized, invested with a simulacral dimension. The past being for us something past, its return—and that of the national—takes place in a spectral mode, like a ghost. Put very briefly: the hypothesis of postliteracy allows us to give national languages the status of dead languages. The concept of postliteracy—which I understand to mean that literature is something of the past for us, that literature itself has become a dead language—is a tool that very efficiently produces the opposite of that reality effect for which Barthes had become so famous. Let us call it the irreality effect: the numbing citationality that gives rise to a kind of generalized Pompeiization. It's what Jameson deploys when he writes of Perec's *Life: A User's Guide*, "It is as though the text and its dead model look back on all the agitation of human history from the standpoint of a geological epoch in which human life had become extinct on the planet" (149).

Why are these effects so seductive, so efficacious? I am tempted to say that it's because the motif of a postliterate age cuts two ways. Undoubtedly it announces that we've left the literary space. That everything no longer exists, as in the time of Mallarmé, to end up in a book. These days we are happy with a film clip, a sound bite, an interview. But, for starters, I will take note of the fact that the self-proclaimed enemies of literature don't have exclusive rights to this theme. A large number of recently published novels in France dramatize, in one way or another, the extinction of the language in which they are written.

If for a postliterate reading the medium is the message, for a literary one it works the other way round: the message has become the death of the medium. This theme is recurrent in recent works of Renaud Camus, Marie Redonnet, Sollers, and Pascal Quignard, who in one of his "little treatises" dwells on the destruction of "the last ritual murmur of a centuries-old language." And elsewhere he imagines an Egyptian sage hearing someone mention a new language: "Why do you want me to care about an emerging dialect? Greek, is that how you called it?"[9] Literature is not necessarily on the loser's side when treated as a dead language. Perhaps literature will begin precisely with this linguistic defamiliarization that allows the language it speaks to appear as something dead. Literature is what permits the dead to return. Ghosts, in other words, are not romantic; they are classical.

In this sense I am tempted to say that the concept of postliteracy is a particularly effective literary theme. And that its current pervasiveness might be the symptom of a paradoxical return to the classical model of literary history, the one according to which a literature is never competing with a vernacular, but always with a dead language. And, when Latin is gone, one treats the vernacular itself as a dead language.

I will close, as I began, with Benedict Anderson. *Imagined Communities* gives spoken languages an important role to play in the genesis of nations, but it's a negative one. It associates the nationalization of space with the desacralization of the imaginary community constituted by medieval Christianity, a community that was united through a language its members didn't speak. The progress of prints, in instituting the written language as a transcription of the spoken one, led to the unidimensional flattening of the medieval literary space that characterizes the vernacular territorialization of literature. The nationalization of literature thus begins when literature, forgetting its connection to the dead language, enters the romantic regime of what Girard has called internal mediation. The classical concept of literature, the inher-

[9] Quignard, *Petits traités*, vol. 4 (Paris: Maeght, 1990), 70, 49.

itor of this two-tiered linguistic space, always returns in one way or another to a dead language, anterior to the nationalist and vernacular territorialization of writing. The irreality effect produced by the literary uncanny produces the impression that the vernacular itself has been transformed into a dead language, which gives the strange feeling of being part of a restored sacred community called literature.[10]

[10] See "How Can One Be French?" the essay I added to the paperback edition of *A New History of French Literature* (Cambridge, Mass.: Harvard University Press, 1994).

More Speech
on Free Speech

Annabel Patterson

Give me the liberty to know, to utter, and to argue freely according
to conscience, *above all liberties.*—Milton[1]

It is style which makes it possible to act effectively, but not
absolutely; it is style which enables us to find a harmony between
the pursuit of ends essential to us, and a regard for the views, the
sensibilities, the aspirations of those to whom the problem may
appear in another light; it is style which is the deference that action
pays to uncertainty; it is above all style through which power defers
to reason.—Robert Oppenheimer[2]

I write from an old but still-growing conviction that there is one category of writing that literary history must adopt as not only within
its province but, in ways that we are just beginning to grasp or are
grasping for the second time, constitutive of it. I refer to the complex
idea comprising the two quotations at the head of this essay and everything they encompass, separately and together: that is to say, to the
legal and political history of libertarian thought, and to the manner
in which that history has been not simply recorded but made by the
verbal power of superior minds in the service of something larger
than themselves.

I propose here to challenge an argument recently made by Stanley
Fish, under a title typical of Fish in its well-considered tactics of shock:
"There's No Such Thing as Free Speech and It's a Good Thing Too."[3]
Fish speaks evidently for the movement that has been stigmatically des-
ignated "political correctness," but that might neutrally be described as

---

[1] *Areopagitica*, in *Complete Prose Works*, ed. Don M. Wolfe et al., 8 vols. (New
Haven, Conn.: Yale University Press, 1953–82), 2:560.

[2] Cited in Walker Gibson, "Literary Judicial Style," *New York University Law
Review* 36 (1961): 924.

[3] *Boston Review* 17, no. 1 (1992): 3, 23–26, rpt. in *Debating P.C.: The Controversy
over Political Correctness on College Campuses*, ed. Paul Berman (New York: Dell, 1992).

a defensive league of minorities of all sorts. Its proponents sometimes argue for the right to assert their identity without themselves becoming the targets of insulting speech (it hurts their feelings) by those who think differently. Fish begins by noting that "many on the liberal and progressive left have been disconcerted" to find the concept of free speech invoked by neoconservatives;[4] he therefore attempts to nullify the usefulness of First Amendment thinking for *either* side, a move that, were it to be taken seriously, could have disastrous consequences.

As someone whose interest in the history of censorship has largely centered on early modern England, I have been encouraged in the formulation of this response by the appearance of Anthony Lewis's *Make No Law*, a history of the civil libel case of *New York Times v. Sullivan*, which was successfully appealed before the Supreme Court in 1963.[5] This work, part legal history, part political persuasion, and part *literary history*, brings to readers outside the legal profession not only an account of the contribution made to First Amendment theory by the Sullivan case itself, but also the compelling story of what happened between 1791, when the First Amendment was added to the Constitution, and 1963, when its central purpose was clarified.

One of the classic articulations of free speech doctrine that Lewis appropriately recycles was that of Oliver Wendell Holmes in the 1929 case *United States v. Schwimmer*. Rosika Schwimmer was a pacifist who emigrated from Hungary and applied for United States citizenship. In her interview with immigration authorities, she refused to say that she would take up arms to defend her new country; her application was rejected, and the Supreme Court upheld the denial of citizenship. Holmes wrote into his dissenting opinion words that should reverberate now more than ever: "Some of her answers might excite popular

[4] This argument is to be distinguished from the leftist critique of an Enlightenment concept of free speech on the grounds that it is anachronistic to the social structures of late capitalism, where ever more complex property rights have overtaken the simple confrontation, if it ever existed, between the state and the individual. Cf. Alan Hutchinson: "The question of whose entitlements are to be protected from whose interference becomes a contested matter of political choice rather than the correct application of abstract principle" ("Talking the Good Life from Free Speech to Democratic Dialogue," *Yale Journal of Law and Liberation* 1 [1989]: 21).

[5] Lewis, *Make No Law: The Sullivan Case and the First Amendment* (New York: Random House, 1991).

prejudice, but if there is any principle of the Constitution that more imperatively calls for attachment than any other it is the principle of free thought—*not free thought for those who agree with us but freedom for the thought that we hate*" (88). Now that we have coined the phrase *hate speech* to refer to what, for Fish and others, constitutes the primary exception to First Amendment principles, such reminders that "freedom for the thought that we hate" is the final test of those problematic abstractions, "freedom" and "liberty," are particularly desirable. As another immigrant to this country, and one who grew up in Milton's, I share his conviction that freedom of speech is "above all liberties" or, as it would today be argued, that it is the *fundamental* liberty, undergirding and enabling the others. Milton would have agreed with the distinction drawn by Ronald Dworkin between the instrumental justification for First Amendment principles, a sort of "collective bet that free speech will do us more good than harm over the long run," and the "constitutive" justification that, in classical liberal terms, defines responsible moral agents as those who insist "on making up their own minds about what is good or bad in life or in politics, or what is true or false in matters of justice or faith."[6] Like Dworkin, Milton clearly believed that the two justifications, means and ends, were not incompatible but intertwined.

The role of the liberal in contemporary academic culture is a thankless task, since one must be prepared to use terms like *fundamental* unironically, in full anticipation of the mockery that deconstructive modes of analysis and other skepticisms have established as the normative sign of cleverness. I would not have risked this exposure had I not been provoked by Fish's use of Milton's *Areopagitica*, which clarified for me two dilemmas at the heart of liberalism that are here, with respect to Milton, structurally related. The first is the proclivity of any right or "liberty" to run into difficulties at the point where it moves from abstraction to application, where it becomes vulnerable to such tests as the seemingly inarguable exception, competing entitlements, or entropic vagueness; the second, that human idealism seems to retain an illogical confidence in the persuasive and educative power of

---

[6] Dworkin, "The Coming Battles over Free Speech," *New York Review of Books*, 11 June 1992, 56–57.

certain abstractions, a belief that does not so much overlook their vulnerabilities as imagine a talking cure. This second dilemma operates partly in the realm of law and politics and partly in the realm of rhetoric and style, revealing the link between my two epigraphs. For by Oppenheimer's claim that style makes for effective action in the territory of rights (effective *because* persuasive), and in his brilliant proposal that style is "the deference that action pays to uncertainty," we can recognize the foresight and temerity of Milton's *Areopagitica* and other expressive acts whose ancestor it became.

The *Areopagitica* is probably still regarded as one of the founding documents of libertarian thought, its obvious limitations notwithstanding. Those limitations begin with the fact that Milton, attacking the 1643 Licensing Act of the Long Parliament for reinstating in the republic the worst features of monarchical censorship, focuses only on prior restraint of the press, or prelicensing; and they end with a single sentence toward the end of the long pamphlet, where Milton, seemingly as an afterthought, admits certain exceptions to the new freedom to publish for which he is arguing: "I mean not tolerated Popery, and open superstition . . . that also which is impious or evil absolutely either against faith or maners no law can possibly permit, that intends not to unlaw itself" (2:565). It is customary to criticize Milton for the religious intolerance in this exception;[7] whereas the more problematic statement occurs, as it does in First Amendment debate today, at the point where Milton grapples with what is "impious or evil absolutely either against faith or *maners*." Strictly speaking, Milton is excepting speech crimes against customs, rather than taste; but the clash between his own "absolutely" and the relativism of "maners" is only a microinstance of the clash between the exception as a whole syntactical unit and the grand sonorities of the *Areopagitica*. Milton registers the deference that action pays to uncertainty, both epistemologically ("Yet is it not impossible that [Truth] may have more shapes than one" [2:563]) and socially, in terms of an idealized image of what motivates sectarianism; that is to say, diversity of *conviction*:

> A little generous prudence, a little forbearance of one another, and
> som grain of charity might win all these diligences to joyn, and unite

---

[7] Of course such criticism can come from any quarter (see Lewis, 52–53).

into one generall and brotherly search after Truth; could we but forgoe this Prelaticall tradition of crowding free consciences and Christian liberties into canons and precepts of men. . . . As if, while the Temple of the Lord was building, some cutting, some squaring the marble, others hewing the cedars, there should be a sort of irrationall men who could not consider there must be many schisms and many dissections made in the quarry and in the timber, ere the house of God can be built. And when every stone is laid artfully together, it cannot be united into a continuity, it can but be contiguous in this world; neither can every peece of the building be of one form; nay rather the perfection consists in this, that out of many moderat varieties and brotherly dissimilitudes that are not vastly disproportionall arises the goodly and the gracefull symmetry that commends the whole pile and structure. (2:554–55)

This vision of persons of opposed convictions busy, despite themselves, building the Temple of a seventeenth-century theocracy has utopian force that far exceeds the religious constraints of its own moment. Fish, however, does not begin with an account of Milton's tract as a whole, still less by taking cognizance of the extent to which it was ahead of its time conceptually, or of the role it has played historically in creating a liberal rhetoric that penetrated seventeenth- and eighteenth-century culture in England both consciously and subliminally, and passed from there to the early American republic. He begins instead with Milton's exception of "Popery, and open superstition," which, he argues, opens the door logically to exceptions of *all* kinds (and those incapable of advance specification). Milton's exceptions (which might have been local blindnesses, or might equally have been last-minute precautions against the censorship of his own pamphlet) are made the basis for an argument that it is theoretically impossible *not* to discover exceptions to protected speech. However, instead of taking the hard road of jurisprudence, which has fought through that question with respect to obscenity, defamation, and "fighting words" (those kinds of insulting speech that are deemed likely to provoke immediate violence in the community), Fish chooses to carry the idea of exceptionality to its deconstructive conclusion. "I want to say," he writes, "that all affirmations of freedom of expression are like Milton's, dependent for their force on an exception that literally carves out the space in which expression can then emerge":

I do not mean that expression (saying something) is a realm whose integrity is sometimes compromised by certain restrictions, but that restriction, in the form of an underlying articulation of the world that necessarily (if silently) negates alternatively possible articulations, is constitutive of expression. . . . The exception to unregulated expression is not a negative restriction, but a positive hollowing out of value— we are for *this*, which means we are against *that*—in relation to which meaningful assertion can then occur.

This deconstructive logic is then applied to the one exception that First Amendment jurisprudence has recognized, though only briefly: the category of fighting words. This too, like exceptionality more generally, becomes infinitely expansive. Fish invokes as support for this argument Oliver Wendell Holmes:

As Justice Holmes said long ago (in Gitlow v. New York), every idea is an incitement to somebody. . . . every sentence is potentially, in some situation that might occur tomorrow, a fighting word and therefore a candidate for regulation. . . . If the category is not a formal one, but one that varies with the varying sensitivities of different groups, there is no utterance that it does not include, and we are led to the conclusion that there is nothing for the First Amendment to protect, no such thing as "speech alone" or speech separable from harmful conduct. (23)

But in fact Fish's point about speech that may theoretically offend some group at some time in the future ignores the powerful legal doctrine, within the history of First Amendment interpretation, of "clear and present danger" to the society, and the gradually increasing specificity of what must be meant by both "present" and "danger." This doctrine was, moreover, created by Oliver Wendell Holmes himself, in relation to the 1919 case *Schenck v. United States*, which was prosecuted under the reprehensible Espionage Act passed in the atmosphere of rabid patriotism generated by the First World War. Although in *Schenck* Holmes did not use the doctrine to support the appellants, he subsequently, in *Abrams v. United States*, also heard in 1919, restated his "clear and present danger" doctrine and brought it explicitly into line with libertarian principles. "If you have no doubt of your premises or your power," Holmes wrote then, "and want a certain result with all your heart you naturally [wish to] express your wishes in law and sweep away all opposition":

But when men have realized that time has upset many fighting faiths, they may come to believe even more than they believe the very foundations of their own conduct that the ultimate good desired is better reached by free trade in ideas—that the best test of truth is the power of the thought to get itself accepted in the competition of the market. . . . That, at any rate, is the theory of our Constitution. It is an experiment, as all life is an experiment. Every year if not every day we have to wager our salvation upon some prophecy based upon imperfect knowledge. While that experiment is part of our system I think that we should be eternally vigilant against attempts to check the expression of opinions that we loathe and believe to be fraught with death, *unless they so imminently threaten immediate interference with the lawful and pressing purposes of the law that an immediate check is required to save the country.* (Lewis, 78)

Now, a reader who knows his *Areopagitica* as well as Fish must do should recognize in Holmes's peroration precisely those ideas of Milton's that established the premises (and much of the rhetoric) of libertarian theory. Compare, for instance, Holmes's emphasis on the need for a "free trade in ideas" with Milton's own commercial metaphor: "Truth and understanding are not such wares as to be monopoliz'd and traded in by tickets and statutes and standards. We must not think to make a staple commodity of all the knowledge in the Land" (2:535–36). And again, with respect to Holmes's emphasis on our "imperfect knowledge," we should remember Milton's warning: "The light which we have gain'd, was giv'n us, not to be ever staring on, but by it to discover onward things more remote from our knowledge" (2:550); or again: "Yet if all cannot be of one mind, as who looks they should be? this doubtles is more wholesome, . . . that many be tolerated, rather than all compell'd" (2:565). Indeed, Holmes's statement that "every day we have to wager our salvation upon some prophecy based upon imperfect knowledge" brilliantly encapsulates the journey taken by libertarian thought since the Reformation to the stage we have now reached in the West, where the secularization of religious choice and duty into the options of democracy is now widely acknowledged, however much we may dispute what role economics has played in that story.

It has been shown by Richard Polenberg that prior to his dissenting opinion Holmes had been reading, among other works on free-

dom of speech, John Locke's *Two Treatises on Civil Government.*[8] Among
those other works, we might well imagine that Holmes had found time
for Milton's *Areopagitica*, and was able to discover the central proposi-
tions of free speech that survive its historically specific or prudential
limitations. Indeed, Holmes's own proposition, that "men have realized that time has upset many fighting faiths," which gave Polenberg
the title for his book, suggests that his reading included the documents
of a time when competing religious faiths were the central issue.

Toward the end of his essay, Fish replays a rhetorical move familiar
from his previous writings—to offer a critique of his own position, but
only in order to rebut it:

> It could be said, however, that I myself mistake the nature of the work
> done by freely tolerated speech because I am too focused on short-run
> outcomes and fail to understand that the good effects of speech will be
> realized not in the present, but in a future whose emergence regulation
> could only inhibit. . . . This forward-looking view of what the First
> Amendment protects has a great appeal, in part because it continues in
> a secular form the Puritan celebration of millenarian hopes, but it
> imposes a requirement so severe that one would expect more justifica-
> tion than is usually provided. The requirement is that we endure what-
> ever pain racist and hate speech inflicts for the sake of a future whose
> emergence we can only take on faith. In a specifically religious vision
> like Milton's this makes perfect sense . . . but in the context of a poli-
> tics that puts its trust in the world . . . it raises more questions than it
> answers and could be seen as the other prong of a strategy designed to
> de-legitimize the complaints of victimized groups. (24)

It is reasonable to suspect this move as an indirect answer to the
prophetic strain in Oliver Wendell Holmes, whose authority Fish had
invoked in the opposite direction.[9] In a way, it confirms my inference
that Holmes had been reading Milton and had produced his own

[8] Polenberg, *Fighting Faiths: The Abrams Case, the Supreme Court, and Free Speech*
(New York: Viking, 1987), 224–27.

[9] In fact Fish cites Holmes mistakenly. Rather than supporting Fish's position,
Holmes's statement that "every idea is an incitement" appears as part of his *dissenting*
opinion in *Gitlow v. New York* and is followed by this critical qualification: "*But* whatever
may be the thought of the redundant discourse before us it had no chance of starting
a *present* conflagration. If in the long run the beliefs expressed in proletarian dictatorship are destined to be accepted by the dominant forces of the community, the only
meaning of free speech is that they should be given their chance" (italics added).

secularized version of Milton's liberationist vision for a society that, at least in the northeastern states, had been created not only in escape from English religious repression and later defiance of English government but also in the spirit of the religious and political dissent that early modern English thinkers like Milton and Locke had dared to articulate.

But Fish is unconcerned with history, whether it be the circumstances in which Milton and Locke and other early modern Englishmen challenged the censorships of their day, at considerable risk to themselves, or the equally threatening circumstances (retold by Anthony Lewis) that led to the gradual emergence in American legal and political culture of First Amendment protections as we now know them. Fish recommends that we abandon the past. "People cling to First Amendment pieties," he writes disparagingly, "because they do not wish to face what they correctly take to be the alternative":

> That alternative is *politics*, the realization . . . that decisions about what is and is not protected in the realm of expression will rest not on principle or firm doctrine, but on the ability of some persons to interpret—recharacterize or rewrite—principle and doctrine in ways that lead to the protection of speech they want heard and the regulation of speech they want silenced. . . . When the First Amendment is successfully invoked the result is not a victory for free speech in the face of a challenge from politics, but a *political victory* won by the party that has managed to wrap its agenda in the mantle of free speech. (25)

Such a political free-for-all can ultimately be resolved (though he does not say this) only in the ballot box. I doubt that those groups for whom Fish claims to speak (even if a statistical majority) would in fact profit from such an eventuality.[10] The consequences of *not* maintaining free-

---

[10] As proof of his claim that the hollow space inside the First Amendment is filled only with a Hobbesian politics, Fish cites a recent advertisement placed in the Duke student *Chronicle* by a group that denies the occurrence of the Holocaust. The fact that the advertisement was subtitled "The Case for Free Debate," and that the student editor supposed an obligation to print it, is offered as support for the general contention that all proponents of the First Amendment are unprincipled. The incident *was* freely debated. But rather than focus, as he might have done, on the student editor's confusion about what is and is not covered by the First Amendment (which certainly does not require a newspaper to accept a paid advertisement); rather than provide the kind of clarification that Lewis's *Make No Law* does; rather

dom of speech as the liberty that undergirds all the others can be considered by observing other countries, past and present, that have not done so. Anthony Lewis is correct in observing that English jurisprudence today offers far less protection, especially for newspapers, than does that of the United States; and it is no coincidence that the landmark decision concerning Joyce's *Ulysses* (to which Fish will eventually allude) took place in the United States and not in the United Kingdom.

Fish's conclusion, once the First Amendment has been emptied of content, is that it is up to "us" all to "take responsibility for our verbal performances—*all* of them—and not assume that they are being taken care of by a clause in the Constitution." "Of course," he continues smoothly, "with responsibility come risks, but they have always been our risks and no doctrine of free speech has ever insulated us from them. They are the risks of either allowing or policing the flow of discourse. They are the risks, respectively, of permitting speech that does obvious harm and of shutting off speech in ways that might deny us the benefit of Joyce's *Ulysses* or Lawrence's *Lady Chatterley's Lover* or Titian's paintings." But this is no conclusion at all. Who is "we" in this case—a question that, after his seminal work on "reader response," one might have expected Fish to anticipate? How, precisely, are "we" to assume this responsibility, and by what communal mechanisms shall we agree when harm is "obvious," or when the contested expression is a "benefit" rather than an offense to certain sensitivities? Whose sensibilities will count for most in these arguments, when there are no judges, with First Amendment principles to guide them, to adjudicate between us? None of these procedures, required to replace the current (admittedly imperfect) reliance on ubiquitous protection for speech, are even sketched; and the long, arduous journey from more or less complete government control of the press in early modern England—the position from which Milton revolted—to the more or less complete tolerance by the governing institutions of the United States of all forms of public critique goes unmentioned.

But to return to the question of style: one of Lewis's insights in *Make No Law* is that often it is the *dissenting* or minority opinions that

---

than perform a service in the arena in which universities *are* supposed to occupy a leading role, that is to say, education; Fish merely scorns the student editor and identifies as "hatemongers" the persons who placed the ad.

move society forward. In 1927, in *Whitney v. California*, Louis D. Brandeis delivered a separate opinion on the appeal of Anita Whitney, convicted under a California statute aimed at suppressing the Wobblies. She had helped found the Communist Labor party of California and was sentenced to one to fourteen years in San Quentin. Her conviction was upheld by the Supreme Court; however, Brandeis's opinion, concurring in law but not in spirit, was probably influential in her being pardoned by California's governor. Brandeis said (in terms that Dworkin recognizes as combining the instrumental and constitutive justifications for First Amendment protections, and that have themselves become constitutive of First Amendment thought as we now know it):

> Those who won our independence believed that the final end of the state was to make men free to develop their faculties; and that in its government the deliberative forces should prevail over the arbitrary. They valued liberty both as an end and as a means. They believed liberty to be the secret of happiness and courage to be the secret of liberty. They believed that freedom to think as you will and to speak as you think are means indispensable to the discovery and spread of political truth; that without free speech and assembly discussion would be futile; that with them, discussion affords ordinarily adequate protection against the dissemination of noxious doctrine; that the greatest menace to freedom is an inert people; that public discussion is a public duty; and that *this should be a fundamental principle of the American government.* They recognized the risks to which all human institutions are subject. But they knew that order cannot be secured merely through fear of punishment for its infraction; that it is hazardous to discourage thought, hope and imagination; that fear breeds repression; that repression breeds hate; that hate menaces stable government; that the path of safety lies in the opportunity to discuss freely supposed grievances and proposed remedies; and that the fitting remedy for evil counsels is good ones. . . .
>
> Fear of serious injury alone cannot justify suppression of free speech and assembly. Men feared witches and burnt women. It is the function of speech to free men from the bondage of irrational fears. To justify suppression of free speech there must be reasonable ground to fear that serious evil will result if free speech is practiced. There must be reasonable ground to believe that the danger apprehended is imminent. . . . If there be time to expose through discussion the falsehood and fallacies, to avert the evil by the processes of education, the remedy to be applied is more speech, not enforced silence. Only an emergency can justify repression. (Lewis, 85–86)

"If the words of Holmes and Brandeis were no more than beautifully expressed protests against the intolerance of their day," Lewis remarked (in re-recording them for a wider audience), "they would not be remembered except perhaps as literary exercises. But they were much more. To an extent exceptional in our constitutional history, those dissents became the law. The Holmes-Brandeis views of free speech persuaded the Country, and, in time, the Court. . . . Holmes and Brandeis had no political or judicial power beyond their votes on the Supreme Court, two of nine. *Their power was in their rhetoric*" (89; italics added).

Their power was in their rhetoric because their rhetoric was informed by a certain kind of power that we can call "literary" in a larger and less dismissive sense than Lewis here employs. The clearest sign of literary intention is Brandeis's invocation of "thought, hope and *imagination*" as conjoined qualities that help sustain and advance civilized negotiations; and anyone can recognize the aphoristic, satiric, and protofeminist bite of "Men feared witches and burnt women." But more "fundamental" to the persuasive power of Brandeis's rhetoric (and it is much to the point that he himself uses the term as a political principle grounded in American history) is the use of what Bruce Ackerman has called "liberating abstraction."[11] Almost every word in Brandeis's famous statement is, in fact, an abstraction, but an abstraction grounded in the convictions of real persons ("those who won our independence") in the past and perpetually capable of being reinhabited, not anachronistically, by convictions of our own.

Finally, it is in the spirit of Brandeis's advice, that "the remedy to be applied is more speech, not enforced silence," that I have chosen to argue in public with a colleague and longtime friend. That we should fight over John Milton is surely a sign that, whatever else happens, both our hearts are in the right place.

---

[11] Ackerman, "Liberating Abstraction," *University of Chicago Law Review* 59 (1992): 317–47; this argument was opposed by Frank Easterbrook, "Abstraction and Authority," *University of Chicago Law Review* 59 (1992): 349–80. In the opening pages of Ackerman's article, in which he debates how expansively judges should interpret the abstract language of the Bill of Rights, the term *fundamental* occurs with unashamed frequency.

TEXTUAL CONQUESTS: ON READERLY COMPETENCE AND "MINORITY" LITERATURE

Doris Sommer

How clever and well trained the reader feels with a novel like Cirilo Villaverde's *Cecilia Valdés* (1882) in hand! Although the heroine's obscure background is blocked and delayed for the narrator, readers have always understood it immediately and have until now enjoyed a condescending grandeur. But on my reading, the white narrator's clumsiness is purposefully theatrical. More than merely dramatize the unreliability of a modern storyteller, his bumbling brings into focus a racially coded resistance to the clear information that black informants can and finally do tell. Each time the narrator or a pale protagonist turns a deaf ear to the slaves' stories, it is as if not listening were an effort to keep the text of Cecilia's life (and theirs) blank, white. The gesture is one of those defensive denials that end self-destructively. To defend the illusory privilege that comes with whiting out her history, Cecilia must ignore the details that make her so compromisingly colorful, so available for the final tragedy of misfired affairs. And to protect the privilege of our expert reading, we are also tempted to ignore colorful competitors for narrative competence. Rather than defer too soon to black rivals, we flatter ourselves by sparring with the obscurely informed narrator who frames the novel.

Who suspected that he is framing our reading, too? Readers to date have suspected no such trap, but suspicion may wedge itself in if we notice an interpretive problem: paradoxically, it is the apparent lack of problems for interpretation in a narrative that seems to beguile the narrator. It is the facile competence that makes the textual conquest so ridiculously easy that the conqueror without contenders may find himself at the butt of an interpretive joke. Competent readers compete with the narrator, who knows himself to be incompetent. He makes a spectacle of his own ignorance because he knows, unlike us, how difficult it is to know anything about others. My purpose as a student of Villaverde's brilliantly benighted narrator is to call attention to our presumptive, facile understanding. I want to argue that a readerly will to knowledge has been trespassing signs of social difference (in books like Villaverde's) and overstepping the Keep Out signs erected in some "minority" writing. Were these signs respected, they might contain the self-flattering claim to competence by privileged readers and so perhaps restrain the social power that follows from presuming to know.[1]

The very fact that I am able to call self-critical attention to our culturebound limitations is to position myself in a history of reading; it is to historicize an interpretive option (to stop short of confident comprehension) available now that universalizing and homogenizing discourses have become suspect. The relevance of history for literary criticism, in other words, can go beyond appreciating the contingent practices of producing literature that are featured in most of the articles that compose this special issue of *Modern Language Quarterly*. History can, and should, also attend to the contingencies of reading.[2] Until now, Villaverde's admirers have not noticed his narrator's purposeful self-demotion in deference to black informants, if the interpretive literature about his novel is any indication.[3] Instead, readers

---

[1] A more developed reading of the novel, "Who Can Tell? Filling in the Blanks for Villaverde," is forthcoming in *American Literary History*.

[2] Some provocative work in this direction is offered by Pierre Bourdieu, "Reading, Readers, the Literate, Literature," in *In Other Words: Essays towards a Reflexive Sociology*, trans. Matthew Adamson (Stanford, Calif.: Stanford University Press, 1990), 94–105; and by David Perkins in this volume. See especially Marianna Torgovnick: "I do not object to the 'we' voice in and of itself. What I object to is the easy slide from 'I' to 'we' that takes place almost unconsciously for many users of the first-person plural or its equivalents—and is often the hidden essence of cultural criticism. This slide can make the 'we' function not as a device to link writer and reader, or as a particularized group voice, or even the voice of 'the culture,' but rather as a covert, and sometimes coercive, universal" ("The Politics of the 'We,'" *South Atlantic Quarterly* 91 [1992]: 48–49). I am grateful to Marshall Brown for these suggestions.

[3] See the literature review by Imeldo Alvarez García, prologue to *Cecilia Valdés*, by Cirilo Villaverde, 2 vols. (Havana: Editorial Letras Cubanas, 1981), 1:5–46; also Roberto Friol, "La novela cubana del siglo diecinueve," *Unión*, December, 1968: 178.

have been praising the novel's sociological information, its local color, and praising themselves for garnering this intelligence from the storyteller's spotty accounts. Readerly satisfaction has followed from assumptions of hermeneutic competence, as if this racially refracted narrative offered no enduring resistance to competent interpretation.

But postmodern readers "are growing wary of the hermeneutic circularity," in George Steiner's words.[4] The old habits have a way of violating the messages moved from one social and cultural context to another, while interpreters are loath to acknowledge the remainder lost in asymmetrical translation (let us say in the transaction between a Cuban slave and his master). The problems raised by presumptive, masterful understanding are both epistemological and ethical, and they ring familiar now that postmodern skepticism has lowered the volume on masterly discourses to hear some competing, even incommensurate voices.

Obviously, the kind of partial deafness, or readerly incompetence, I can advocate for today's self-critical reader is not the kind that Allan Bloom and others have lamented as a failure of education. Incompetence for me is a modest-making goal. It is the goal of respecting the distances and the refusals that some texts have been broadcasting to our still-deaf ears. Here my language feels the lack of a transitive verb derived from *modesty*. Perhaps *to chasten* comes close, although the morality that *chastity* suggests may be more self-denying than attentive to limitations. *To constrain* is an available verb, but it carries a coercive rather than an ethical charge. Modesty's intransitive nature to date may be no surprise for those of us who inhabit carefree, or careless, languages of criticism and who can easily name the contrary movement: to approach, explore, interpret, freely associate, understand, empathize, assimilate.

It is a movement that some minority narrators decide to frustrate. One is Rigoberta Menchú, in her testimonial narrative about the Maya Quiché struggle in Guatemala.[5] Her 1984 account, ranging from daily ritual to military strategies, is a response to the evidently

---

[4] Steiner, *After Babel: Aspects of Language and Translation* (London: Oxford University Press, 1975), 355.

[5] Menchú, *I, Rigoberta Menchú: An Indian Woman in Guatemala,* ed. and intro. Elisabeth Burgos-Debray, trans. Ann Wright (London: Verso, 1984).

friendly interrogations of a Venezuelan anthropologist. But Menchú's quincentennial experience with Spanish-speaking conquerors taught her not to share communal secrets with outsiders. And the anthropologist's respectful rendering of the testimony keeps the declarations of secrecy on the page, even though they remain unthematized in her interpretive introduction. Ill prepared and/or unreliable, outsiders cannot [and should not] know too much.[6] After almost four hundred pages, filled with the most detailed information, the informant insists that secrets meant to cordon off the curious and controlling reader from the vulnerable objects of attention, have been kept. Menchú will repeat, with Villaverde's contraband dealer in slaves, "Not everything is meant to be said." But her discretion is more subtle than his, since it is very possible that she is hiding very little. Perhaps Menchú's audible silences and her wordy refusals to talk are calculated not to cut short our curiosity but to incite and then frustrate it, leaving us to feel the access closed off and to wonder at our exclusion.

Even a conservative Mexican American like Richard Rodriguez, who chooses not to identify with an ethnically marked "community" of Chicanos, stops Anglos in their reading tracks. For example, he will give deliberately empty information about his grandmother to say, in effect, that the linguistic (and ethnic) medium is the message, that translatable information is beside the point: "This message of intimacy could never be translated because it was not *in* the words she had used but passed *through* them." To read, then, to make the very effort of approaching the autobiographical author, is to reveal one's unbridgeable distance from him. "You who read this act of contrition should know that by writing it I seek a kind of forgiveness—not yours. The forgiveness, rather, of those many persons whose absence from higher education permitted me to be classed a minority student. I wish that they would read this. I doubt they ever will."[7]

But perhaps the most subtle performance of differential distancing that we have today is Toni Morrison's orchestration of various read-

---

[6] See Doris Sommer, "No Secrets: Rigoberta's Guarded Truth," *Women's Studies* (Tulsa, Okla.), 20–21 October 1991, 51–73.

[7] Rodriguez, *Hunger of Memory: The Education of Richard Rodriguez* (New York: Bantam, 1983), 31.

ers for her *Beloved*. "She and Baby Suggs had agreed without saying so that it was unspeakable; . . . Even with Paul D, who had shared some of it and to whom she could talk with at least a measure of calm, the hurt was always there."[8] Distinguishing levels of identification among *Beloved*'s characters works to distinguish among readers, too. The concentric, ever-weakening circles of experience-based understanding expand outside Morrison's novel to contemporary readers, those who share the historical burden of slavery and, at a farther remove, those who do not.[9] And while readers desire more and more information to piece together a story that is already painfully clear, the narration stops dramatically and repeatedly to confront a danger in that desire. It is an ethically and ethnically encoded danger that may have gone unperceived by those of us at a far and safe remove, the danger that historical narration itself may reinscribe humiliation and loss:

> My greedy brain says, Oh thanks, I'd love more—so I add more. And no sooner than I do, there is no stopping. . . .
> But her brain was not interested in the future. Loaded with the past and hungry for more, it left her no room to imagine, let alone plan for, the next day. . . . Other people went crazy, why couldn't she? Other people's brains stopped, turned around and went on to something new. . . .
> "I didn't plan on telling you that."
> "I didn't plan on hearing it.". . .
> Maybe. Maybe you can hear it. I just ain't sure I can say it.
> (Morrison, 70)

Reflective and protective reticence should bring other cases to mind once we learn to recognize the posture as a strategy for con-

---

[8] Morrison, *Beloved: A Novel* (New York: Knopf, 1987), 58.

[9] Without entering the debate on whether or not experience is a reliable "ground" for theorizing, I should mention it in the current reevaluation of what one might call inescapable essentialism. A necessary corollary, it seems to me, is the inescapable conditioning of experience. Tania Modleski, for example, rejects Jonathan Culler's and Peggy Kamuf's suspicions of experience, and especially Culler's pretense of imagining how a woman reads ("Feminism and the Power of Interpretation: Some Critical Readings," in *Feminist Studies, Critical Studies*, ed. Teresa de Lauretis [Bloomington: Indiana University Press, 1986], 133). But Diana Fuss points out that the project of poststructuralism has been not to make experience anathema but to refuse "the hypostatization of experience as *the* ground" of knowing ("Reading Like a Feminist," *Differences* 1, no. 3 [1989]: 86).

fronting the readerly will to appropriate a writer's position through unexamined empathy and demands for candor. In Villaverde's Cuba, there is the well-known case of slave autobiographer Juan Francisco Manzano. Many remember that Manzano had agreed to record his memoirs for abolitionist Domingo del Monte, whose support could mean freedom for the author. But on reflection, the slave changed his mind about what to write and what to keep silent. A second letter to del Monte explained that frankness about certain incidents would be impossible. One reason may have been the retaliation he feared in a still-slavocratic country; another, as Sylvia Molloy notes, was the developing sense of control that came with Manzano's project of self-authorship.[10] I want to speculate, though, that a third reason may have been some skepticism about the possibility of sharing the pain specific to slavery without trivializing it. Typically, the narrative locates a threshold and stops: "But let's leave to silence the rest of this painful scene," pointing to the private parts of the narrative but refusing to expose them to a voyeur.[11]

Remembering Manzano's precautions against required intimacy, or attending to them for the first time, we may begin to doubt a whole series of competent readings we have performed, embarrassingly easy readings. What if other nineteenth-century (and earlier) texts have been performing their unavailability without our having noticed before? Privileged readers have never been (res)trained to stop at signs of resistance. Instead, we have read protests of privacy as the coquettish modesty calculated to incite conquest. Nevertheless, a small effort may remind many readers how Harriet Jacobs interrupts her otherwise intimate confessions of *Incidents in the Life of a Slave Girl* (1861) to stop her

---

[10] "While the first letter gave full power to del Monte over Manzano's story, the second establishes a line between what has been promised to the critic . . . and what Manzano keeps for himself. The previous letter, marked by subservience, waived Manzano's rights to the text by 'giving' it to del Monte; the second letter, marked instead by resistance, has Manzano keep the text for himself" (Molloy, "From Serf to Self: The Autobiography of Juan Francisco Manzano," in *At Face Value: Autobiographical Writing in Spanish America* [Cambridge: Cambridge University Press, 1991], 43).

[11] Quoted by Susan Willis, "Crushed Geraniums: Juan Francisco Manzano and the Language of Slavery," in *The Slave's Narrative*, ed. Charles T. Davis and Henry Louis Gates Jr. (Oxford: Oxford University Press, 1985), 208–9.

white readers from presuming to judge her. You "whose purity has been sheltered from childhood, who have been free to choose the objects of your affection, whose homes are protected by law, do not judge the poor desolate slave girl too severely!"[12]

These books resist the competent reader, intentionally. By marking off an impassable distance between reader and text, and thereby raising questions of access or welcome, writers ranging from Harriet Jacobs and Juan Francisco Manzano to Toni Morrison, Richard Rodriguez, and Rigoberta Menchú practice strategies to produce the kind of readerly incompetence that more reading will not overcome. At issue is not the ultimate or universal impossibility to exhaust always ambiguous literature through interpretation. Ambiguity, unlike the resistance that interests me here, has been for some time a consecrated and flattering theme for professional readers. It blunts interpretive efforts and thereby invites more labor, so that ambiguity allows us to offset frustrated mastery with a liberating license to continue endlessly. Nor do I mean resistance as the ideally empty or even bored refusal to narrate that Flaubert apparently pioneered when he would stop a story to contemplate some diegetically insignificant detail.[13]

The issue to be considered is neither the final undecidability of interpretation nor the novel's pauses over what is or is not relevant to tell. It is, rather, the rhetoric of selective, socially differentiated understanding. Announcing limited access is the point, not whether or not some information is really withheld. Resistance does not necessarily signal a genuine epistemological impasse; it is enough that the impasse is claimed in this ethico-aesthetic strategy to position the reader within limits.[14] The question, finally, is not what "insiders" can know as

---

[12] Jacobs, *Incidents in the Life of a Slave Girl*, intro. Walter Teller (New York: Harcourt Brace, 1973), 54.

[13] Gérard Genette mentions several theorists on this issue: Roman Jakobson, Valéry, John Crowe Ransom, William Empson, among others (*Figures of Literary Discourse*, trans. Alan Sheridan, intro. Marie-Rose Logan [New York: Columbia University Press, 1982]).

[14] Among other critics concerned with related issues, see Tobin Siebers, *The Ethics of Criticism* (Ithaca, N.Y.: Cornell University Press, 1988). In general, Siebers offers an almost shrill rejection of contemporary criticism, from the New Criticism to poststructuralism, for assuming that decisions in reading literature are necessarily oppressive, totalitarian, and unethical. From a narrow reading of Kant, and then of

opposed to "outsiders"; it is how those positions are constructed as incommensurate or conflictive. And professional readers who may share some social space with a writer, enough to claim privileged understanding and explanatory powers, may miss, or hastily fill in, the constitutive gaps these texts would demarcate.

These are not the ethnically marked books that invite empathy and that can turn out to be translations or imitations of the real thing, as Henry Louis Gates, Jr., shows in "'Authenticity,' or the Lesson of Little Tree." His critique hovers around the always suspect claim of authenticity, since imitations are often indistinguishable from more presumptive fictions. Therefore he concludes that "no human culture is inaccessible to someone who makes the effort to understand, to learn, to inhabit another world."[15] But resistant texts don't seem to fret over the snare of transparent authenticity that can reveal visible inventions. They are determined to offer opacity, not to make it evaporate. Resistant texts thematize what is lost in translation. They hesitate to play musical chairs, a game of easy substitutions designed to eliminate all but one position. Hesitation doesn't mean that the music stops so that authenticity can sit down securely and leave us standing; it signals skepticism about the process of elimination. Gates tracks the mistakes incurred by empathetic readings that inevitably, I think, fuse self with other and melt down differences. That simplifying fusion is what some texts foil.

If we learn to stop at signs of obstinacy to interpretation, we may notice that they sometimes calculate a problem of division: to discriminate between the authorial community (which will not read Menchú, is guiltily avoided by Rodriguez, and is hardly the sole reader of Morrison) and the authorial audience of perhaps predominantly curious outsiders. Obstinacy targets those who would read in the presumptuous register of "If I were a . . . ," failing to assimilate lessons about

---

Nietzsche, New Critics insist on the autonomy of art and then of language, free from considerations of intentionality. For them, society and art are opposing terms; the undecidability of art gives the realm of freedom that society tries to limit by law. For an informed review and evaluation of the critical literature, see Adam Zachary Newton, "Narrative Ethics: The Intersubjective Claim of Fiction" (Ph.D. diss., Harvard University, 1992).

[15] Gates, "'Authenticity,' or the Lesson of Little Tree," *New York Times Book Review*, 11 November 1991, 30.

how positionality helps constitute knowledge.[16] Yet the asymmetry of positions restricts travel from one to the other, despite the fantasies of mutuality that motivate some studies of "multiculturalism," which assume that their own effort to understand an ethnically inflected text is somehow commensurate with the writer's decision to perform in an imperial language. A competent reader can acknowledge that a novel like *Tangi,* by the Maori Witi Ihimaera, "shows how a strategic refusal to accommodate the reader can stand at the very core of a work's meaning." And yet the same reader can assume an equivalence or reciprocity between writing and reception, an interchangeability that allows for the ultimate identifications between self and other that override differences. "At the *tangi* and in the novel *Tangi,* we are on Maori ground, and, for a change, we have to do the accommodating and the adapting. As we do so, we experience the kind of shifting and adapting a Tama undergoes every day in his life."[17] But "ideal" or target readers for resistant texts are hardly the writer's egalitarian counterparts. They are certainly not the coconspirators or allies who putatively share experiences and assumptions, as we have presumed in our critical vocabulary.[18] They are marked precisely as strangers, incapable of—or undesirable for—conspiratorial intimacy. Discrimination here takes for granted that differences in social positionality exist and that they effect (or require, for safety's sake) various degrees of understand-

[16] Michel Foucault gives a strong formulation in *The Archaeology of Knowledge,* trans. A. M. Sheridan Smith (New York: Pantheon, 1972). For a critique of presumptive "empathy" and identifications, see Gloria Anzaldúa, ed., *Making Face, Making Soul: Creative and Critical Perspectives by Women of Color* (San Francisco: Aunt Lute Foundation Books, 1990).

[17] Reed Way Dasenbrock, "Intelligibility and Meaningfulness in Multicultural Literature in English," *PMLA* 102 (1987): 16–17. On the one hand, Dasenbrock claims that foreign words or unfamiliar uses signal cultural differences "and that difference must be respected" (18). But on the other hand, the differences are read as invitations to work at extracting meaning, to assimilate oneself into the other's culture, just as the other has had to work at negotiating mainstream English.

[18] Peter J. Rabinowitz, *Before Reading: Narrative Conventions and the Politics of Interpretation* (Ithaca, N.Y.: Cornell University Press, 1987). Rabinowitz reviews the generally accepted notion of authorial audience as one the writer could have predicted. Not that all readers are ideal, but they are "deformed" in ways that the writer would have known and shared. They are "members of the same cultural community" (22, 26, 28).

ing.[19] Written from clearly drawn positions on a chart where only the powerful center can mistake its specificity for universality, these "marginal" or "minority" texts draw boundaries around that arrogant space.

These texts continue to protest, long after Cirilo Villaverde's self-critical staging, because they neither assume nor welcome comprehension by the reader who would still assimilate them. It may surprise some well-meaning readers to find that particularists are not always accommodating, that assimilation rhymes more with cultural annihilation than with progressive *Aufhebung*. The ecumenical gestures to reduce otherness to sameness suggest that difference is a superable problem rather than a source of pride or simply the way we are in the world.[20] Unyielding responses to the liberal embrace, the responses that I am tracking here, range from offering up a surrogate self whose absorption is no real loss, the "featherbed resistance" that Zora Neale Hurston described as the Negro's polite refusal, to striking the pose of an intransigent, unaccommodating self from the place "competent" readers have associated with the other. This pose may not need to construct a stable, coherent speaking subject, whom readers, after all, could then presume to know and to represent. The purpose of what Gayatri Spivak and Diana Fuss, among others, have been calling "strategic essentialism" is to cast doubts on the reader's capacity to know, without allowing incapacity to float into the comforting, unmanageable mists of ambiguity.[21] But intransigence can be dismissed as

[19] For an earlier and very astute exploration of this inscribed difference, see Marta·Sánchez, "Hispanic- and Anglo-American Discourse in Edward Rivera's *Family Installments*," *American Literary History* 1 (1989): 853–71.

[20] For the collusion between the apparently opposite projects of universalizing (saming) and subordination of the other (othering), see Naomi Schor, "This Essentialism Which Is Not One: Coming to Grips with Irigaray," *Differences* 1, no. 3 (1989): 38–58. Comparing Beauvoir's call for equality with men to Irigaray's celebration of female difference, Schor observes the limitations of both. "If othering involves attributing to the objectified other a difference that serves to legitimate her oppression, saming denies the objectified other the right to her difference, submitting the other to the laws of phallic specularity. If othering assumes that the other is knowable, saming precludes any knowledge of the other in her otherness" (45).

[21] Spivak's work is associated with this idea, although Robert Scholes suggests that John Locke came upon it some time ago. He apparently distinguished between real and nominal essences, the former being the Aristotelian irreducible and unchanging core of thing and the latter merely a linguistic convenience, a classifica-

inauthentic, and featherbedding can be lost on those who presume to know. The very markers of resistance are often disregarded or overlooked and thus cannot constrain the intimately possessive knowledge that passes for love.

To make a parenthesis, I should confess that my last project depended on just this kind of knowledge and intimacy. I asked a historical question about writing rather than reading, specifically, how nineteenth-century foundational novels intervened in Latin American nations. Then I traced back from a galvanizing effect to the beguiling strategies that slipped allegorically between passion and patriotism.[22] From those hegemonizing (homogenizing) books I could (correctly) assume that readers were being invited in as participant observers in the love affairs that generated countries. Identification with the frustrated lovers whose union could produce the modern state was precisely the desired effect on the tenuous citizenry of newly consolidated countries. It was a mirror effect that survived mass distribution to required readers, who were told, in that dangerously democratic embrace of compulsory education, that their differences from the elite lovers did not really matter. My project, in other words, was to read foundations with a foundational theory that conjugated imagined communities with dreams of love. Rather than refuse the programmatic clarity of those novels in favor of decon-

---

tory fiction (Scholes, "Reading like a Man," in *Men in Feminism*, ed. Alice Jardine and Paul Smith [New York: Methuen, 1987], 208; Locke, *An Essay Concerning Human Understanding* [London: Printed by Elizabeth Hold for Thomas Bassett, 1690], esp. 2.31, 3.3, 3.6, 3.10, 4.6, 4.12). Spivak's formulation doesn't dismiss the essentialism; it's "a *strategic* use of positivistic essentialism in a scrupulously visible political interest" ("Subaltern Studies: Deconstructing Historiography," in *In Other Words* [New York: Methuen, 1987], 205). Allying themselves with the subaltern is an "interventionist strategy" (207). For a more cautious consideration, "within a personalist culture," where essentialism can be smuggled in again to serve the powerful, see Spivak's interview with Ellen Rooney in the special issue of *Differences* entitled "The Essential Difference: Another Look at Essentialism" ("In a Word: Interview," *Differences* 1, no. 2 [1989]: 124–56). In the same issue, Diana Fuss anticipates some of these concerns. It is one thing for the subaltern to use essentialism, another for the hegemonic group to use it. "The question of permissibility . . . is therefore framed and determined by the subject-positions from which one speaks" (86).

[22] Sommer, *Foundational Fictions: The National Romances of Latin America* (Berkeley: University of California Press, 1991).

structive unravelings that can show how any text wavers and contradicts its apparent message, I chose to address the books in their own ideal terms.

But to read resistant fictions in *their* ideal terms calls for a paradigm shift. How could a theory derived from narrative foundations of inclusive communities manage to read books that show and stretch the cracks at the base of society? To follow these defiant books, our critical vocabulary will strain after antifoundationalist terms. It will struggle because their characteristic rhetorical strategies have evidently seemed unremarkable. In the vicious circle of familiarity and predictability that describes some hermeneutical habits, the unanticipated lessons these texts could teach seem hard to read. How can the books teach reading effectively if our readerly training is precisely to ignore their lessons? There is so much that one must ignore anyway, especially in long works, that it would be rather easy to continue our inattention.[23] If our training assumes that learning is a progression, that it is always learning something, how does interpretive reticence make sense? At our most modest we have been assuming, with the New Critics and then more radically with deconstruction, that ambiguity cannot be conquered. But distance from the object of desire? Confessed ignorance of that object? Prohibition against trespassing? We have yet to recognize those purposefully offputting enticements. Yet these limiting lures are worth noticing if privileged readers hope to engage "minority" literature instead of offering sycophantish praise, rejecting the political posturing or liberally assimilating the differences. Reading otherwise will reveal texts that refuse to flatter the competent reader with touristic invitations to intimacy but instead produce what we can call the "Cordelia effect," which cripples authority by refusing to pander to it.[24] Unlike so many opportune books (at least since the time of the Inca Garcilaso de la Vega) that have parlayed the author's "exoticism" into classical norms—in a wager to confuse boundaries and win some

[23] "As Michael Riffaterre's criticism of Jakobson makes abundantly clear, readers need to ignore or play down many textual features when they read lyric poetry; they need to *ignore* even more in longer works like novels" (Rabinowitz, 19).

[24] In George Steiner's pithy indictment: "Like murderous Cordelia, children know that silence can destroy another human being. Or like Kafka they remember that several have survived the songs of the Sirens, but none their silence" (35).

space at the center—these uncooperative texts declare their intransi-gence. They locate traditionally privileged readers beyond an invio-lable border on the fragmented map we call postmodernity. From that border we can be "ideal," paradoxically, to the extent that we are excluded. We can be competent to the extent that we cannot conquer.

The Hum of Literature: Ostension in Language

Paul H. Fry

As an avid student of literary history, I know just how unwelcome it must be to read the opinion, in this collection of essays on literary history, that literature as such is not historical. But having once let the pigeon out of the bag, all I can do is put it among the cats. Both the historical character of literature and its marked features in literary history are exhausted in and by the moment of *predication*. Undoubtedly, those aspects of all uttered language which narrate, describe, or explain can only be properly grasped—that is to say, differentially grasped—as the product and producer of history. In view of my opposition, here and throughout the argument of the book, to the "strong version" of historicism, which ascribes all phenomena whatsoever to cultural construction, it is crucial for me to avoid misunderstanding or quarrel about this first proposition: language in its predicative moment, I repeat, is culturally conditioned without exception or qualification. The strong or "new" historicists will remain unsatisfied with this conciliatory gesture, to be sure. They will respond that what stands behind it, the essentialization of an entity I call "literature," here redefined as nonpredicative language, merely intensifies when this entity is no longer defined as this or that invariant social, psychological, or aesthetic concretization (journalistic homily aside, there is a growing consensus that no such definition can survive demystification) but rather as a glimpse beyond the boundaries of concretization itself.

In other words, the shift in focus I am attempting more than ever requires a refutation of the argument that literature, even when so defined as to include each and every form of popular and oral culture, is a wholly contingent form of expression linked to material interest of some sort wherever it is found. If, as Peter Stallybrass argued in a recent public discussion, literature is something that gets produced through successive "technologies" of writing and reading, and if its very durability raises a suspicion that it is sustained artificially in accordance with superstructural interests,[1] then literature in no sense answers an authentically species-specific need (if indeed, after Foucault, we are allowed to suppose that any species-specific needs, or even species, remain to contemplate). Rather, it exists as one of those commodities disguised as "perennial necessities" whereby supply-and-demand economies mystify their enabling logic.

The anti-essentialist critique of the concept *literature* has fortified itself and gained widespread currency, I believe, owing to the self-evident artificiality of existing definitions of literature, canon-authorizing definitions that supporters and detractors in fact *share*. The suspiciously easy defeat of "literature" by multiculturalism in the academy has been accomplished because the attackers have shrewdly chosen to agree with the defenders' obviously weak definitions of the thing attacked. Many believe that diverse cultural expressions will gain in exuberance and force as soon as the term *literature*—of comparatively recent vintage itself, after all[2]—is buried and forgotten; and this belief will seem legitimate as long as literature continues to be understood as formal representation. But nothing of that sort, I agree with its critics, is "essential" to it. The impulse or drive that really does inhere in animals that look before and after, and in fact ultimately defines such animals, is neither *Formtrieb* nor *Stofftrieb* (to borrow Schiller's terms), although the very intensity with which those impulses are gratified and exhausted in "works of art" is an important signal of its presence.

Even if we think of the predicative moment as entailing a recognizable intentional structure, there is still nothing specifically literary in the notion of conditioned predicative language, no ground on which to decide what literature is or—what is of still greater interest—

---

[1] Stallybrass made these remarks at a 1993 MLA panel on which we both appeared.

[2] For the history and provenance of this term see, inter alia, Timothy Reiss, *The Meaning of Literature* (Ithaca, N.Y.: Cornell University Press, 1992). Most scholars agree that Robert Southey was the first to use the term roughly as it is still used.

why it perdurably exists. As Wolfgang Iser has suggested, the issue would seem to be an "anthropological" one insofar as it is accessible to reflection at all.[3] We might willingly enough agree, with many of our colleagues, simply to give up formalist, traditional Marxist, and rear-guard humanist efforts to define literature and settle instead for the neopragmatist argument that whatever you want it to be is what it is; but that argument leaves an interesting question unanswered, the question why you do invariably want it to be *something*, and why so many have always wanted to write or speak that something, whatever it is, not just until formal, representational, or vocational aims have been fulfilled but incessantly, with obsessive repetitiveness. From this curious fact it is almost enough to infer that literature is coextensive with human being in defining human being, over against all other forms of sentience, as that which can never say what it wants to say.

It is said that there is always a snob motive for literature, a matter of superstructure or "reproduction" (à la Bourdieu) or cultural capital or the flaunting of leisure. This claim has considerable force, certainly, but it cannot account for the fact that cultural capital has persisted transhistorically, unless it is then said, again demystifying supply and demand, that there is a sucker *created* every minute.[4] William Hogarth saw the serpentine line—the "line of beauty"—and its equivalent the minuet pattern in dance as reflecting the luxury of not having to take

[3] Iser, "Towards a Literary Anthropology," in *The Future of Literary Theory*, ed. Ralph Cohen (New York: Routledge, 1989), 208–28.

[4] I am answered, perhaps, by Louis Althusser's assertion that "ideology has no history" ("Ideology and Ideological State Apparatuses," in *Lenin and Philosophy and Other Essays*, trans. Ben Brewster [New York: New Left Books, 1971], 159) and can only respond that I find the argument of this famous essay structurally valid yet devoid of political merit. Consider the claim—which is brilliantly formulated and fundamentally correct—that ideology is the (transhistorical) subjection of a subject to a Subject (see 179): When I "call" (i.e., "interpellate") my dog, precisely in Althusser's double sense of the word *call*, I dominate the animal unequivocally by some contractual means of its own devising that it is a "subject." It did not invent me and then decide to obey me, whereas there is always some measure of contractualism (i.e., voluntarism) in the agreement of any interpellated human individual to be con-stituted as a subject, no matter how illusory or mystified the other, dominant "party" to the agreement may be. This should suffice to show, contra Althusser, that *dehu-manization begins precisely where ideology is suspended.* (I do not say, be it noted, that this necessarily happens under Communism; but the "party" abovementioned, duly cap-italized, functions very nicely in the place of God or state.)

the shortest distance between two points;[5] and we for our part tend to see the lavish forms of art in Marxist terms as an ostentation of surplus. But in doing so, we still have not identified the purpose of the unnecessary, except perhaps to say that when functionless activities come to be felt as a need, they have taken on the character of what Marx and Freud would agree to call—but in the name of what alternative cultural health?—a fetish. Yet this sort of argument, too, like my own claim, counts as true for all times, or at least until the classless society arrives. The Marxist argument treats literature as Louis Althusser treats ideology, agreeing in effect with me that "literature has no history."

Possibly any conceivable "anthropology of X" will take the high transhistorical road. Iser thinks literature answers a need for shared fictive hypotheses, an argument that could easily be put in other terms: neo-Kantian, as in Ernst Cassirer or Suzanne Langer; apocalyptic, as in Northrop Frye; or Marxist, as in Fredric Jameson's appropriation of Frye on romance. Literature in all these strikingly Arnoldian accounts is an expansive energy that supplements the poverty and entropy of life. I am convinced, on the contrary, that literature is an entropy supplementing the expansive, purposeful energies of life. I do not think, that is, with the various philosophers whose impressive store of thought has lately been trained upon and influenced by literature (Stanley Cavell, Martha Nussbaum, and Richard Rorty, to name diverse exemplars of the trend), that the specific function of literary expression is to shape our social or cultural or even personal identities, simply for the reason that social dialogue in general does that, for better and worse; and to assume for literature a special polysemousness or degree of "dialogism" that shapes identity with a somehow privileged, even ontologically distinct subtlety (making it better for that purpose, in Nussbaum's opinion, than the categorical method essential to philosophy),[6] is to slip back more or less unawares into language-specific doctrines of "poetic function" that the formalist tradition has actually worked out with more rigor. This is not to say that literature does not

---

[5] Hogarth, *The Analysis of Beauty* (1753), ed. Joseph Burke (Oxford: Clarendon, 1955), 151–52, 156–60.

[6] See, inter alia, Nussbaum, "Emotions as Judgments of Value," *Yale Journal of Criticism* 5 (1992): 201–12, together with my "Response" (225–28).

have a claim (*Anspruch*) to make upon us, a call to hermeneutic engagement that discloses ourselves to ourselves; but it is just the purpose of this essay to argue that that disclosure, the disclosure that really is specific to literature, stands at an opposite extreme from any and all forms of "local knowledge."

No, Aristotle's complaint that he had no word to encompass Socratic dialogue, mime, and poetic imitation still has force, and for that reason when we write literary criticism we still do not know what we are talking about. Of course, any number of definitions, including Bentham's ludic anticipation of Wittgenstein (poetry and pushpin are both games; I prefer pushpin), are perfectly usable for heuristic purposes, which is why we feel that despite its handicap a tremendous amount of literary criticism is brilliantly illuminating; and I for one still admire the formalists enough to feel that if we understand some version of the "poetic function" (including, say, Bakhtin's or Pierre Macherey's) to be in place when we read, we are not too likely to write crude criticism. Indeed, to return now to my thesis, it will be very important to recognize from the outset that the invariant and breathtaking simplicity of the literary occasion, which is also its claim, cannot be disclosed except through the folds, the formal implications, of a severe, historically layered complexity.

I spoke earlier of language in its predicative moment, implying that it has other moments. There are two, an indicative (or indexical) moment and a phonic-scriptive moment, and it is in the complex dialectic these moments form in concert with predication that the gesture of ostension in literature can be discovered and defined. It is the function of indication, of saying that something just is, to estrange utterance from its historical situation by refusing to say that that something is predicated upon, determined by, something else, whether in narrative, description, or explanation. Predication differentiates the object, and indication cannot help doing the same insofar as it coincides grammatically with predication; but it differs intentionally from predication in perceptibly resisting its grammatical function. It is in thus suspending the instrumentality of language that indication brings into view the phonic-scriptive aspect of a text, its material character as uninterpreted sound (hence neither music nor phonation) and as uninterpreted trace (hence neither image nor phoneme).

This is the moment, completing the structure of ostension, which reduces the estranged, necessarily "situated" utterance to sound and trace and thus returns it to the unsignifying sphere of actuality, of things in themselves, from which history for its part is by nature forever estranged. Literature, then, is that mode of utterance which lays bare the irreducible distance between history and actuality from the *parti pris* of the latter. By suspending our purposeful engagement with the world, it reattaches itself to the world. Literature is that dimension of verbal utterance which is unhistorical in itself yet constitutes by its very existence a critique of history. The ontological nature of its occasion, as opposed to the historical nature of its intentional structure, can be understood anthropologically as the need to disclose the being that is normally suppressed by doing—and if that sounds like Hogarth all over again, anticipating the Marxists, it should be noted that the serpentine and the minuet are not in the least ostensive; they are elaborations of activity, not suspensions of it.

All three stages of this argument must necessarily be kept in mind together in order to distinguish it from what at this point it will otherwise seem to resemble: a formalist, antimimetic methodology for criticism and a modernist, antirealist program for literature. It is very decidedly neither. The grammatical form of indication at its most effective lurks *within* predication as a suspension of semantic closure, not as an avoidance of reference; and by "phonic-scriptive" I do not mean those characteristics normally grouped under the Jakobsonian heading of "poetic function," including so-called self-reference, mise-en-abyme effects, and the whole panoply of devices that make the sign palpable *as a sign*—all of which I take to be covertly predicative: language representing itself as speech, or vice versa. The phonic and scriptive elements of language are those elements that just are (that is, they could not be other than sound and trace) and hence belong in an ontological continuum with the things they are perceived to indicate, things of which one could only say that they "call attention to themselves" *after* one had called attention *to* them by predicating something of them, hence no longer preserving their self-identity. Thus literature is arguably most itself when it is *not* modernist, that is, when it retains the linguistic transparency, the unassumingness, of its historical project.

As I have already acknowledged, indication does not entail a suspension of reference. To say that something "is" (implying: not that it is not and that it is not something else) is undoubtedly to refer. The Peircian index, for all its simplicity, is still a sign.[7] For this reason I have chosen the relatively more precise grammatical term *predication* in place of *reference*, which unquestionably does entail both predication and indication. The relation between predication in grammar and predication in philosophy remains in some ways bewildering (is it with respect to things, concepts, or constraints of linguistic usage that I say a predication is or is not true?), and that is why the term is only "relatively" more precise. But the key to my argument is sufficiently clear and distinct: whereas the *is* of predication is a copula, *a* is *b*, the *is* of indication is a tautology, *a* is *a*; and I want to lay the very greatest stress in everything that follows on the philosophers' contemptuous insistence that a tautology is a meaningless proposition. Exactly: it is nothing other than the meaningless that literature exists to disclose, and in my opinion it was from the awareness of this extraordinarily subversive power and not from envy of literature's rival mode of conceptualization that "the ancient quarrel between the poets and the philosophers" arose. If my own commentary can never escape the interpreter's need to "say something in other words" (in speaking, for instance, as I recurrently do, of "thematization")—if indeed I can never abandon a predicative way of identifying the indicative basis of the literary (indication in this argument can itself never be indicated but only predicated, because my point is not that indication itself just is but that it is functional)—that in itself will show the difference between commentary and literature.

It may appear from the clustering of examples in what follows that the ostensive moment of literature is itself not only historical but period-specific. Even though, again, it is not a modernist phenome-

---

[7] See Charles Sanders Peirce to Lady Welby, 12 October 1904, in *Semiotic and Significs: The Correspondence between Charles S. Peirce and Victoria Lady Welby*, ed. Charles S. Hardwick (Bloomington: Indiana University Press, 1977), 33.

non, it is undeniably a prominent feature of late romanticism and hence, by implication, of that crisis surrounding "the meaninglessness of existence" that can be variously associated with Darwin and with the commodification of surplus value in late capitalism. I myself, with my seemingly unexamined presupposition about the unsignifying nature of actuality, would seem to be rewriting ("inscribed within") the post-mortem on the typological tradition that belongs very much to that moment. (One could imagine being asked, is there any hint of sheer ostension in Blake?) But there is no self-refutation in these emphases: while the indicative and the phonic-scriptive moments are not histori-cal in themselves, they nevertheless do ebb and flow through history. To revert again to the categories of Russian formalist literary histori-ography, we can say that in the age of Victoria, of the biedermeier, of the Second Empire, and of the rethinking of manifest destiny in Amer-ica, the self-identity of literature became the "dominant," the marked feature, in literary discourse. The thematization of sound and of visual tracery upon which the ensuing remarks focus belongs to the same era in which there was a fashion for the evocation of music as sheer sound and for ecphrases in prose and verse evoking the alleged meaningless-ness of painting. But that there were always and will always be such underdeterminations of meaning in literary discourse is not just a necessary condition for the general force of my argument, to be left in the hands of inference and called, for example, a logic implicit in the structure of the literary occasion (though I do think that that is what it is); it can and will be demonstrated as a simple fact spanning recorded literary history, exemplified with telling complexity by the Virgilian trope of the bees.

No doubt there would be advantages in beginning with a hard case, with a recalcitrant example of the audible tracery in literature—with a Balzacian novel, say, in which engagement with history, politics, and society is clearly the marked literary-historical feature. But that is what I hope to do in the end with the muted hum of Virgil's bees. In the meantime, an obviously central example (but not necessarily an easy one) seems best.

I heard a Fly buzz—when I died—
The Stillness in the Room
Was like the Stillness in the Air—
Between the Heaves of Storm—

The Eyes around—had wrung them dry—
And Breaths were gathering firm
For that last Onset—when the King
Be witnessed—in the Room—

I willed my Keepsakes—Signed away
What portion of me be
Assignable—and then it was
There interposed a Fly—

With Blue—uncertain stumbling Buzz—
Between the light—and me—
And then the Windows failed—and then
I could not see to see—[8]

"I heard a Fly buzz—when I died" is a predication that is properly—that is to say, differentially—understood only with respect to its
historical moment. The period of civil war (like many of Dickinson's
most morbid poems, this one bears the probable date of 1862), of
frontier or forest peril (the "Heaves of Storm" beyond the room),[9] of
the sensationalist turn in piety signaling the breakdown of a securely
theocratic social order ("when the King / Be witnessed": is he God or
death?), of the preoccupation with illness as contagion or plague pre-
conditioning the paradigm of inoculation in the history of medicine
(flies *carry* things), and of the domestication of both culture and the
life rituals by women ("I willed my Keepsakes")[10]—this period is exemplified equally well by Twain's Emmeline Grangerford, by her proto-
type Lydia Sigourney, and by the Dickinson of poems like this one.

---

[8] *The Complete Poems of Emily Dickinson*, ed. Thomas H. Johnson (Boston: Little,
Brown and Co., 1950), no. 465 (223–24). All references to Dickinson's poems are to
this edition, by number.

[9] See Shira Wolosky, *Emily Dickinson: A Voice of War* (New Haven, Conn.: Yale
University Press, 1984), xviii.

[10] See Ann Douglas, *The Feminization of American Culture* (New York: Avon,
1978), 240–72.

We accord Dickinson a superior regard within this constellation by saying that her sleight of hand or perspective trick of speaking from the grave is what sets her apart;[11] and we say further that her conscious denial of consciousness ("I could not see to see"), itself denying her denial, anoints her a unique spokesperson for that historical moment in which "secularization" is helplessly stranded, equidistant between religious and scientific rationalizations of death, and is thus constantly teased by death in the form of a riddle, a grim parlor game or *Fort-Da* compulsion to be enacted over and over on the very site of its future occurrence—

> Faith is a fine invention
> When gentlemen can see!
> But microscopes are prudent
> In an emergency!

> . . . That bareheaded life, under the grass, worries one like a wasp[12]

—and produces with its buzzing, partly at the phonic-scriptive level, what Debra Fried has called "the repetitious stalling that is characteristic of many utterances from the tomb."[13]

These are the historical contours of Dickinson's predication, fine-tuned sufficiently to entail questions of form and even a certain specificity with respect to the "author function." There is more: the house with "screenless"[14] glass windows meant to keep out flies but only serving to place the persistent intruders in visual relief (Dickinson's recorded dislike of flies[15] is a fastidiousness no doubt unavailable to

---

[11] For a good account of this stratagem see David Porter, *Dickinson: The Modern Idiom* (Cambridge, Mass.: Harvard University Press, 1981), 9ff. For the claim that the "epitaph of the self" is actually a traditional gesture see Vivian R. Pollak, *Dickinson: The Anxiety of Gender* (Ithaca, N.Y.: Cornell University Press, 1984), 193–98. But as this convention is confined almost exclusively to funerary inscription, we can say that Dickinson was needed to put it to serious use.

[12] Dickinson to Samuel Bowles, c. 1860, *The Letters of Emily Dickinson*, ed. Thomas H. Johnson, 2 vols. (Cambridge, Mass.: Harvard University Press, 1956), 2:364.

[13] Fried, "Repetition, Refrain, and Epitaph," *English Literary History* 53 (1986): 615.

[14] See Jerome Loving, *Emily Dickinson: The Poet on the Second Story* (Cambridge: Cambridge University Press, 1986), 63.

[15] This is thoroughly documented by Robert Weisbuch, *Emily Dickinson's Poetry* (Chicago: University of Chicago Press, 1975), 188n.

ladies of an earlier time who had no means of keeping them at a distance), a house with rooms set aside for birth, living, and dying, with its gloomy mahogany furniture and its "Keepsakes" ready to hand for redistribution;[16] and that age of "natural history" in which the Linnaean preoccupation with taxonomy (literary realism repudiates Dr. Johnson and numbers the streaks of the tulip) domesticates the name of the bluebottle, here by metonymic allusion, for literary discourse.[17]

The literary-historical markers are equally significant. Recurring here are the abrupt openings of Donne ("I wonder, by my troth"), with the addition of trick perspective, and the deathbed scenes of Donne's "Valediction: Forbidding Mourning" and Browning's "Childe Roland," with the significant difference that whereas in Donne the scene is the comparative term of a simile and in Browning a sustained parenthetical simile, in Dickinson it expands to fill the poem. There is also this, introduced—as in Donne—by way of comparing the conveyance of grim tidings to a deathbed scene, from Barrett Browning's *Aurora Leigh* (6.1079–87):

> For something came between them, something thin
> As a cobweb, catching every fly of doubt
> . . . .
> To hold it buzzing at the window-pane
> And help to dim the daylight.[18]

What is most important, though, is Dickinson's sustained ironic revision of Keats's "Ode to a Nightingale," which also has an incidental deathbed scene ("Here, where men sit and hear each other groan"). Setting aside as an implied future referent Dickinson's reduction of

---

[16] On the furnishing of the Homestead and on the vogue for distributing mementos (at least in popular literature) when dying, see Barton Levi St. Armand, *Emily Dickinson and Her Culture: The Soul's Society* (Cambridge: Cambridge University Press, 1984), 310, 61.

[17] This solution of the "Blue" riddle was first suggested by Brita Lindberg-Seyersted, *The Voice of the Poet: Aspects of Style in the Poetry of Emily Dickinson* (Cambridge, Mass.: Harvard University Press, 1968), 90. Earlier, Byron uses the word *bluebottle* as a synonym for *bluestocking* in *Beppo*, stanza 74.

[18] Cited by Jack L. Capps, *Emily Dickinson's Reading, 1836–1886* (Cambridge, Mass.: Harvard University Press, 1966), 85. For the relevance of Donne's sermons (his poetry is not cited here) see the ingenious but startlingly pious reading by Katrina Bachinger, "'I Heard a Fly Buzz,'" *Explicator* 43 (1985): 12–15.

Keatsian birdsong ("Fled is that music") to an undifferentiated hum, there remain to consider the drowsy numbness of her opening compared with Keats's and the comparable confusion in the end—but with higher stakes—about whether she wakes or sleeps, prefigured in Keats by the moment when he "cannot see" the world he has left unseen and can no longer hear "the murmurous haunt of flies on summer eves." Dickinson's fancy *can* temporarily cheat well; hence to the uncertain, stumbling buzz of the fly she has not yet become a sod. True to her historical moment, then, Dickinson has obscured—riddled—Keats's relatively clear distinctions among life, death, and his third term, immortality.[19]

But what of the fly? It is not that I have kept it out of this discussion, holding it back for a grand entrance; on the contrary, I have tried to show that flies are very historical little creatures. In bringing it now to the forefront, in fact, I will no longer think of it as a fly but as a hum. Sharon Cameron's important reading of "I Heard a Fly Buzz" can be said to falter only in undervaluing this fly by treating it as a historical agent. In her book about temporality in Dickinson and in lyric, Cameron describes the poem as a scene of instruction, an education in the meaning—or lack of meaning—of death that can only be passed along posthumously. In this account the fly belongs to a narrative chiasmus in which it is seen first as "a triviality" contrasted with the speaker's foolish expectations about the coming of a king, and then as the mentor by whom she is "schooled" to realize her mistake.[20]

There is so much truth in this reading, with its quietly efficient gendering of Dickinson's perceptions, that the greatest care must be taken in explaining how important it is to shift its focus. For one thing, we know from many accounts, most amusingly from the hapless Thomas Wentworth Higginson's,[21] that Dickinson never let herself be

---

[19] For a relevant discussion of Dickinson's relation to Keats see Joanne Feit Diehl, *Dickinson and the Romantic Imagination* (Princeton, N.J.: Princeton University Press, 1981), 68–121, which concludes: "Dickinson refuses to embrace Keats's hard-won vision, for she prefers to remain in the dark—still questioning, torn by doubt" (120–21).

[20] Cameron, *Lyric Time: Dickinson and the Limits of Genre* (Baltimore, Md.: Johns Hopkins University Press, 1979), 113, 114.

[21] See the account reprinted in *Selected Poems and Letters of Emily Dickinson*, ed. Robert H. Linscott (New York: Doubleday Anchor, 1959), 14.

taught anything. And not, quite obviously, because she thought well of herself (indeed, what follows from what I am about to say is what appears to have been the case, namely, that she had no opinion of herself at all); rather, she evidently did not believe in teaching except as something that it was ladylike to ask for and pretend to accept at the hands of a man—a fact that reveals a strikingly radical skepticism about what can be known. She speaks from the grave, then, not to offer any knowledge about death or even about dying, however true it may be that there is nothing exalted about it and that that is worth saying, but rather to situate a suspicion about the zero-degree somatic actuality of being alive. This is much more clearly what she is doing in poems like "After Great Pain" (no. 341) and "There's a Certain Slant of Light" (no. 258; "None may teach it"), in which she is unquestionably comparing life to death rather than the other way around.

In the narrative logic of the poem the fly is introduced proleptically as part of the bustle, the busy-ness, of the agents in the room, hence in contrast with "The Stillness in the Room" where it later "interposed." It is this logic that motivates Cameron's developmental reading. But in the ordering of preliminary affect the buzz and the silen*ce* that continues its sound are almost indistinguishable, constituting a unified interval between the "Heaves" of agency: efforts such as gathering breath firm for an onset, final willing, and above all *signing*. In giving away everything concerning herself to which a transmissable sign can be attached, everything that has meaning (and not just in the sentimental sense of this expression), in giving away "What portion of me be / Assignable," she is also freeing herself from the inauthentic, the merely cultural and melodramatic, as Cameron I think would agree.[22] What remains, in life *or* death, is that hum of existence which is what literature, in this powerful embodiment, wishes to *sound*. And then it wuzz. "The fly," writes David Porter, is "the buzz of ceaseless consciousness" (239).

We are now in a position to say, for this instance, in what sense the ostensive moment in literature is not just transhistorical but in fact a

---

[22] In a transcendentalizing reading, E. Miller Budick lays comparable stress on the word *assignable* (*Emily Dickinson and the Life of Language: A Study in Symbolic Poetics* [Baton Rouge: Louisiana State University Press, 1985], 172−73).

critique of history.[23] Any scrupulously historical reading of this poem *must* conclude, as I did earlier, that Dickinson approached death as a riddle and that she devised a perspective which enabled her to see farther into it (as we imagine) than others. If, however, her poem is a sounding of the existent, the buzz of silence, then we should suspect rather that she entertained a quite definite view of death, a view that is consistent (the paradox is only superficial) with her resistance to any viewpoint concerning life. If consciousness prior to ideation (the "Assignable": "internal difference, / Where the Meanings, are" ["There's a Certain Slant of Light"]) is a sensation just exceeding the insentience of somatic being, intelligible perhaps as the sensitivity of the body or as the neurological activity of those insects whose hum is its signal, then perhaps the soul with its valves of stone is neither eternal nor annihilated by death but decays slowly, like the body, resulting in a dwindling half-life of sentience. This is not a novel idea, especially in literature, where it figures in various ways, notably in ghosts that seem more like walking corpses—from Virgil's Hector to Keats's Lorenzo in *Isabella*—whose putrefaction extends even to the difficulty they have speaking and to their gradual estrangement from their former passionate concern for the affairs of the living. And while this idea does not appear to have surfaced in Dickinson scholarship, it did influence at least one of her readers, the Thornton Wilder of *Our Town*.

There are some Dickinson poems in which the idea seems incontestably present, for instance, in another 1862 poem (no. 449) that is an even more savagely ironic revision of Keats's "Ode on a Grecian Urn" than "I Heard a Fly Buzz" is of the Nightingale ode (which is audible at the end of this poem as well):

I died for Beauty—but was scarce
Adjusted in the Tomb
When One who died for Truth, was lain
In an adjoining Room—

---

[23] Wolosky describes Dickinson's overall relation to "history" as follows: "The turmoil of events that claimed to be made in a universal pattern led her, not to project providential schemata into historical events, but to question such eternal patterns [invoked] in the name of history" (63).

He questioned softly "Why I failed"?
"For Beauty", I replied—
"And I—for Truth—Themself are One—
We Brethren, are", He said—

And so, as Kinsmen, met a Night—
We talked between the Rooms—
Until the Moss had reached our lips—
And covered up—our names—

The interchangeability of being alive and being dead is suggested not just in the domesticity of the setting but in the word *failed*, which suggests a long disease rather than any abrupt terminus—as it does also in "I Heard a Fly Buzz." Our talking heads signifying remembrance and our headstones remembering what is "Assignable" to us are fused in a complex metonymy even as they are fused shut, both sound and trace being lost together. The relentless materiality of Dickinson's fusions, enforcing the decay of signs, drains any residual Platonism from the pronouncement of Keats's urn—another speaking mineral form. Dickinson's "Beauty" stands demystified as sheer *aisthesis*, while "Truth" is that which indicates and is indicated by the radioactive half-life of consciousness; and it is only in those registers that "themself are One."

Body and voice do not always decay at the same rate in Dickinson: on one occasion voice takes longer, as we infer from the "Centuries" that have passed since death stopped his carriage for the speaker (see no. 712); and on others it is very quickly silenced, as when the "soldered mouth" of a housewife withholds speech even before her release from frantic activity into "Indolence" has become an accustomed condition (no. 187; note that only when she is no longer housekeeping can the sound and trace of consciousness be disclosed: "Buzz the dull flies—on the chamber window—," which is now "freckled" with grime); or again when her "Granite lip," were she dead, would struggle in vain to speak, even though a "Memorial crumb" (assignable to her) can still be given to her favorite robin (no. 182). But no variation on the theme of gradual decay, with death a mere point of transition along the way, can alter its contribution to the project of Dickinson's poetry, which is the disclosure of the insignificant in the very sound of signification.

What is insignificant, what none can teach, is "nature," as Dickinson says so often and so forthrightly that we take it to be a humbly pious homily, one that can be read perhaps most ambitiously as a critique of Emersonian hubris: "those who know her, know her less / The nearer her they get" (no. 1400). It is worth quoting in full a poem of the happiness-is-a-warm-puppy variety to which Dickinson was prone, a poem in which the negative creed is stated outright, thus leaving signification no scope for activity, in order to show why the peculiarly literary moment of ostension must declare itself in and through a dialectic arising from cognitive predication:

> "Nature" is what we see—
> The Hill—the Afternoon—
> Squirrel—Eclipse—the Bumble bee—
> Nay—Nature is Heaven—
> Nature is what we hear—
> The Bobolink—the Sea—
> Thunder—the Cricket—
> Nay—Nature is Harmony—
> Nature is what we know—
> Yet have no art to say—
> So impotent our Wisdom is
> To her Simplicity.

Here is the whole Keatsian "poetry of earth," an attempted poetry of pure indication, pointing to sounds and traces, bestowing on the "art"-lessness of children's verse the homage of its cloying imitative form.[24] (My answer to the imaginary critic abovementioned would be: Blake does this better because he juxtaposes it with "experience.") But because of course there is no such thing as pure indication (it is impossible to say, in language, that *a* is really only *a*), because pure indication can only be implied as that state of nature, itself the occasion of literature, which is always betrayed by the writing of sentences, Dickinson's poem falls back in the other direction toward predication, and her Dame Nature turns out to resemble Spenser's, except that it is far

---

[24] I am here expressing measured agreement with the indictment of Yvor Winters, "Emily Dickinson and the Limits of Judgment," in *Emily Dickinson: A Collection of Critical Essays*, ed. Richard B. Sewall (Englewood Cliffs, N.J.: Prentice-Hall, 1963), 28: "Her diction, at its worst, is a kind of poetic nursery jargon."

less enigmatic. And yet, only a contemporary of Marx, propounding a materialism as canny as his, would have put "Nature" in quotes, making it a name not yet covered up.

Indolence, a Keatsian theme, modulates into languor and world-weariness and becomes more classbound as the century wears on toward Wilde, but it retains its function as the seedbed of literature. In the suspension of action, reflection occurs (Nietzsche calls it "history"), but beyond or prior to reflection there is that astonishment at the simple being-situated of the self among things, according no special privilege to the self among things, out of which reflection arises and toward which, perhaps, it also gradually sinks. It is solely in the suspended time of *rêverie* that poets and the rest of us too are aroused from blankness by the humming of the world, with no way or wish to decide whether it is in fact the world or our own circulatory system that hums, and in that moment we notice existence in itself (the Being of beings, if you will, but there is no need for the portentous capital of Heidegger translation), which is the ground of literature.

   This moment cannot occur except as a suspension of labor, of historical being; hence it is an interesting and—on the face of it—troublesome fact that we find its literary origins in the epic and georgic genres, where *otium* is impossible except when it is a betrayal of historical destiny. In the *Odyssey*, the sound of being is a siren call—and Tennyson writes one of his earliest characteristic poems about a closely linked episode ("The Lotos-Eaters," in *Poems* [1832]). But in Virgil, to approach him more nearly, the interdependency of work and the suspension of work in the flourishing *civis* is more subtly drawn than it ever would be again, despite the literary persistence of his bees. It is hard to resist remarking here that everywhere along the Mediterranean one does not need to stop working to hear the cicada, the only steady sound there is in rural areas and in the islands; and it is the same, in many places, with the "Hyblaean bees." The spirit of such sounds is embodied in the poem to be found among the Anacreontea called "The Cicada." There may then be at least this one natural reason why our own alternations of doing and being seem awkwardly compartmentalized by contrast. But it is chiefly owing to cultural developments that for us the *fourmi* works without pause in silence, the *cigale* makes a steady but short-lived racket, and the Protestant ethic stipulates two weeks for vacation.

It seems doubtful that there was any siesta for the laborers raising the walls of Dido's Carthage ("Instant ardentes Tyrii"), and it is by assimilation to their industriousness at least as much as in illustration of it that the bees become a paradigm for the cooperative work of historical communities:

> qualis apes aestate nova per florea rura
> exercet sub sole labor, cum gentis adultos
> educunt fetus, aut cum liquentia mella
> stipant et dulci distendunt nectare cellas,
> aut onera accipiunt venientum, aut agmine facto
> ignavum fucos pecus a praesepibus arcent;
> fervet opus redolentque thymo fragrantia mella.[25]

Virgil does not need to overplay the humming sounds in these lines, because in the quality his diction chiefly imitates here, the smoothness of "mella" (honey), there is also the liquidity of "melos" (song). The sense of honeyed indolence that might well seize upon the reader (the scent of thyme that makes bees work harder makes people drowsy) is exorcised in Virgil's text with the lazy drones. The smoothness Virgil wants to emphasize is not honeyed peace but a fluency of civic cooperation. The heat of the sun lends ardor, fervor, but not stupor to the occasion. And yet, after all, the heat, the honey, the drones, and the fragrance are still there, neither canceled nor even diminished in their intense lassitude by negation. They are indicated, in short, counterindicated within their predication; and once in view, they are made present in the unlabored liquefaction of the writing—which is at the same time, however, Virgil's *opus* and *labor*, the historical mural on which he represents the actions of his heroes.

And also their inaction. Almost from this point forward in the "tragedy of Dido," things fall apart. When Aeneas and Dido become lazy drones, making the cave into which they first withdrew a symbol of their social dereliction and rechanneling *ardor* unproductively, the walls stop rising. For Virgil it is inconceivable that virtue can stand out-

[25] *Aeneidos*, in *P. Vergili Maronis Opera*, ed. F. A. Hirtzel (Oxford: Clarendon, 1963), 1:423, 430–36.

side history, which he understands as destiny; and it is therefore necessary for that critique of history that we are calling literature and that
surfaces everywhere in his poem as the pathos of being *fato profugus*,
hounded by history, to appear in the undertones and negations of the
text. Thus for him, existence as such can be heard not in the inter-
stices of labor but in the very rhythms of labor itself. This fact, for
which the Marxist will feel nostalgia, belongs crucially to history and
sets the integrated nature of the text which T. S. Eliot called "the classic"[26] firmly apart from the much later dissociations of the period—
that of Dickinson and Tennyson—in which "literature" becomes the
dominant in literary discourse. But the feeling of pastoral leisure in
the "florea rura" with which the simile of the bees is saturated (let *them*
work, and we'll have a nap) is still at odds with destiny's obligations,
even in Virgil. Very interestingly, there is a consensus among modern
critics that Aeneas loses his "humanity," not only because one by one
his family and friends, pieces of himself, fall away from him, but also
because he has lost his right to come to rest.[27] In choosing the word
humanity, we surprise ourselves. We do not refer to his historical identity, which he not only preserves but fulfills. We refer to the freedom
from history which is human, which precisely defines the human
because, when it is not lost, it is knowingly shared with the unknowing
bees.

[26] Eliot, "What Is a Classic?" in *Selected Prose of T. S. Eliot*, ed. Frank Kermode
(New York: Harvest, 1975), 115–31.

[27] On Aeneas's "loss of humanity" see, for example, Traugott Lawler, "The
Aeneid," in *Homer to Brecht: The European Epic and Dramatic Traditions*, ed. Michael Sei-
del and Edward Mendelson (New Haven, Conn.: Yale University Press, 1977), 71.
Lawler acknowledges his debt to the reading of the Palinurus episode by Michael C.
J. Putnam, who concludes: "Aeneas is to a great extent released from any human
attachment as he prepares to meet his father in the land of the dead" (*The Poetry of
the Aeneid: Four Studies in Imaginative Unity and Design* [Cambridge, Mass.: Harvard
University Press, 1966], 99). The emphasis of Brooks Otis on the *humanitas* of
Aeneas concerns the definition of a specifically Roman concept and does not really
stand opposed to the emphasis on human loss (*Virgil: A Study in Civilized Poetry*
[Oxford: Clarendon, 1964], esp. 391–94).

Charles Altieri teaches in the English department at the University of California, Berkeley. His most recent books are a paperback edition of *Painterly Abstraction in Modernist American Poetry* and *Subjective Agency* (1994). He is now writing a book on contemporary poetry and beginning a project attempting to use classical aesthetics for contemporary concerns.

Jonathan Arac is professor of English at the University of Pittsburgh and a member of the *boundary 2* editorial group. Author of *Critical Genealogies* (1987), he is completing two other books: one concerning *Huckleberry Finn* and the functions of criticism, the other tentatively titled *Impure Worlds: Genre, Language, and Politics in the Emergence of "Literature."*

R. Howard Bloch is professor of French at Columbia University. He is author of *Medieval French Literature and Law* (1977), *Etymologies and Genealogies* (1983), *The Scandal of the Fabliaux* (1986), *Medieval Misogyny and the Invention of Western Romantic Love* (1991), and *God's Plagiarist: Being an Account of the Fabulous Industry and Irregular Commerce of the Abbé Migne* (1994). He is currently working on a book about Buffalo Bill in Paris.

Marshall Brown is professor of English and comparative literature at the University of Washington and editor of *Modern Language Quarterly*. He is author of *The Shape of German Romanticism* (1979), *Preromanticism* (1991), and the forthcoming *Turning Points: Essays in the History of Cultural Expressions*. He is currently working on a book about Kant and the gothic novel.

Richard Dellamora, who lives in Toronto and teaches at Trent University, wrote this essay while a visiting fellow in the Department of English at Princeton University. He is author of *Masculine Desire: The Sexual Politics of Victorian Aestheticism* (1990) and *Apocalyptic Overtures:*

Sexual Politics and the Sense of an Ending (1994) and editor of *Postmodern Apocalypse: Theory and Cultural Practice at the End* (1995).

Paul H. Fry is professor of English at Yale University. He is author of *The Poet's Calling in the English Ode* (1980), *The Reach of Criticism: Method and Perception in Literary Theory* (1983), *William Empson: Prophet against Sacrifice* (1991), *A Defense of Poetry: Reflections on the Occasion of Writing* (1995), and numerous articles on literary theory, the history of criticism, and British romanticism.

Geoffrey H. Hartman is Sterling Professor of English and Comparative Literature at Yale University and project director of its Fortunoff Video Archive for Holocaust Testimonies. He has recently published *Minor Prophecies* (1991) and edited *Holocaust Remembrance: The Shapes of Memory* (1994). *The Longest Shadow: In the Aftermath of the Holocaust* is due to appear early in 1996.

Denis Hollier is chairman of the Department of French at Yale University. He is general editor of *A New History of French Literature* (1989), whose French translation appears under the title *De la littérature française* (1993). The translation of his last book, *Les Dépossédés (Bataille, Caillois, Leiris, Malraux, Sartre)*, is due to be published by Harvard University Press in 1996.

Donna Landry is author of *The Muses of Resistance: Laboring Class Women's Poetry in Britain, 1729–1796* (1990) and, with Gerald MacLean, of *Materialist Feminisms* (1993) and *The Spivak Reader* (1995). Professor of English at Wayne State University, she is currently pursuing a study of landscape, gender, and field sports in the eighteenth-century British countryside, funded by a Guggenheim fellowship.

Lawrence Lipking is Chester D. Tripp Professor of Humanities at Northwestern University. This essay returns to some themes addressed in "The Genie in the Lamp: M. H. Abrams and the Motives of Literary History," which appeared in his edited volume *High Romantic Argument: Essays for M. H. Abrams* (1981). His most recent book is *Abandoned Women and Poetic Tradition* (1988).

Jerome J. McGann is John Stewart Bryan Professor of English at the University of Virginia. His book on the conventions of sentimental poetry—*Poetics of Sensibility: A Revolution in Literary Style*—was due to be published by Oxford University Press in late 1995. His major current project remains *The Complete Writings and Pictures of Dante Gabriel Rossetti: A Hypermedia Research Archive.*

Walter Benn Michaels is professor of English and the humanities at Johns Hopkins University. He is author of *The Gold Standard and the Logic of Naturalism* (1987) and *Our America: Nativism, Modernism, and Pluralism* (1995).

Rukmini Bhaya Nair is associate professor of humanities and social sciences at the Indian Institute of Technology, Delhi. She has published one book of poems, *The Hyoid Bone* (1993). Her forthcoming publications, all due out in 1996, are *Gargi's Silence*, a second collection of poems; *Narrative Gravity: Conversation, Cognition, Culture*; *Essays on the Poetics of Postcoloniality*; *Impliculture; or, How We Might Maximize Metaphor*; and *Technobrat: Thinking through Technology, Cultural Cross-Examinations*, an "interactive" volume, written in collaboration with Nair's students, that explores the cultural anthropology of the engineer.

Virgil Nemoianu is William J. Byron Distinguished Professor of Literature at the Catholic University of America. He is a secretary general of the International Comparative Literature Association and a member of the European Academy for Arts and Sciences. Among his books are *The Taming of Romanticism* (1985) and *Theory of the Secondary* (1989).

Annabel Patterson is Karl Young Professor of English at Yale University. Among her publications are *Censorship and Interpretation* (1984, 1990), *Pastoral Ideology, Virgil to Valéry* (1988), *Shakespeare and the Popular Voice* (1989), *Reading between the Lines* (1992), and *Reading Holinshed's Chronicles* (1994).

David Perkins is Marquand Professor of English and American Literature, Emeritus, at Harvard University. He is author of *A History of Modern Poetry* (1976–87) and *Is Literary History Possible?* (1992) and editor of *Theoretical Issues in Literary History* (1991).

Marjorie Perloff's books include *The Futurist Moment: Avant-Garde, Avant-Guerre, and the Language of Rupture* (1986), *Poetic License* (1990), and *Radical Artifice: Writing Poetry in the Age of Media* (1992). Her *Wittgenstein's Ladder: Poetic Language and the Strangeness of the Ordinary* is forthcoming in 1996 from the University of Chicago Press. She is Sadie Dernham Patek Professor of Humanities at Stanford University.

Meredith Anne Skura is professor of English at Rice University. She is author of *The Literary Use of the Psychoanalytic Process* (1981) and *Shakespeare the Actor and the Purposes of Playing* (1993).

Doris Sommer, professor of Latin American literature at Harvard University, is author of *One Master for Another: Populism as Patriarchal Rhetoric in Dominican Novels* (1984) and *Foundational Fictions: The National Romances of Latin America* (1991) and coeditor of *Nationalisms and Sexualities*. Thanks to grants from the Guggenheim Foundation and from ACLS, she is writing a book tentatively titled *Telling Limits*, which develops the issues of ethnically marked resistance to readerly collaborations that are suggested by her essay in this volume.

Peter Stallybrass is professor of English and chair of the Cultural Studies Committee at the University of Pennsylvania. He is author, with Allon White, of *The Politics and Poetics of Transgression* (1986) and editor, with David Scott Kastan, of *Staging the Renaissance* (1991).

Susan Stewart is author of a new volume of poetry titled *The Forest* (1995) and of two earlier books of poetry, *Yellow Stars and Ice* (1981) and *The Hive* (1987). Her literary criticism includes *Nonsense* (1979), *On Longing* (1984), and *Crimes of Writing* (1991).